UNJUSTIFIED

UNJUSTIFIED

The Freedom Convoy,
The Emergencies Act,
And The Inquiry That Got It Wrong

RAY MCGINNIS

Praise for *Unjustified*

"Often, when momentous national events of questionable motivation occur, people simply want a down-to-earth common-sense assessment. Just give me the facts. In today's world, objective facts are hard to come by as society spirals toward a totalitarian, hazy moral future.

Enter Ray McGinnis to the rescue. In a fast-paced yet methodical manner, Ray sifts through the political spin and facts and exposes the falsity of the Canadian federal government's invocation of the Emergencies Act to quell a fictitious national emergency supposedly created by a peaceful truckers' protest. Along the way, he astutely implies and describes how the public were duped and science and our Constitution were hijacked by the high priests of leadership in government, health research and policy, big tech, and big media.

Ray's credibility is enhanced by his own experience of being at the beginning on the 'other side,' and that he had already written a book on the 9/11 Commission Report entitled 'Unanswered Questions.'

This book is a valuable contribution to the truth, hopefully assisting in restoring Canada's democracy."

~ Honourable A. Brian Peckford P.C., last living First Minister who signed The Patriation Agreement, *the basis of* The Constitution Act 1982, *which includes* The Charter of Rights and Freedoms

"McGinnis has crafted the ultimate expose on the West's campaign against dissent. With careful reporting, he blows up the false propaganda narrative that the trucker convoy was dangerous. But he also reveals a whitewash clean-up by the POEC on behalf of the government's invocation of the Emergencies Act against peaceful protestors."

~ Trish Wood, an award-winning investigative journalist with CBC's The Fifth Estate *and* As It Happens, *author of a critically acclaimed book on the Iraq War, and host of the podcast* Trish Wood Is Critical.

"I first met Ray in Ottawa during the POEC. We spoke at length about the things we had heard during the testimony, compared to what really happened during the Freedom Convoy. I've been following Ray's work and sharing it on all of my social media. He has consistently captured the truth with an in-depth comparison of those in the federal government apparatus, who have painted a very different picture of the actual reality that happened on the ground in Ottawa last year. Ray's work serves as a historical record of the catastrophic thinking of government officials, who from the very beginning of the Convoy aimed to demonize Canadians. The Convoy was filled by ordinary Canadians who only wanted to peacefully assemble and have their objections counted in a way envisioned by the Constitution and as members of a law-abiding citizenry."

~ Tom Marazzo was a Freedom Convoy volunteer in daily contact with the Ottawa Police Service Police Liaison Teams during the protest. He testified at the POEC. His forthcoming book is The People's Emergency Act: The Freedom Convoy.

"Ray brilliantly illustrates how ordinary Canadians went to Ottawa to hold their government to account because the institutions designed to protect them, including the mainstream media, failed them. He further provides many examples where the government did everything in its power to divide, vilify, and crush its own citizens rather than speaking with them. He leaves the reader with many important questions that need to be answered about the strength of our democracy. He still has me questioning, 'When did the government become so afraid of its own citizens?'"

~ Eva Chipiuk is a Canadian civil liberties lawyer who represented a number of the lead Freedom Convoy participants in Ottawa and at the Public Order Emergency Commission, where she cross-examined Prime Minister Justin Trudeau.

"Ray McGinnis has done a great service in documenting the truth about the Canadian trucker's convoy and Trudeau's unjustified invocation of the Emergencies Act to forcefully suppress it. The picture that emerges from his careful analysis of the facts bears little resemblance to the propaganda deployed to vilify the truckers' protest. This peaceful protest continued for weeks without a single violent incident. That is, until Canadian police roughed up some of the truckers in Ottawa when Trudeau sent in his shock troops to force the truckers out of the city. Corporatist and statist Canadian media labored to vilify the truckers, slandering them as, at worst, neo-Nazis and, at best, the unwashed refuse of society. The reality on the ground, as McGinnis documents here, belied these libelous smears. Even as authoritarian police confiscated fuel that the truckers were using to stay warm at night, the protestors' responses remained uniformly nonviolent.

The protestors and their allies showed exceptional fortitude and restraint in response to the massive state and corporate powers arrayed against them. Unwilling to face the truckers himself and meet with his own aggrieved citizens, Prime Minister Trudeau invoked the Emergency Act for the first time in Canadian history. Armed thereby with unprecedented powers, he sent in police to forcibly remove the truckers from the city. In a move of astonishing hubris and overweening authoritarian control, without a court order Trudeau also froze the bank accounts of the protestors, and even of Canadians who donated money to the convoy. Private banking and investment firms complied with this directive, not grudgingly but eagerly, turning on their own clients to do the government's bidding and rid society of these "unclean" elements.

The true story of what happened to the truckers should not be forgotten. McGinnis' *Unjustified* sets the record straight on an event that was of extraordinary importance not only for Canada but for the entire world. I warmly recommend this book to all who care about the protection of our civil liberties from authoritarian encroachments."

~ Aaron Kheriaty, MD, fellow and director of the Bioethics and American Democracy Program at the Ethics and Public Policy Center in Washington, DC. He formerly taught psychiatry at the UCI School of Medicine, was the director of the Medical Ethics Program at UCI Health, and was the chairman of the ethics committee at the California Department of State Hospitals. He is the author of The New Abnormal: The Rise of the Biomedical Security State.

"Twenty years from now, when we look back on this moment in history, we will wish that more people wrote about what they were seeing, not just the facts of government collusion, institutional corruption, and our deep culture of silence, but how those things translated into our lived experiences as citizens, spouses, parents, and friends. *Unjustified* makes a valuable contribution to the record of events related to the Freedom Convoy. By offering a day-by-day, blow-by-blow account of the events of a month in 2022 that refused to be ignored, McGinnis brings to life the indomitable truth that freedom might be able to be suppressed for a while but there will always be people who are willing hold it in their hearts until the world is ready to listen."

~ *Julie Ponesse, PhD, author of* My Choice: The Ethical Case Against COVID-19 Vaccine Mandates, *chief of biomedical ethics at The Wellness Company Canada, and professor of ethics at Huron University College for twenty years until placed on leave and banned from accessing her campus due to the vaccine mandate.*

"Ray McGinnis was not convinced by the legacy media portrayal of the Trucker Convoy as a sinister crusade by seditious, ignorant racists. Disturbed by the inflammatory rhetoric, McGinnis made the decision to travel from his home in Vancouver to attend the November 2022 hearings of the Public Order Emergency Commission in person. McGinnis has written a comprehensive synopsis of the Commission hearings. In particular, he shines a spotlight on the testimony of the government agents responsible for intelligence gathering and public security during the weeks of the Convoy. That testimony, by the Ottawa Police Service, Ontario Provincial Police, RCMP, Canada Border Services Agency, and Canadian Security Intelligence Service, corresponded to the experience of so many of us who were present in Ottawa in those days. The representation of the Convoy by politicians and journalists as violent and dangerous bore no resemblance to the reality on the ground."

~ *Anna Farrow is a columnist-correspondent for* The Catholic Register. *She has written for the* C2C Journal *and several other publications, including Catholic World Report and Convivium magazine.*

"The confrontation between the Freedom Convoy and Canadian authorities in 2022 is a seminal event in the Covid-biosecurity regime saga. Powerfully and intelligently, McGinnis details the smears and the lies leveled at the protesters, the antidemocratic and disingenuous stance of the authorities, and the whitewashing of the Canadian government during the follow-up inquiry. Always rigorous and carefully argued, and always empathetic toward the people involved in these tumultuous events, McGinnis' *Unjustified* tells the compelling story of what happens when democracy fails and the people rise. An essential contribution to the historical record and a warning as to where our democracies are heading."

~ *Dr. Piers Robinson, Organisation for Propaganda Studies, is lead author of* Pockets of Resistance: British News Media, War and Theory in the 2003 Invasion of Iraq.

"During the pandemic, politicians around the world saw an opportunity to turn a legitimate public health emergency into an abuse of political power. Nowhere was this more evident than in Canada, where the Trudeau Government decided to stigmatize the Canadian Trucker Convoy. A spontaneous movement whose members protested forced vaccinations and violations of the Canadian Charter of Rights and Freedoms . . . McGinnis's work during the pandemic is vital to bring to public attention the lies that were being told in Canada under the guise of media cover, the abuse of political power, the consequence of catastrophizing in politics, and the subsequent farce that was the Public Order Emergency Commission."

~ *Paris-based writer and YouTube podcaster Hügo Krüger is a structural nuclear engineer who has worked on nuclear, oil and gas, and renewable energy infrastructure projects. His writing has appeared in* Rapport, Newsweek, Unherd, Spiked, Quilette, *and* Rational Standard.

"If you're looking for an authoritative account of the Freedom Convoy protest, and what the testimony at the Public Order Emergency Commission revealed regarding the government's flawed justification for invoking the Emergencies Act, you've found it!"

~ Keith Wilson is an Alberta litigator who led a team of lawyers on the ground advising the Freedom Convoy participants in Ottawa. He testified before the Public Order Emergencies Commission and was part of the Freedom Corp. legal team at the inquiry.

"This brilliantly researched analysis of the propaganda surrounding the 2022 trucker freedom convoy shows how badly Canadians were misled by the bullying and cover-ups of the Trudeau administration.

When, in the depths of their January winter, Canadians lined the country's major national highway to cheer on the beleaguered truck drivers who had been subjected to singularly punitive Covid-19 mandates, "the mainstream media told Canadians the protesters were white supremacists, Nazis, insurrectionists, and hillbillies. Politicians claimed the protesters were converging in Ottawa to overthrow the government. The CBC told its viewers that "Russian actors" were instigating the protest."

When the trucks arrived in Ottawa, the federal government, instead of rising to the occasion and negotiating with the organized, disciplined, and safety-conscious convoy leaders, chose to invoke and mis-apply the *Emergencies Act*, which is authorized to deal with threats to national security and sovereignty.

By statute, the use of the *Emergencies Act* legally requires a public inquiry after the fact. Author Ray McGinnis travelled to Ottawa to directly witness testimony of the extensive evidence of administrative cowardice and incompetence during the six weeks of the hearing.

McGinnis's book belatedly reveals to Canadians the unreported facts of the whole disgraceful saga: the shameful disregard for Canadian political traditions, and the failure of Trudeau's bought-off media—especially the CBC—to investigate and report both sides of the protest."

~ Elizabeth Woodworth is a former medical librarian, and author/ co-author of books and articles on nuclear disarmament, climate policy, 9/11 evidence, Covid-19 policy, and corporate control of the media.

"Unjustified is one of the most important books of our time. Ray does a deep dive into the false narratives created and perpetrated by Canada's ruling Liberal Party in partnership with the legacy media, and shows how the judiciary system is being weaponized against everyday Canadian citizens who voice their concerns. It's a must read for anyone seeking the jaw dropping truth around the Freedom Convoy, the POEC, and the ongoing persecution of Canadian political prisoners."

~ Tamara Lich is author of Hold the Line: My story from the heart of the Freedom Convoy. *As a volunteer with the Freedom Convoy Tamara was in frequent contact with members of the Ottawa Police Service.*

"As a journalist you have to always remember that you are a public servant. If you back down, if you don't try to find the truth, then you aren't doing your job. It's a huge responsibility."

~ Kristina Borjesson

Unjustified: The Freedom Convoy, The Emergencies Act,
And The Inquiry That Got It Wrong

Foreword by Rodney Palmer

Frontier Centre for Public Policy
203-2727 Portage Avenue
Winnipeg, Manitoba, Canada
R3J 0R2

Printed in Turkey
Cover design by Shalomi Ranasinghe
Typeset by Karl Hunt

Library and Archives Canada Cataloguing in Publication
Title: Unjustified : the Freedom Convoy, the Emergencies Act,
and the inquiry that got it wrong / Ray McGinnis.
Names: McGinnis, Ray, author.
Identifiers: Canadiana 20240373057 | ISBN 9781998365029 (softcover)
Subjects: LCSH: Freedom Convoy (2022 : Ottawa, Ont.) | LCSH: Canada.
Emergencies Act. | LCSH: Public Order Emergency Commission (Canada) |
LCSH: Vaccine mandates—Canada. | LCSH: Protest movements—Canada. |
LCSH: Truck drivers—Political activity—Canada.
Classification: LCC HM883 .M34 2024 | DDC 303.48/40971—dc23

ISBN 978-1-998365-02-9
eBook 978-1-998365-03-6

CONTENTS

FOREWORD

When the Freedom Convoy rolled into Ottawa on January 28, 2022, I had been out of journalism for twenty years. A call came from the Canadian Covid Care Alliance for which I'd been volunteering as communications advisor. "There are thousands of trucks in a convoy driving toward Ottawa to protest the Covid vaccine mandates. There is a filmmaker documenting their trek across the country. He needs someone on the ground in Ottawa to film the trucks when they roll in." Suddenly I was a foreign correspondent again, covering the largest news event on the planet but this time in my own country. I filmed the first day as tens of thousands of jubilant Canadians flooded the streets in front of Canada's Parliament to support the truck drivers. The truckers had just been handed a deadline, and potentially a death sentence, to get a Covid vaccine or be fired. They were the first group in the world to say "No. We've had enough." The heart and soul of our country was coming to our rescue.

On that first day, I had a hard time holding my camera still as countless sights of unbridled love and joy swirled around me. There were nurses standing with their colleagues who were suspended because they refused to be vaccinated. Veterans warning against the signs of creeping tyranny in Ottawa. Off duty police officers and Armed Forces voicing their support. This was Canada on display. There was free food and music. There were people handing out bibles and cooking hot dogs. Everywhere young children walked, strolled, or sat in wagons behind their parents as families joined peacefully to support the nation's largest labor protest in history.

If you were there, you'd see that the earnest protest had transformed into a joyous celebration. It was like Canada Day in the winter. But if you watched it on the television news you saw a different story. After covering dozens of developing news events like this around the world for CTV News, I knew the obvious script: "In the midst of a globally coordinated lock down, Canada's truck drivers saved the world today by being the first to say, "enough is enough."

But the news didn't report the news that day. The CTV morning show in Ottawa said the lead organizers were white supremacists. Prime Minister Trudeau called them "a fringe minority." Jagmeet Singh said they promoted "pure bloodlines".

I knew they couldn't all be that wrong. I easily identified the broadcasts as a coordinated misdirection. Classic propaganda. There were a hundred thousand witnesses on the streets of Ottawa. It clearly had nothing to do with race. Every race including indigenous was represented in the faces of the truckers and their supporters. I saw it with my own eyes, and filmed it hourly for the first five days. The wildly popular movement became known as the Freedom Convoy. So many Canadians sent them $5 to $50 that they raised more than $20 Million in a few weeks. It was the most swift and successful peaceful campaign for change that any living Canadian could recall.

However, The CBC, CTV, *Globe & Mail,* and *Toronto Star*—all news outlets I've worked for—lied to their audience and readers about the Freedom convoy. The media's betrayal of its audience, to me, was irrefutable. Canada was sliding into the behaviour of a totalitarian state. The CBC was being transformed from a public broadcaster into a state broadcaster to propagandize on behalf of the government. Soon we fell even further into the practice of dictators when our media publicly broadcast the physical punishment meted out to the most visible dissenters.

When I worked for CTV News in China in 2003, that totalitarian government had phased out public executions in Beijing. Now in Canada I watched dissenters being beaten by police on the CBC like a broadcast warning to all who objected to government policies. At this moment, Canada entered a new era of totalitarian rule. Hundreds of Canadians who funded the convoy with $50 donations had their bank accounts frozen. On Feb 15, 2022 Finance Minister Chrystia Freeland announced that Canadian Banks were being deputized to freeze the accounts of any Canadian for any reason. In her chilling dictatorial debut, Freeland gleefully announced that the new law giving banks control over human behaviour would become permanent.

In this moment, the concept of Canada as I understand it was finished.

It was the Senate that saved us. An antiquated redundancy built into our democratic machinery stopped the boy Prime Minister from executing a totalitarian coup over his people. Another failsafe, designed by wiser leaders of the past, is that triggering this virgin Emergency Act also triggered a built-in public inquiry, the Public Order Emergency Commission. On Feb 17, 2023, a year after Minister Freeland hid behind the Emergency Act to anoint Canadian bankers as the thought police of Canada, the Commission issued its long-awaited report. Unfortunately, it failed to reach the obvious conclusion that invoking the Emergency Act was not necessary. On that day many Canadians, myself included, exhaled their last whisper of hope for our democracy.

Almost a year later another of our great institutions woke up. A Federal Court ruled in a multipronged lawsuit against the government that the invocation of the Emergencies Act by Trudeau was not justified. The plaintiffs whose bank accounts were frozen under the brief invocation of the Act, were told the Government had no right to do it. Days later Trudeau's Justice Minister David Lametti resigned from his Cabinet post and in a further display of shame, resigned his seat as a Member of Parliament, covered his tracks by deleting the official Justice Minister Twitter (X) account, and slithered off into Canadian infamy.

The following examination of the toothless Public Order Emergency Commission, which failed to determine the obvious—there was no reason to invoke the Act—is required reading for anyone seeking to reclaim the democracy of Canada. Ray McGinnis is a great Canadian who has stepped forward to dissect the deeply flawed Emergency Act Inquiry, on our behalf. In this report, he has created an historic analysis of one of the most important moments in modern Canadian History. The failure of the Public Order Emergency Commission to escape political influence and deliver an unbiased condemnation of the consistently described "unnecessary" use of the Act.

This book is a natural progression of other citizen led investigations such as Canada's National Citizen's Inquiry, where I was called to testify on how the CBC transformed from a newsgathering organization which I worked for from 1988 to 1996, into a propaganda organization on behalf of pharmaceutical marketing and government agendas during the time of Covid. Even when Health Canada admitted on its website that hundreds of Canadians were reported to have been killed by the COVID-19 vaccines, the nationally trusted CBC announcers suppressed this fact, and falsely claimed COVID vaccines are safe for everyone, no doubt with catastrophic impacts for many who believed their lie.[1] With the undeniable risk of injury and death from COVID-19 vaccines documented by Health Canada, I was certain the CBC was using its best broadcasters as weapons of the state, aimed at our citizens.

This is how the government was able to lock down bank accounts and incarcerate the convoy's spokesperson Tamara Lich for thirty days on charges that were later dropped. It paid the media to collaborate in the campaign, and abandon its traditional role of questioning government policy. The entire sordid affair wreaks of the totalitarian, military, and dictatorial nations I was assigned to work in as a foreign correspondent. China, North Korea, and Syria commonly employ the tactics now adopted by Canada's previously trusted media.

When our Prime Minister called the truckers' peaceful labour protest a radical occupation, our news media repeated it with glee. We lost our democracy. We were left with liars controlling our thoughts. This is Canada's current political reality. As a nation we think we still form opinions and make our decisions willingly, in agreement with a majority. But that agreement is based on the idea that COVID-19 vaccines are safe, and the Freedom Convoy was a racist occupation. Neither are true. This leaves us only with a façade of democracy, long after it was effectively killed by those who quietly euthanized journalism.

The good news is more people are finally talking about it, writing about it, and creating documents like this book on which we can all agree, or disagree. But if you're going to form an opinion at all, you're first going to have to read the truth.

– Rodney Palmer worked as a journalist in Canada for twenty years. He was a general assignment reporter for the Globe & Mail newspaper. He worked as a producer and investigative reporter at CBC Radio and Television. Rodney was the foreign correspondent and bureau chief for CTV News based in India, then Israel, and finally China. He has also been a reporter at the Toronto Star, and a daily news reporter at the Vancouver Sun.

INTRODUCTION

The point of modern propaganda isn't only to misinform or push an agenda. It is to exhaust your critical thinking, to annihilate truth.
~ Garry Kasparov, political activist and former world chess champion

In January–February 2022, Canadians were treated to a spectacle of media hysteria and heated political rhetoric. In apparent urgency, headline news stories rivaled those of the internment of Japanese-Canadians in World War II and the 1970 FLQ Crisis. The Liberal government of Prime Minister Justin Trudeau required all truck drivers to get vaccinated in order to enter Canada. President Joe Biden's administration in Washington, DC, required vaccine mandates for truck drivers, but *only* in companies with one hundred or more employees. Along the Canada–US border, customs agents uniquely scrutinized truck driver vaccine status. Meanwhile, independent, self-employed truck drivers across the rest of the world continued to drive by themselves and deliver goods to international destinations unencumbered. In response to the Canada–US border measures, 32,000 truck drivers were thrown out of work when the January 15, 2022, deadline arrived.

A protest instantly materialized against the rationale for the vaccine mandates for truck drivers. On January 23, 2022, truck drivers and other citizens began a journey to Ottawa, arriving as early as January 28. As the trucks began to roll, the mainstream media told Canadians the protesters were white supremacists, Nazis, misogynists, homophobes, racists, insurrectionists, and hillbillies. Politicians claimed the protesters were converging in Ottawa to overthrow the government. The CBC told its viewers that "Russian actors" were instigating the protest. Freedom Convoy leaders like Tamara Lich had been under surveillance prior to the start of the protests against the government's pandemic measures and vaccine mandates.[2] Out of thin air, a tolerant society—heralded by the Democracy

Unjustified

Index as among the healthiest democracies around the globe—had hatched a hoard of a deplorable "feral mob" intent on fomenting a coup. As it approached Ottawa, local residents watching the news awaited Freedom Convoy protesters with horror, fear, and disgust.

However, the Canadian Armed Forces, the Canadian Security and Intelligence Service (CSIS), and the Royal Canadian Mounted Police (RCMP) sounded no alarm. No military checkpoints were erected along the TransCanada Highway to stop truckers in their tracks on the Rocky Mountains, Saskatchewan, Manitoba, or Ontario borders. No roadblocks were erected to stop seditionist truckers from heading west from Nova Scotia, Prince Edward Island, New Brunswick, and Quebec into Ottawa. Tamara Lich and others who became the face of the protest were not apprehended en route. Those in charge of the police, intelligence, and military watched the protest grow with a collective shrug.

When people commit acts of arson, they should be charged with that offense. But testimony at the Public Order Emergency Commission (POEC) found no protester in Ottawa committed arson. When people call in bomb threats to a hospital, they should face consequences for their actions. But no protester in Ottawa made bomb threats to any hospital. When people smash windows, loot shops, or commit acts of physical violence, they should be charged for these offenses. But no protester has been charged with or faces pending charges in relation to these kinds of acts. If there had been a plot to overthrow the government, this writer would support the prosecution of individuals involved to the fullest extent of the law. But no one connected with the protests faces charges of treason, sedition, conspiracy, or terrorism. There were off-color placards that read "F*CK Trudeau." But these did not meet the threshold for invoking the Emergencies Act. The disconnect between the long list of serious allegations made against the protesters—too numerous to name in this introduction— and what testimony at the POEC revealed is sobering and troubling.

Our media lied to us. Our political leaders lied to us. But many citizens, faced with an onslaught of incendiary depictions of protesters by the government and the media, believed what they were told. The emotional affect and media hype were arguably unrivaled in Canada's history. And the emotional reaction itself, to the stories in the media, has taken on a life of its own that fuels outrage to this day.

Canadians have generally thought of their country as among the healthiest democracies in the world. In 2019, the Democracy Index

Introduction

ranked Canada among the healthiest of nations, designated as having a "full democracy." The report published by the Economist Intelligence Unit detailed how "Canada has scored consistently well in the Democracy Index, thanks to its history of stable, democratic government. It continues to occupy sixth place in the global ranking, and has never fallen outside of the top ten." Canada was given full marks for "freedom of expression and religious and cultural tolerance," among the key pillars of determining a healthy democracy. In contrast with its other North American trading partners, the United States and Mexico, Canada was a beacon on a hill, exemplifying how democracy should work. In 2019, the United States was ranked twenty-fifth on the Democracy Index and designated as a "flawed democracy." Mexico was ranked seventy-first on the list.[3]

In February 2021, the Democracy Index ranked Canada as the fifth-healthiest democracy in the world. Norway was far ahead of the other countries, where it remained in the top spot. Iceland was alone in second place. A cluster of nations were ranked between third and seventh place in this order: Sweden, New Zealand, Canada, Finland, and Denmark. The United States was again ranked twenty-fifth on the list. Mexico had dropped to seventy-second place, just below Albania—in the bottom tier of "flawed democracies." Mexico was just above "hybrid democracies" like Guatemala, Pakistan, Turkey, and Lebanon.[4]

In 2021, notwithstanding the pandemic measures in place here and across most of the planet, Canada's democratic health remained in sync with the Democracy Index ranking for the nation that spring. On May 9, 2021, in an interview during the Brandon Gonez Show, Prime Minister Justin Trudeau addressed the matter of mRNA vaccine hesitancy, saying, "What do you do with someone with an allergy? What do you do with someone who's immunocompromised, or someone who for religious reasons . . . or deep convictions, decided that no, they're not going to get a vaccine? We're not a country that makes vaccination mandatory."[5] Canadians needed to be compassionate and empathize with those who were hesitant to take an experimental vaccine into their body that hadn't gone through standard trials that take years to evaluate safety and effectiveness. In May 2021, there was no plan to require mandatory vaccination or pressure citizens to get vaccinated or else suffer consequences for not getting vaccinated. There was no talk of the unvaccinated facing consequences of getting fired from their jobs or being denied employment insurance.

xvii

Despite the lockdown mandates, masking, and social distancing, Canadians were, for the most part, going along with the Liberal government in Ottawa. As seen in the prime minister's statements in May 2021, there was still a veneer of classical liberalism in the language and tone of the government.

Classical liberalism began with the invention of the printing press, the flowering of culture in the vernacular (non-Latin) languages among the commoners, and widespread educational reform. It advanced the need for noninterference and independence of citizens under the rule of law. The word "liberal" comes from the Latin *liber*, which means "free." In his book, *Liberalism*, John Gray writes that classical liberalism consists of four pillars.

The first pillar of liberalism stressed the primacy of the person against any collectivity. Talk of what is best for the "collective good" went against the rights of the individual. Second, liberalism stressed egalitarian values, granting citizens and noncitizens the same basic moral status. The third pillar of liberalism embraced universal inclusion of all persons, regardless of any distinguishing features. Each person had the same moral worth, regardless of the property they owned, their personal wealth, their status in society, and their sexuality, gender, race/ethnicity, creed, ability, or health status. The fourth pillar of liberalism encouraged the general public to participate in the march of human progress. This could be achieved through critical thinking in order to advance social well-being.[6]

In the eighteenth and nineteenth centuries, liberal politicians championed causes that included the six-day/forty-eight-hour workweek, welfare, child labour laws, public schooling, freedom of speech, freedom of the press, universal suffrage, unemployment insurance, social security, and the abolition of slavery. Liberalism also advanced the value of bodily integrity. This included (i) a woman's right to choose whether or not to have an abortion, (ii) the right to not be sold into slavery or forced labour, (iii) the right not to be tortured, (iv) the right not to be sexually assaulted, and (v) the right to the security of one's person. The latter included informed decisions about medical treatments and procedures.

Following Justin Trudeau's election in 2015, many Canadians looked forward to the "Sunny Ways" the new prime minister had campaigned on. The door was open to an ever-widening culture of inclusion and openness. Canada liberalized its laws to make possession of cannabis legal. There were strides being made to follow up on pledges of reconciliation with the indigenous peoples of Canada. September 30 was designated as a National Day for Truth and Reconciliation, marking a new holiday.

Introduction

On New Year's Day 2020, Canadians glimpsed a horizon of seemingly unstoppable promise. Our self-perception was that we Canadians were a force for good. We sent peacekeepers to war-torn areas. We were among the first tier of humanitarians. Where there was injustice, we made efforts to let justice reign. Where there was wrong done, we stepped up to the plate to make things right. At home we were tolerant. We listened to each other. We searched to find a middle ground and a way forward. We aired our differences of opinion on the CBC's *Cross Country Checkup*. We learned that talking to people with whom we disagreed was a way to learn and grow. It was also a way to understand people instead of othering them and rushing to pass judgment.

As Canadians, our sense of our own nobility was often one we contrasted with Americans. Ranked at number twenty-five by the Democracy Index, the United States was among the "flawed democracies" in need of improvement and correction. In Canada, many of us looked on in horror at the Trump candidacy for president and his pledge to "build a great, great wall." During the 2016 campaign, Donald Trump exclaimed, "We will build a great wall along the southern border—and Mexico will pay for the wall. 100 percent. They don't know it yet, but they're gonna pay for the wall."[7] But liberals objected to the idea that walls, like the Berlin Wall, were symbols of restriction on freedom of movement. In 2016, it was a rallying cry for self-described liberals and progressives in America to keep Trump out of office. Most of us in Canada were rooting for whoever the Democrats put forward, Bernie Sanders or Hilary Clinton.

There were other examples going back decades. For better or worse, we Canadians prided ourselves on being above the political hysteria seen by the McCarthyism of the late 1940s and the mid-1950s. During that era, one person after the next appeared before either the House Un-American Activities Committee or the US Senate's Permanent Subcommittee on Investigations, chaired by Senator Joseph McCarthy. Individuals were asked, "Are you now, or have you ever been, a member of the Communist Party?" Careers in politics, the military, government, and Hollywood were ended. There was a "Lavender scare," where those "suspected of being homosexual" lost their jobs. Between 1947 and 1950, over 1,700 applicants to federal jobs were denied the positions due to allegations of homosexuality.[8] Though "homosexuality" was illegal in Canada until the Criminal Law Amendment Act of 1968–1969 was passed, Canadians could congratulate themselves for advancing the rights of sexual minorities.

This included Canada being among the first nations to legalize same-sex marriage.[9]

Growing up in Canada, I felt fortunate to turn on the CBC and listen to *As It Happens, The National, The Journal,* and *The Fifth Estate.* I knew that the news I listened to didn't always get the story right. But I also knew there were other countries where people were constantly told lies. In 1988, I read an article in the *Washington Post* describing how whole chapters of Soviet history had been airbrushed to make the Soviet Union look good. All references to the purges of political and military adversaries, and famine in Ukraine, disappeared. Any suggestion of the appearance of failure, violence, corruption, or misrule had been removed from textbooks and exams for students of Soviet history. The *Washington Post* detailed how the chickens had come home to roost:

> The Soviet Union has canceled final history examinations for elementary and high school students because the textbooks used in schools, according to the government newspaper *Izvestia,* are collections of "lies." . . . "The guilt of those who fooled generation after generation is gigantic and without measure," *Izvestia* said in a front-page article last night. "They poisoned with lies the minds and souls" of Soviet students. . . . *Izvestia* said that articles now being published in the press contradict what students are forced to learn in school. "The history exam can be canceled," *Izvestia* said, "but no one has a right to cancel history itself, no matter how painful. It continues, and everyone now living must take part in its creation. . . . Today, we are reaping the bitter fruit of our own moral compromises and are paying for those things that we mutely accepted and supported and now do not know how to explain to our children."[10]

The distortion by the Soviet Union of its own history took many decades for the nation to confront. It was only in the final decade of the USSR under Mikhail Gorbachev that the nation began to confront its difficult past.

In the past decades, Canadian prime ministers have sought to admit past mistakes and seek to reconcile our nation with the skeletons in our own closet. This has included Prime Minister Brian Mulroney's apology for the "internment of Japanese-Canadians during World War II." He later issued an apology to Italian-Canadians declared "enemy aliens" when Italy declared war on Canada in 1940, and many Italian-Canadians were detained during World War II. Prime Minister Stephen Harper issued an apology in the House of Commons for the head tax imposed on Chinese immigrants between 1885 and 1923. In 2008, he gave an apology for Canada's residential-school system, which more than 150,000 indigenous children attended from the 1840s to 1996. In 2016, Prime Minister Justin Trudeau issued an apology for the Komagata Maru incident, in which a shipload of migrants from India was turned away from Vancouver in 1914. And in 2018, Justin Trudeau gave an apology for Canada's decision in 1939 to reject an asylum request from more than 900 German Jews aboard the MS St. Louis, 254 of whom died in the Holocaust.[11]

It is laudable that federal governments have apologized for various harms done to different peoples throughout our nation's history. One might hope that such apologies would inform the course of future conduct by the government toward its citizens. Sadly, the story of the Freedom Convoy illustrates how quickly our nation can succumb to finding scapegoats, to fearing the stranger. The official account of the nature of the protests in January and February 2022 and the justification for invoking the Emergencies Act require perspective. A good place to begin is by paying attention to police testimony at the Public Order Emergency Commission. We need to separate the facts on the ground from the received media narrative. Some future retrospectives may record that in these times Canadians reaped "the bitter fruit of our own moral compromises and are paying for those things that we mutely accepted and supported and now do not know how to explain to our children."

The chapters of this book begin with the Freedom Convoy protest from the point of view of the protesters. I describe the official narrative broadcast that the media presented and politicians pitched in response to the protest. Attention is given to the reasons for the invocation of the Emergencies Act and the testimony of a variety of witnesses before the POEC. Testimony from the city of Ottawa staff details that a plan was reached with the protesters. On the morning of February 14, 2022, city officials were taking photos of the license plates of over a hundred protest vehicles that left a four-by-five block area in downtown Ottawa. Police testimony demonstrates there was no credible threat to the nation's security. Testimony by senior government bureaucrats and politicians reveals how the language of "threat to national security" was made fungible. The POEC Report itself watered down the language of *threat*, broadened the definition of *violence*, and defanged the triggers for invoking a national emergency. This should concern Canadians of all political stripes.

The official story about what happened during the protest is a case study in propaganda. This is not a word I use lightly. In the past few years, Canadians have witnessed the collapse of liberalism in Canada and the emergence of an illiberal society. We have learned not to question any premise made by government leaders, public health officials, or the media. This is not good for our democracy. Until we examine what happened, we won't have a common language for understanding what we've been through. We need to get this story straight before another virus comes along. We cannot risk having our democratic rights hobbled again by the state in the name of keeping us safe with coercive measures when 99.75 percent of the population survives infection.

The Emergencies Act needs to have a high threshold that must be met in order for a national emergency to be declared. The four specific triggers named in the Act need to be retained. The POEC Report recommends removing espionage, sabotage, serious acts of violence, and a plot to overthrow the government as thresholds for triggering a national emergency. With a blank slate, the executive branch is given too much room to invoke an emergency based solely on ungrounded assumptions. On February 14, 2022, all the border points were ranked at their lowest threat level. Police intelligence reports stated that protesters in Ottawa posed no credible threat to the nation. This should have provided a solid basis for those in government to calm down. Instead, they catastrophized about worst-case scenarios that were not materializing. What a threat to national security means should be strictly defined.

Going forward, Canadians need to ask themselves what they expect from political leadership. On February 14, 2022, the federal government had the option to deal with the Freedom Convoy protest under the very considerable powers that exist under the laws of Canada. Our collective understanding of what constitutes a threat to national security has suffered. It has not been aided by a political establishment whose default position, when citizens ask them to be accountable for their costly decisions, is to run around yelling, "the sky is falling." The definition of "threat to the security of Canada" has been made fungible. Some in the press have lauded the POEC recommendations in its report. But these do not offer the remedy we require. As the pandemic eases, one of the patients remaining in the hospital is Canadian democracy. However, the Judicial Review by Justice Richard Mosley ruled the government's proclamation of the Emergencies Act was illegal. This paves the way to restore peace, order and good government in Canada.

Introduction

We have shifted from an open society where people can have difficult civil discussions about challenging issues. We are becoming a closed-down society where people know not to voice opinions or raise issues when they are met with silence, shaming, or vitriol. Russian chess master Garry Kasparov said in 2017, "The point of modern propaganda isn't only to misinform or push an agenda. It is to exhaust your critical thinking, to annihilate truth." The propaganda of the past few years in Canada has impaired the lure of engaging in critical thinking. And truth? Do we really care about the truth anymore? In these proto-authoritarian times, what is taking its place? Have we become afraid of democracy?

CHAPTER ONE

PROTEST OR INSURRECTION?

At any given moment there is an orthodoxy, a body of ideas which it is assumed all right-thinking people will accept without question. It is not exactly forbidden to say this, that or the other, but it is "not done" to say it, just as in mid-Victorian times it was "not done" to mention trousers in the presence of a lady. Anyone who challenges the prevailing orthodoxy finds himself silenced with surprising effectiveness. A genuinely unfashionable opinion is almost never given a fair hearing, either in the popular press or in highbrow periodicals.

~ George Orwell, "Freedom of the Press"

In January 2022, Canadian mainstream media and politicians described an unruly mob headed for Ottawa. On January 26, 2022, Prime Minister Justin Trudeau told Canadians there was a "fringe minority" with "unacceptable views" coming to Ottawa in a "so-called freedom convoy."[12] Protesters began arriving in Ottawa on January 28, with the majority arriving the following day.

Protest leaders worked with Ottawa Police Service Police Liaison Teams to ensure emergency lanes in downtown Ottawa remained open. On two occasions, an Ontario court ruled the protests in Ottawa could proceed. The second ruling, on February 16, 2022, took into account the protesters adhering to the February 7 injunction against honking of horns. There was no looting, no acts of actual physical violence, and no smashing of windows. Police and intelligence agencies testified to the lack of criminal activity. Nonetheless, inflammatory rhetoric coming from politicians and the media depicted the protesters as "terrorists," "mercenaries," and "insurrectionists."

1

Protest leaders held press conferences, welcoming an opportunity to meet with government leaders, including public health officials. They wanted to have a discussion about the pandemic measures. Could dialogue lead to a breakthrough, a win-win? Even when unions and management are in tough negotiations during a strike, there can be a breakthrough with an unexpected way forward to resolve matters. Face-to-face dialogue was always the first step to learning if there was a path forward. A seventy-three-page plan by the Ontario Provincial Police included recommendations that the federal government enter into dialogue with the protesters. The government did so in 2020 when First Nations protesters disrupted rail service, ferry sailings, and pipeline construction and blockaded an Ontario highway. But in 2022, the Liberal government was in no mood for dialogue. Policing agencies and even the Ontario Attorney-General had suggested the federal government engage in dialogue with the protesters. But the protesters were depicted as impossible, unreasonable people incapable of participating in discussion.

Yet, in an effort to defuse the situation, on February 12, 2022, protest leaders came to an agreement with the City of Ottawa to remove 75 percent of protest vehicles from the city between February 14 and 16. By 12 p.m., February 14, 102 vehicles had been removed. Hours later, at 4:30 p.m., February 14, Justin Trudeau invoked the Emergencies Act to crush the protest. The bank accounts of some hundreds of protesters were frozen. In Windsor, Ontario, protesters and police were able to reach an agreement to clear the blockade at the Ambassador Bridge by late on February 13. Concerning conspiracy charges against four protesters in Coutts, Alberta, were dealt with under the existing laws of the land on the night of February 13 and into February 14.

After the February 18 police crackdown on protesters, Bill Blair, the minister of emergency preparedness, said it was "textbook" police action. "It restored my pride in my profession." Blair continued, ". . . what I witnessed (was) . . . an entirely professional proportional, measured response. They moved slowly, methodically, respectfully. . . . I've never seen it done better than what I witnessed here in the City of Ottawa as they . . . peacefully as possible, brought this to a resolution."[13] Cell phone and livestreaming video of the police action on February 18 told a different story.

On February 22, the Liberal–NDP coalition ratified the invocation of the Emergencies Act. But a day later, the Act was rescinded. The invocation was before the Canadian Senate, and based on senators' statements, it looked like the Act might be defeated. Attorney General David Lametti warned in memos presented as evidence before the POEC that the government "had to get ahead of the NDP," who were starting to show signs of discontent in the face of the "emergency" having evaporated. The Emergencies Act legislation of 1988 required that, on the occasion of its use, an inquiry must be held to determine if it was justified.

CHAPTER TWO

WHAT SPARKED
THE PROTEST?

The biggest thing for me was that informed consent was being absolutely ignored. . . . The lockdowns made absolutely no sense. The vilification of Canadians by the Prime Minister was shocking.
~ Tom Marazzo, Freedom Convoy volunteer, POEC, November 2022

During the pandemic, truck drivers were designated as essential service workers, transporting groceries, hospital supplies, factory parts, and other critical goods. In March 2021, Justin Trudeau called them "heroes." On Twitter, Trudeau offered, "While many of us are working from home, there are others who aren't able to do that—like truck drivers who are working day and night to make sure our shelves are stocked. So, when you can, please #ThankATrucker for everything they're doing and help them however you can."[14]

But in November 2021, the Canadian government announced the truck driver exemption from vaccination would end. Drivers would soon be required to show proof of vaccination in order to cross back into Canada from the United States. The Canadian Chamber of Commerce, the Canadian Manufacturing Coalition, the Canadian Trucking Alliance (CTA), and the Private Motor Truck Council of Canada (PMTC) were among those urging the government to reverse policy.

The PMTC warned that "over 31 thousand cross-border truckers will leave the industry." The CTA had similar estimates of drivers who would exit the industry. The PMTC estimated that if the government postponed its regulation until at least April 15, 2022, only "22,800 drivers would exit the cross-border industry if given the extra time" to decide whether to get vaccinated.[15]

The government didn't produce any statistics proving truck drivers, who travel alone in their trucks, were a source of COVID-19 infection in Canada. One could infer, by the governments' hard line, that there was a solid basis for fearing truck drivers were spreading COVID-19 when crossing the international border. But not when they travelled inter-provincially.

When asked in January 2022 by the House of Commons health committee, "Neither Health Minister Jean-Yves Duclos nor Chief Public Health Officer Dr. Theresa Tam were able to provide any data about COVID-19 and truck drivers."[16] It was not enough for the Public Health Agency of Canada to advise all truck drivers who were ill with any symptoms to stay home. It was not enough to simply require truck drivers to take a PCR rapid test before a trip across the border, allowing drivers who tested negative to proceed. It didn't matter that truck drivers were not interacting with the most vulnerable seniors in living assisted facilities. Or that the overall infection fatality rate for COVID-19 was about 0.25 percent, with 99.75 percent of the population who got Covid surviving infection.[17]

There were no vaccine requirements for truck drivers entering Mexico. At the US–Mexico border, there were very few long-haul drivers that crossed into the United States. It had already been the custom for long-haul drivers to remain in Mexico and for crossing carriers with B-1 visas to drag the trailers across the border into the United States.[18]

For truck drivers entering the United States, Labor Secretary Marty Walsh clarified the Biden administration's new regulations. There was a lot of pushback from the trucking industry in response to news headlines about what Biden was planning. "The ironic thing is most truckers are not covered by this, because they're driving a truck, they're in a cab, they're by themselves, they wouldn't be covered by this," Walsh said. Though they were often framed as equivalent to the Trudeau mandates for truck drivers, the Biden administration mandates were less restrictive compared to the new Canadian regulations.

The US administration mandate exempted workers "who do not report to a workplace where other individuals such as coworkers or customers are present." This included truck drivers alone in their cabs, according to the US Department of Labor.[19]

Further eroding the Biden administration's vaccine mandate regulations was a ruling by the United States Supreme Court on January 13, 2022. The high court ruled that Biden was not allowed to force larger companies to require their employees to get vaccinated, undergo weekly PCR testing, or wear masks. The new regulation gave permission for the Occupational Safety and Health Administration to overstep its authority. The Supreme Court wrote, "Although Congress has indisputably given OSHA the power to regulate occupational dangers, it has not given that agency the power to regulate public health more broadly. Requiring the vaccination of 84 million Americans, selected simply because they work for employers with more than 100 employees, certainly falls in the latter category."[20]

Canadian truck drivers were not being deprived of making a living due to regulations in the United States. It was entry back into Canada that was now at issue. Canada was an outlier. In Africa, Europe, South America, the Middle East, and Southeast Asia, truck drivers were deemed essential service workers. Concerned about supply chains and economic well-being, other nations retained the same exemptions for truck drivers that were suddenly denied them when entering Canada at the US–Canada border.

Among those who joined the protest were several who later testified under oath before the POEC. Tom Marazzo served for twenty-five years in the Canadian Armed Forces, achieving the rank of captain. After retiring from the military, he lost his job at Georgian College in Barrie, Ontario, after he declined to get the mRNA vaccine. He was motivated to come to Ottawa based on his fears about what was happening to Canada. He came to Ottawa from Napanee, Ontario.

Marazzo testified, "The biggest thing for me was that informed consent was being absolutely ignored. . . . The lockdowns made absolutely no sense. The vilification of Canadians by the Prime Minister was shocking . . . I knew things were fundamentally upside-down with the approach that the government was using . . . shut down a store that sells kids clothing, but you can go to a store and get a case of beer . . . A kid in Calgary was playing hockey outside and police were threatening to Taser him." Marazzo told the inquiry protesters came to Ottawa to get the government to explain their policies. "We were trying to nudge them, to do anything to get them to talk to us. And to this day they've never spoken to us. . . . We wanted no part of being the government. We wanted the government to do the governing, but to listen to us."[21]

Tamara Lich came from Medicine Hat, Alberta. Lich testified, "At the time of the convoy there was rumblings of stopping . . . interprovincial . . . travel if you were unvaccinated. My parents live in Saskatchewan and my grandmother is in Saskatchewan and I have a daughter and a granddaughter in Manitoba. So, I found that incredibly alarming."[22]

Minister of Transport Omar Alghabra told the CBC on January 30, "No one should be surprised that there is work being done to get us there," regarding interprovincial vaccine mandates. But the chair of the Canadian Pork Council, Rick Bergmann, objected. He told the House of Commons agriculture committee on February 14, "Implementation of that rule will set us up for guaranteed failure. The reality is we're experiencing a significant shortage of trucks and trailers to haul hogs across Canada and the situation is worse than publicly stated." Bergmann insisted that such a policy would be "the straw that breaks the camel's back."[23]

Asked why she travelled to Ottawa, Lich said:

> I was hoping that somebody would come and listen to us and listen to the concerns that we had . . . about the mandates. . . . We wanted to be heard. We wanted to have discussions. We wanted to end the mandates . . . open a dialogue. . . . I heard from families that were living in vehicles because they had lost their jobs . . . and lost everything. I have the tears of thousands of Canadians on my shoulder, who everyday told me that we were bringing them hope. I saw little old ladies praying on their knees on the side of the road and I saw little children holding signs saying, "Thank you for giving me back my future."[24]

Daniel Bulford was a former RCMP fifteen-year-career officer who had been part of the security detail for the prime minister. He testified:

> I spoke out publicly against the federal government vaccination mandate for COVID-19 vaccines . . . after speaking out publicly, my security clearance was revoked. . . . I made the decision to resign. . . . We lost neighbours and friends who were perfectly fine to have relationships with us until the vaccine passport deadline kicked in . . . then we were no longer worthy to speak to . . . There was a very heightened state of anxiety about how much further the situation in Canada would degenerate. . . . The dehumanization effort had begun. . . . The ultimate problem was that the Canadian people . . . (were) led to believe that people like myself and my family were a threat to other people and their children, which was not true, by his (Justin Trudeau's) own admission in July 2021 on camera.

Bulford stated that prior to the convoy, he was ready to leave the country. "Seeing the convoy and the rallying of support behind it all across Canada restored my faith in Canadians. That they weren't going to let Canada degenerate further." During the Ottawa protest, Bulford became a key police liaison for the convoy. He had communications "regularly with the Ottawa Police Service, the Parliamentary Protective Service, the OPP, and the RCMP."[25]

Margaret Hope-Braun, a mother of two children in Peterborough, Ontario, was troubled by the hysteria in the media. "We were reading . . . Global News . . . about (not having) received a police report yet on how many . . . additional rapes had taken place in the city since the convoy arrived." Hope-Braun testified how she felt completely "safe" and "treated with respect" among the other protesters.[26]

Christopher Deering, a decorated Afghan War veteran in the Canadian Armed Forces, testified that he was wounded in Afghanistan. He came to Ottawa to protest because he felt it was his duty. "I couldn't grieve my comrades in Nova Scotia because I wasn't allowed to cross the border in my own vehicle, by myself to a cemetery where no one was living, and lay my flowers for my mental health. And I was denied that for two years."[27]

Independent journalist Rupa Subramanya interviewed over a hundred protesters in Ottawa to learn why they made the journey. She spoke to a forty-six-year-old protester named Ivan who emigrated with his wife, Tatiana, from Ukraine to build a new life in New Brunswick: We came to Canada to be free—not slaves. . . . We lived under communism, and, in Canada, we're now fighting for our freedom. Subramanya heard similar stories:

> Kamal Pannu, thirty-three, is a Sikh immigrant and trucker from Montreal. He doesn't believe in vaccinations; he believes in natural immunity. He had joined the convoy because the Covid restrictions in the surrounding province of Quebec had become too much to bear. He said that he and his wife used to do their grocery shopping at Costco until the government decreed that the unvaxxed would be barred from big-box stores. Since then, their monthly grocery bill has jumped by $200. 'Before, he said, 'we didn't look at the price of what we were buying. Now, we sometimes put items back because we don't have that much money.'
>
> Matt Sim, forty-three, who immigrated to Canada from South Korea, is director of operations of an IT startup in Toronto and came to Ottawa with his wife to join the protests. He'd had Covid, and then

he'd recovered, and he was skeptical of all the hysteria surrounding the vaccines. His family, back home in Korea, had lived through the Asian financial crisis of 1997, and that had made him skeptical of the media, the government, and powerful people in general. 'There's a group in power that always manages to create panic among the masses . . .' Sim said."[28]

As the convoy headed east into Manitoba during January's freezing temperatures, truckers themselves reported what was unfolding. Said one:

The convoy is 100 km long and growing all the time. The support people have is overwhelming. Coming into Winnipeg yesterday was pretty emotional. The com radios went pretty quiet because no one could find words to express what we felt . . . people packed on the shoulders of the streets. Cars parked and people for miles and miles on the ring road around the city. On the four-lane going out of Winnipeg . . . ended up driving 5 to 20 km/hour for hours and hours. People had camp fires going in the ditches, fireworks. . . . Crane trucks with the booms up with signs, lights flashing, and [Canadian] flags. The shoulders of the four-lane packed with people and cars. Overpasses packed with people. Tons of families, little kids all bundled up. Everyone was jumping, dancing, waving signs, flags, and flashlights. All in -30C.[29]

CHAPTER THREE

THE OFFICIAL STORY

*Given Canada's support of Ukraine in this current crisis with Russia
... there is a concern that Russian actors could be continuing to fuel
things as this protest grows, perhaps even instigating it from the outside.*
                                                    ~ *CBC, January 28, 2022*

But as truck drivers headed from the British Columbia coast on January 23, 2022, a media narrative instantly emerged. It depicted protesters headed for Ottawa as the worst of the worst. On January 25, a CTV headline screamed: "'So many angry people': Experts say online conversation around trucker convoy veering into dangerous territory." CTV interviewed Kurt Phillips, founder of Anti-Racist Canada, who warned that he'd "seen people online calling the trucker convoy Canada's version of the US Capitol insurrection on January 6, 2021, for the truckers to ram their trucks into Parliament, and people encouraging the hanging of politicians."[30] It turned out that on no occasion during the Ottawa protest did any trucks ram into the parliament buildings. No politicians were lynched.

On January 26, Global News carried a report by Marie Woolf and Joan Bryden warning of violence by protesters in Ottawa. Protesters heading to Ottawa were referred to as the "so-called Freedom Convoy." They referred to an anonymous video of someone purporting to be a Freedom Convoy protester. "One online video includes a man expressing hope the rally will turn into the Canadian equivalent of the Jan. 6, 2021, riot at the U.S. Capitol by supporters of former president Donald Trump."[31] This was in reference to a January 24, 2022, tweet by CTV reporter Glenn McGregor at 10:27 p.m. He had provided a link to a YouTube video where an unnamed potential Ottawa protester, according to McGregor, described themselves as a bigot and urged a "Capitol Hill Jan. 6-type assault on Parliament Hill." The YouTube video in question was soon taken down and its contents were unavailable for commentators to scrutinize. Aware of McGregor's tweet, Alexander Cohen, director of communications for Public Safety Minister Marco Mendicino, sent a text to Mary-Liz Power, issues and policy advisor to the office of the prime minister. At 9:22 a.m. on January 25, 2022, Cohen let Power know, "I've put Marie Woolf onto it. She's obsessed with this kind of stuff."[32] And by coincidence, Marie Woolf penned her scary news story a day later about the violent protesters converging in Ottawa.

The Convoy was next framed as an inspiration for Russian president Vladimir Putin. "Russian actors" had instigated the convoy. On January 28, CBC reporter Nil Koksal mused, "Given Canada's support of Ukraine in this current crisis with Russia . . . there is a concern that Russian actors could be continuing to fuel things as this protest grows, perhaps even instigating it from the outside." The CBC quietly retracted the statement on February 4.[33]

In October 2022, CBC Ombudsman Jack Nagler concluded that the broadcaster had breached its own journalistic standards. CBC reportage alleging Russian influence in connection with the protests was based entirely on wild speculation. Nagler stated, "there should have been evidence backing the claim" and advised CBC programmers to be "aware of the impact of [their] work."[34]

On January 29, CTV journalist Mackenzie Gray posted a photo of an individual carrying a confederate flag. Gray tweeted above the photo, "We've got our first confederate flag of the day here on Parliament Hill." Florida governor Ron Desantis' press secretary Christina Pushaw responded on Twitter to Gray's tweet, observing, "You claim to be a journalist, so why don't you interview him? You can ask him who he is—and why he is flying a Confederate flag. If you just post a picture like this with no context, it looks like you're implying the entire convoy are racists. How do you know he isn't a plant?"[35]

The *Toronto Star* reported, "The appearance of a Nazi flag at the 'Freedom Convoy' in Ottawa drew widespread condemnation from across the political spectrum. Opponents of the protest said it was proof of white supremacist sympathies lurking beneath the movement's surface, while supporters said it was unfair to paint the entire convoy as hateful because of a few bad actors."[36] The media chose not to focus on the hundreds of thousands of Canadian flags lining highways from the Pacific Ocean to the Atlantic Ocean and on Parliament Hill. One swastika trumped a sea of Canadian flags. However, the bearer of the Nazi symbol was not the subject of police or intelligence attention. For all the concern being expressed about ideologically motivated violent extremists, when one person appeared with an incendiary flag, no one asked the individual to come to a police station for questioning. No one thought to follow them to their vehicle and write down their license plate. When asked if he knew who the Nazi flag-bearer was, CSIS Director David Vigneault said he could not answer because of national security concerns.

Before the first protesters began to assemble on Parliament Hill on January 28, prescient Public Safety Minister Marco Mendicino warned Nazi and Confederate flags would appear at the protest.

Numerous tweets and posts online underscored the ethnic diversity of the convoy protesters. Indigenous drummers were leading the crowd by Parliament Hill in singing "O Canada."[37]

On January 29, it was reported that a woman was yelling "freedom" and dancing on the tomb of the unknown soldier. The *National Observer* asked the chief of the Canadian defence staff, General Wayne Eyre, for a comment. He responded, "I am sickened to see protesters dance on the Tomb of the Unknown Soldier and desecrate the National War Memorial. Generations of Canadians have fought and died for our rights, including free speech, but not this. Those involved should hang their heads in shame."[38]

On the morning of February 6, Matias Munoz alleged two arsonists came to an apartment building lobby in downtown Ottawa at 5 a.m. Munoz tweeted: "One of them taped the door handles so no one could get out." This apparently included the arsonists. According to the story, a tenant saw the arsonists lighting a fire in the lobby and asked if they were truckers. Then the tenant decided to go to bed without calling 911. Which is what you'd do if you knew you were in a building that was on fire. Ottawa Mayor Jim Watson held an emergency meeting of the city council, condemning the "malicious intent" of the convoy protesters. "Yesterday we learned of a horrific story that clearly demonstrates the malicious intent of the protesters occupying our city."[39]

On April 8, Rex Murphy reported in the *National Post*:

This week, we found out that the attempt to burn down an apartment building in Ottawa, which was so widely and wildly heralded during the Freedom Convoy protest, had nothing to do with the truckers. Please let this sink in. At the time, such was the volume of assumption, innuendo and outright allegation that everyone from Nanaimo, B.C., to Nain, N.L., formed the impression that this despicable action, an outrage by any standard, was the work of the truckers. Not true. False. Nothing to do at all with the protesters. It was allegedly the work of two Ottawa miscreants who were working alone.[40]

Convoy protesters were also accused of being terrorists. Ottawa City Counsellor Diane Deans referred to the protest as part of a "nationwide insurrection," and the protesters themselves were "terrorists" and "mercenaries."[41] A repeated talking point was that the protesters intended to orchestrate their own version of the events of January 6, 2021, in Washington, DC, here on Parliament Hill. Deputy Prime Minister Chrystia Freeland, Justin Trudeau, and others in the Liberal cabinet inferred a plot to overthrow the government was in motion. When crowdfunding efforts raised over $14 million combined in regular and cryptocurrency donations, media commentators alleged it was the work of domestic and foreign terrorism and supporters of Donald Trump. However, Barry MacKillop, deputy-director of FINTRAC, the federal organization that goes after terrorism funds and criminal money-laundering, told the Commons finance committee that there was not a shred of illegal activity associated with the trucker convoy.[42] The protests had nothing to do with domestic terrorism or money-laundering.[43]

Trucker Freedom Convoy lawyer, Keith Wilson Q.C., recalled that during the first week after the trucks arrived, they were vandalized.

Groups of Antifa were coming through at night in their black hoodies and backpacks and black jeans. And they would come when the truckers were sleeping and knife their tires and cut their air lines and spray paint the trucks. They would vandalize the trucks. So, each block had a block captain for that area of trucks. And they had a watch system so that when an Antifa person would show up, the trucker would grab them, call 911 and the police would come, arrest that guy and take him away. That would happen three instances in the night. Guess what the police chief would do the next day? He'd say 'we had three arrests for property damage in the downtown core last night.' The arrests were Antifa, the 911 calls were from truckers.' But Ottawa police left it to the media to infer that the vandals, those responsible for 'property damage,' were convoy protesters.[44]

In early February, Bernie Farber, chair of the Canadian Anti-Hate Network, decried an anti-Semitic flyer alleged to be the work of Ottawa protesters titled "Every Single Aspect of the COVID Agenda Is Jewish." It turned out the offending flyer was from a photo taken in Miami, Florida, two weeks before the Ottawa protest began.[45]

In addition, the truckers were painted as delinquent parents whose children should be taken away from them. "I can only say that there have been ongoing reports regarding child welfare concerns, and that we consider all information received to determine the best response," said a spokesperson for the Ottawa Children's Aid Society. After the Emergencies Act was invoked on February 14, bringing children to the demonstrations was prohibited. If a child was in the cab of a truck, it would result in a potential fine of $5,000 or up to five years in prison. Ottawa police said roughly 25 percent of the vehicles in the blockades had children in them.[46]

In an opinion piece to the *Globe and Mail*, former chief justice of the Supreme Court of Canada, Beverley McLachlin wrote, "The Ottawa truck convoy has revealed the ugly side of freedom." McLachlin wondered, "what does this vaunted 'freedom' mean? The answer is, everything and nothing. Everything: the right not to wear masks in public places; the right not to be vaccinated; the right to hold Ottawa's downtown residents and businesses hostage; the right to malign public officials and call for the Prime Minister's death; the right to shout epithets at people of colour." To date, no protesters connected to the Freedom Convoy have been charged, or face pending legal action, in relation to uttering death threats against Justin Trudeau.[47]

Freedom Convoy protester Pat King suggested that someone might shoot at Justin Trudeau in the future. As ill-considered as his comments were, they didn't result in King himself being arrested for uttering death threats against the prime minister. King was arrested at the end of the Ottawa protest. He was charged with mischief, counseling to commit mischief, counselling to commit the offense of disobeying a court order, and counselling to obstruct police.[48]

There were also suggestions in the media that protesters threatened to bomb the Children's Hospital of Eastern Ontario. These allegations were shown to be false, as reflected in the POEC testimony given by City of Ottawa staff Kim Ayotte.[49] Politicians lined up to rebuke a protest they described as "illegal." Yet, on February 7, 2022, Ontario Chief Justice McLean ruled the protest was legal. He wrote, "the defendants and other persons remain at liberty to engage in a peaceful, lawful and safe protest." McLean also issued an injunction against the honking of horns, which residents and businesses understandably took issue with.[50] He issued another ruling on February 16, again declaring the Ottawa protest legal. The February 16 order where the judge determined that the protest could continue its legal right to public assembly was due, in part, to his being satisfied that his horn-honking injunction of February 7 had been adhered to by the protesters.[51]

Public Safety Minister Marco Mendicino stated that "threats of rape" by truckers in Ottawa was one of the catalysts for the Liberal government invoking the Emergencies Act.[52] He also alleged protester trucks in Ottawa contained weapons.

Yet Mendicino's own staff were telling him the protests were peaceful. The Director General of the Government Operations Centre Deryck Trehearne confirmed that "the majority of the event was peaceful . . . disruption of government activities is minor." Ottawa senior Public Safety officials advised Mendicino that convoy organizers were encouraging participants to keep lanes obstruction-free, clear vehicles out of residential areas, and be respectful of the police.[53]

For a majority of Canadians following the mainstream news, the prime minister had fended off an insurrection. White supremacists, misogynists, homophobes, and transphobes had been sent packing. Nonetheless, the nation would have to go through the perfunctory exercise of determining if there was anything to tweak regarding the Liberals' invocation.

Passed in 1988 to replace the War Measures Act, the Emergencies Act legislation states there are unique circumstances by which the Act can be invoked. These are that "The emergency must be a 'national emergency', which means an 'urgent and critical situation of a temporary nature' that either '(a) seriously endangers the lives, health or safety of Canadians and is of such proportions or nature as to exceed the capacity or authority of a province to deal with it, or (b) seriously threatens the ability of the Government of Canada to preserve the sovereignty, security and territorial integrity of Canada and that cannot be effectively dealt with under any other law of Canada.'"[54]

In late April 2022, Justin Trudeau appointed Chief Justice Paul Rouleau to head the POEC. Rouleau had historic ties to the Liberal Party of Canada, serving in the Prime Minister's Office under Prime Minister John Turner. There was some concern that the government was setting up the inquiry to be a whitewash. Could the government investigate itself? Should the commissioner appointed have been one who received support on both sides of the House of Commons?

CHAPTER FOUR

A GROWING
COUNTER-NARRATIVE

I didn't encounter a single racist, white supremacist, or even a misogynist.
These were some of the warmest, friendliest people I've ever met in my life
(after) two decades here in Canada.

~ Rupa Subramanya, independent reporter
and downtown Ottawa resident

By the time Rouleau was appointed to head the POEC, already there
were articles in the press calling into question the media narrative about
the Freedom Convoy. Indo-Canadian reporter Rupa Subramanya wrote
several articles and was interviewed about her experience speaking with
the protesters.

Subramanya explained:

There was already a received narrative in place even before the convoy
and the protesters arrived in Ottawa. And this was a narrative that
was coming from the Trudeau Government, from the Prime Minister
himself. . . . I live in downtown Ottawa . . . within blocks of where all
of this was happening, about a five-minute walk. I really went there
as a resident of the city . . . I'd read about what all the protests were
going to be about, and all the mainstream media coverage of it. And
so, I had all this stuff in my head. But I wanted to go there and make
up my mind. I didn't want to buy any established official line here. The
reality of these protesters, of the truckers . . . they were not . . . a bunch
of disgruntled old white men—because that's what we were told. There
is this misconception that the protesters are anti-vax. This is another
falsehood. I think some of them are, for sure. But many aren't. Many of

the truckers are actually vaccinated. But they were there in solidarity with colleagues who were unvaccinated.

Subramanya also commented on protesters' concerns about public health officers ignoring people who got COVID-19 and recovered. "Several of the people that I met had actually gotten Covid and had recovered from it, and they felt that was good enough. The question I kept hearing (among the protesters) was 'Why is it something as old as time itself—natural immunity that you get from infection—not being recognized? Why are we doubling down on vaccines or nothing?' She explained, "I wanted to go there and make up my own mind."

> The reality of these protesters, the truckers, starting from Day One, is very different from the received narrative that was already in place—propaganda—because that is really what it amounted to. These people were a cross-section of Canadians. They were mostly working-class. I encountered people of colour. I saw new immigrants. I saw children. I saw women. I saw the old, the young. Franco-Canadians, Anglo-Canadians. A lot of camaraderie. I spent three weeks at the protest every day, several times a day. I didn't encounter a single racist, white supremacist, or even a misogynist. These were some of the warmest, friendliest people I've ever met in my life (after) two decades here in Canada. It was quite unusual that my perspective, as a person of colour who went into the protests, was so different from the mainstream coverage. There was this total disconnect between what was being said and what I personally experienced.[55]

Anna Farrow came from Montreal to attend protests on the first weekend. She published a guest column on January 31, 2022, in the *Catholic Register*. Reflecting on her experience, Farrow wrote:

> On Parliament Hill, I saw hundreds of Canadian flags and an incredibly diverse cross-section of Canadians. Imagine guys wearing hunting camo and an odd group of white boomers trying to drum. Throw in some Sikhs, a lot of little kids all wrapped up in snowsuits and an enormous crowd of Quebecers. Imagine them standing around in delight and bemusement, looking at each other and saying, 'Hello? Do I know you? Is that you, Canada?' For the record, I did not see one

Confederate flag or swastika. . . . We saw a lot of signs. One teenage girl's said: 'I lost my graduation; I lost my prom; Trudeau, you lost nothing.' The police, while we wandered around, did not seem concerned or on guard. I read this morning not one arrest was made. . . .

When I returned to the house, and my fingers had thawed, I turned to Twitter on my phone. I learned that Prime Minister Justin Trudeau and his family were whisked away for safety; that the CBC was speculating that the Freedom Convoy was directed by Russian operatives; that a former press officer for Stephen Harper deleted her account after being hounded for tweeting that the day's events felt like a happy Canada Day; that NDP leader Jagmeet Singh tweeted, 'today Conservative MPs have endorsed a convoy led by those that claim the superiority of the white bloodline and equate Islam to a disease.'

Say what? I felt like a cartoon character giving its head a shake. The friend I went to Ottawa with is the daughter of a Trinidadian-Canadian. She stared as I read out Singh's words. I felt a little sick. There, on my phone, was the mob. . . . Whatever you read about the Freedom Convoy, whatever your stance on vaccine mandates and passports, know this: the narrative being spun that the convoy is a fascist, white supremacist movement is a bald-faced political lie.[56]

Farrow said she didn't see a mob on Parliament Hill. But when she went online, she saw a mob of reporters spinning propaganda and defaming the protesters.

The Ottawa Police Service (OPS) held a press conference on February 8 stating that no protester was under suspicion for the attempted arson of a residential building in downtown Ottawa. The OPS subsequently charged two Ottawa area men with arson in March 2022.[57]

On March 24, 2022, Interim Ottawa Police Service Chief Steve Bell confirmed there were no weapons in protester vehicles in Ottawa.[58] During a press conference on February 17, a reporter pointed out that Public Safety Minister Marco Mendicino had been "insinuating for days" that weapons were being brought to Ottawa or were in Ottawa with the convoy. Mendicino replied, "I am not saying that there is an intelligence saying there are weapons in Ottawa."[59]

These and other allegations about the protesters were discredited in the months following the protests. Protesters had not called in bomb threats against hospitals, threatened, or committed rape. The woman who danced on the Tomb of the Unknown Soldier turned out to be from Quebec and was not involved with the Ottawa protests, despite the good luck of the media to catch her "freedom" yells with the cameras rolling. And video of protesters being beaten with rifles, kicked by police, and trampled by horses put the lie to Bill Blair's pride in the "textbook" police action to crush the protest in Ottawa.[60]

But these news reports challenging the initial headlines dribbled out over weeks and months. They were underreported. The majority of Canadians were still reeling and feeling threatened, disgusted, and agitated by the news reports about the Freedom Convoy protesters. Watching the nightly news, the spectre of seditionist, violent, racist, white supremacist truckers trying to topple the sitting government set in stone an emotional scar that has yet to heal. It was as if the media was depicting the Ottawa protests on purpose based on old talking points from coverage of the August 2017 Unite the Right rally in Charlottesville, Virginia. That protest *did* consist of neo-Confederates, neo-fascists, white nationalists, neo-Nazis, the KKK, and far-right militias. Yet it was clear from hearing persons of colour, who attended the Ottawa protests, that they—like the Sikh truck drivers serving food to other protesters—felt safe and were not threatened with violence during the Freedom Convoy.

For protesters, and those who supported the Freedom Convoy, news coverage confirmed a slanted domestic mainstream media bias resembling textbook propaganda.

An example of propaganda in the media is this news story from 1990 in the United States. A young girl testified before Congress, and her testimony was used to get Americans to back an invasion that launched the Persian Gulf War. On October 10, 1990, a fifteen-year-old Kuwaiti girl named Nayirah Al-Sabah gave riveting testimony before Congress about the horrors inside Kuwait after Iraq invaded. She testified that while she was volunteering at the Al-Adan Hospital in Kuwait, she "saw the Iraqi soldiers come into the hospital with guns. They took the babies out of incubators, took the incubators and left the children to die on the cold floor. It was horrifying."

President George H.W. Bush repeatedly cited her claims. "They had kids in incubators, and they were thrown out of the incubators, so that Kuwait could be systematically dismantled." Three months later, Bush launched the Persian Gulf War. The vote in the United States Senate was fifty-two to forty-seven in support of going to war against Iraq. Statements by many senators cited the testimony of Nayirah as key in persuading them to vote "yes." Amnesty International claimed as many as 300 incubator babies had been left on hospital floors to die. However, *Democracy Now!* and *Harper's* found none of it was true. The story was fabricated. None of the members of Congress hearing her testimony knew Nayirah was the daughter of the Kuwaiti ambassador to the United States. None of the senators questioned the news reports. Nightly news headlines were treated as a secular god presumed to be all-knowing and all-seeing.[61]

The groupthink in the American media convinced the general public that the viscerally powerful story must be true. The surname of Nayirah was never asked for during her testimony. Finally, over a year later, *Harper's* magazine reporter Rick MacArthur phoned the Kuwaiti embassy and asked who Nayirah was. MacArthur reflected, "Any reporter could have done this, but nobody had." He found out that she was the daughter of the ambassador from Kuwait to this country. "I don't think this country would have gone to war, really—sitting there at that point, if it hadn't been for this story, because this was such a powerful story and kept being repeated over and over again." When the testimony of Nayirah was discovered to be a fraud after the invasion of Iraq, Canadians could shake their heads about the state of democracy in America. As MacArthur noted in his book *The Second Front, Censorship and Propaganda in the Gulf War*, President George H.W. Bush "harnessed the fake baby killing story to help drive a reluctant Senate and public into rescuing the Kuwaiti royal family. . . ."[62]

Here in Canada, we have our scandals. But most of us in Canada assumed the news we followed was trustworthy. We could go for a walk down the memory lane of past government scandals and lies. But many Canadians had become conditioned to minimize or ignore unwelcome news about their own political leaders. As Canadians, we tended to tell ourselves that the lies told to us weren't really that bad. Especially if the lies told were by leaders of Canada's "natural governing party," the Liberal Party of Canada. During the Freedom Convoy protests, a majority of Canadians gave the Liberal government the benefit of the doubt.

Yet independent journalists like Rupa Subramanya and Anna Farrow wrote about the disconnect between live reports from the Ottawa protests and mainstream headlines. Here were female reporters encountering no misogyny as they walked for days among the protesters on Parliament Hill. Here was an Indo-Canadiale reporter free from harassment, encountering no racism. Ottawa police at press conferences, and in testimony before a parliamentary committee, confirmed that news headlines were wrong.

In a democracy, the free press is relied upon by citizens to remedy the problem of governments engaging in deception or delusion. The nickname for the media is "the Fourth Estate." This is because the media are supposed to scrutinize in public the words and deeds of the government. But the mainstream media didn't question the prime minister. When he was far away from the protesters, no mainstream reporter asked, "How do you know? Why do you think that the protesters are misogynists when you haven't been there yourself? Where is your proof the protesters have plotted a coup?" Instead, the mainstream media served as courtiers to the powerful. The media amplified every allegation against "an unruly mob." The official narrative about the protesters was viscerally powerful. The media headlines were accepted as unassailable by the Liberal base.

In contrast with the mainstream media in Canada, the international press was critical of the Liberal government. The *Wall Street Journal* (*WSJ*) asked, "Will Canadian Democracy Survive Justin Trudeau? His father invoked emergency powers in 1970—but that was against terrorists, not peaceful protesters." *WSJ* wondered, "Will Canada return to its peaceful, democratic roots? Or will this episode transform into something more sinister and undemocratic? Prime Minister Justin Trudeau has certainly acted like a tinpot dictator. Mr. Trudeau refused to meet with Freedom Convoy organizers or protesters in Ottawa. . . . [T]he PM was nowhere to be seen. Instead of finding ways to diffuse this tense situation, Mr. Trudeau's approach was to throw more gasoline on the fire. The absentee Prime Minister would infrequently grace the nation with his presence to mock and smear his opponents." In another editorial, the paper concluded, "Government's job is to maintain public order while respecting civil liberties. Canada has failed on both scores."[63]

The *Financial Times of London* (*FT*) wrote an editorial titled "Canada's Illiberal Response to Protesters." *FT* warned: "Canadian leader Justin Trudeau's invocation of the Emergencies Act this week in response to the occupation was a step too far. . . . The measures are designed to respond to insurrection, espionage and genuine threats to the Canadian constitution rather than peaceful protest, no matter how irritating and inconvenient. The right to such protest is fundamental to a free society."[64] *The Economist* editorialized that "a wise government would listen to them (Freedom Convoy protesters) and respond politely, taking their complaints seriously and patiently explaining why COVID restrictions, though onerous, are necessary for the time being."

Sensing the historic importance of this unfolding story, I flew from Vancouver to Ottawa to attend public hearings for a week in mid-November 2022.

CHAPTER FIVE

COMMENTS MADE BY PUBLIC FIGURES, MEDIA, NOT PREMISED IN FACT

The (media) narrative about what was happening in Ottawa was being controlled and was one-sided. There were a lot of good things happening.
~ OPP Supt. Carson Pardy

During the Public Order Emergency Commission, a number of police were called to testify. It was revealed that earlier on the day when the *Emergencies Act* was invoked, the Ontario Provincial Police (OPP) issued an internal intelligence briefing memo. Titled "Operational Intelligence Report," it summarized the Ottawa protest. The memo stated, "The mood today was again calm, festive, and family oriented. Speakers were again telling people to walk away from agitators and thanked the police for remaining calm. Many of the speakers were promoting love and peaceful protest, some even taking quotes from the Bible. Speakers were also wishing everyone a happy Valentine's." The memo noted there were "children on Wellington Street playing hockey."[65]

Supt. Patrick Morris, "the foremost authority in the Province of Ontario regarding Intelligence," with the OPP testified before the POEC. He said of the protest, ". . . the lack of violent crime was shocking. . . . If there was an actual threat, then there would have been an investigation, and if it was an actual threat, I assume the Ottawa Police Service would have laid a charge for uttering threats." Morris agreed it was "hard to lay a charge . . . or even to ascertain if it's an actual threat if you can't identify the individual."

Regarding the media coverage and statements by politicians about the protest, Morris stated, "I was concerned by the politicization and I was concerned by hyperbole and I was concerned by the affixing of labels without evidence to individuals' movements et cetera." In a letter entered as evidence at the Commission, TDF lawyer Alan Honner quoted Morris' letter, where it states, "But now the public discourse is dominated by political figures and the media, and the commentary is providing a very different picture from what law enforcement collectively gathered. It is painting a different picture. It speaks to extremism. It offers parallels to terrorism. It speaks of sedition."

Morris elaborated in his testimony that his letter reflected his concern about

> comments made publicly, by public figures and in the media that I believed were not premised in fact. . . . I was leading the criminal intelligence collection of information and the production of criminal intelligence in relation to these events. So, I believed I was in a unique situation to understand what was transpiring. So, when I read accounts that the State of Russia had something to do with it; Or that this was the result of American influence, either financially or ideologically; Or that Donald Trump was behind it; Or that it was un-Canadian; Or that the people participating were un-Canadian, and that they were not Canadian views and they were extremists; I found it to be problematic, because what I ascertained from my role . . . I did not see validation for those assertions. . . . I did not see information that substantiated what was being said publicly and via the media. And I found that the subjective assertions sensationalized . . . and exacerbated conflict. . . . So, the labelling was problematic to me.

Morris further stated in a letter, "I do not know where the political figures are acquiring information on intelligence on the extent of extremist involvement." He was emphatic. "I want to be clear on this. We produced no intelligence to indicate these individuals would be armed. There has been a lot of hyperbole around that."

During his testimony, Supt. Morris confirmed that at no point did he receive any reliable intelligence that there was "any risk to national security due to the Freedom Convoy protests." In cross-examination with Freedom Convoy lawyer Brendan Miller, Supt. Morris confirmed that at no time did any violence against property take place. No arson, no destruction, no vandalism, no bombing.[66] As protester Chris Barber later testified, even slow rolls of trucks on different Ottawa roads during the protests took place with police permission.

OPP Supt. Carson Pardy, testifying on October 21, 2022, stated that the media depiction of the protest in Ottawa was "problematic. The narrative about what was happening in Ottawa was being controlled and was one-sided. There were a lot of good things happening. We heard about the bouncy castles and there were prayer meetings in the morning. . . . This is a family event. Bring your kids. There's a bouncy castle. We can have fun. . . ." Pardy found media rhetoric about protesters being extremists "problematic . . . because I've been involved in events from the past, G-summits . . . where we had a lot of extremist views. There was fringes of it . . . that were not a major concern. . . . The profile of the protester at this event was unlike none that I've seen in my thirty-six-year career. We had everything from grandparents. You know, my first day on this assignment, I was shown a picture of two officers that had worked for me in the past, who were retiring, who were in the crowd with the protesters. We saw children. We saw a lot of crestfallen police officers, military, nurses. So, it wasn't your normal group of people you're dealing with . . . we relied on and trusted the intelligence as it came in on that regard."[67]

Margaret Hope-Braun, a mother of two from Peterborough, Ontario, was at the protest on Valentine's Day. During her testimony before the Commission, she recalled, "I witnessed hundreds of roses being offered to the police officers. There was a lot of love. There was a lot of trying to heal the divide . . . being created between us and the police . . . the streets of Ottawa were covered in roses that day."[68]

OPS, OPP, RCMP, Canada Border Service Agency (CBSA), and the CSIS were pointing away from IMVE (ideologically motivated violent extremist) threats. CSIS reported on the afternoon of February 14 that "Downtown Ottawa . . . was actually quite festive—not threatening to a passerby." CSIS entered as evidence before the Commission that they "had no concern with IMVEs in Ottawa."[69] In the aftermath of the Valentine's Day invocation of the *Emergencies Act*, Supt. Morris reported on February 22 that the Freedom Convoy protest was "not comprised of ideologically motivated violent extremists. The actual leaders are not violent extremists with histories of violent criminal acts."[70]

Former Ottawa police chief Peter Sloly testified before the POEC. He confirmed it was "correct" that at no time before Trudeau invoked the *Emergencies Act* on February 14, 2022, did the OPS issue any form of formal notice to the protesters that they had been deemed to be an unlawful assembly and they must disperse. The protests were not a criminal matter under section 63 of the Criminal Code. There was no declaration that the Ottawa protests constituted a riot or that the public assembly was unlawful.[71]

OPP Commissioner Thomas Carrique, with a specialty in terrorism studies, also testified. He agreed that "based on all OPP intelligence and the intelligence provided by the RCMP and federal intelligence agencies to the OPP . . . there was no credible threat to the security of Canada." Carrique confirmed it "would be my understanding" that in order to invoke the Emergencies Act, there needs to be a "credible threat." He agreed that the Canadian Charter of Rights and Freedoms protected citizens' rights to assemble and protest. He agreed that this includes protesting government policies. Carrique also concurred that the trucks that were arriving in Ottawa in late January 2022 "did so at the direction of police officers."[72]

If the protest in Ottawa had become unlawful, as determined by the OPS or OPP, the Riot Act could have been enforced and the protest declared a riot. Arrests would have ensued, all under the existing laws of the Criminal Code. But prior to the invocation of the Emergencies Act, not a single charge of unlawful assembly was laid against any protester in Ottawa.

On February 12, the cabinet was given a "Proposal: Trucker Protest Engagement" from Deputy Minister of Public Safety Rob Stewart. The proposal was supported by OPP Insp. Marcel Beaudin, who was confident Police Liaison Teams were ready to make contact and negotiate with protesters in order to defuse or end situations. In his testimony before the Commission, Beaudin confirmed that this plan recommended that "the political branch of the Government of Canada . . . agree to a meeting with the protesters."[73]

Beaudin testified that he was in contact with Police Liaison Team program analyst Leslie Jean. It was Jean who pointed out that federal government officials had met with protesters during the rail blockades of 2020, providing an exit strategy for the majority of the rail and pipeline demonstrators. He also suggested another exit strategy to end the protest would be to have Health Canada announce that since the Omicron wave had peaked, restrictions could be lifted according to a set timeline.[74]

What about the operation to clear the streets of protesters around Parliament Hill after the Emergencies Act was invoked? OPS Supt. Robert Bernier testified that "The plan I was developing was based on existing authorities. I was satisfied we were going to have all the authorities we needed to take action."[75] RCMP Commissioner Brenda Lucki testified that it had been her view that not all existing tools had been exhausted to deal with the Ottawa protest.[76] Lucki also regarded the detailed plan signed off by RCMP, OPP, and Ottawa Police as "an amazing plan," as outlined in a closing submission of the OPS legal team to the inquiry. Lucki, confident in the plan, had given it "the green light."[77]

CHAPTER SIX

AGREEMENT BETWEEN THE CITY OF OTTAWA AND PROTESTERS

Ottawa City Manager Steve Kanellakos was shocked at how reasonable and intelligent the Freedom Convoy protest leaders were to negotiate with.

~ Keith Wilson, Freedom Convoy lawyer

Serge Arpin, City of Ottawa Chief of Staff to the Mayor, testified that by noon on February 14, 2022, 102 protest vehicles had been moved out of a four-block-by-five block area in downtown Ottawa. Most of these had left the city. "Photos were taken of each vehicle's license plate as it began to drive away." The protesters were on schedule to remove 75 percent of the vehicles from downtown Ottawa and leave the city by February 16. With so many vehicles scheduled to leave Ottawa voluntarily, the need for tow-truck drivers would be moot. The remaining 25 percent of the protest vehicles were to be confined to Wellington Street along Parliament Hill, taking up their complaint with the Trudeau Government.[78]

Under testimony, Kim Ayotte, General Manager of Emergency and Protective Services with the City of Ottawa, confirmed that the movement of vehicles onto Wellington Street "got stopped by police." Movement out of downtown Ottawa away from the city or onto Wellington Street was not blocked or abandoned by the protesters. It was the police who blocked the movement of protest vehicles. Freedom Convoy lawyer Brendan Miller pointed out, "the difficulty in moving individuals to Wellington Street after the agreement was announced . . . was only stopped because the police wouldn't let them on to Wellington and because the police then also stopped them from leaving the streets they were parked on. . . ."[79]

According to Ottawa City Manager Steve Kanellakos, Freedom Convoy organizers were complying with the agreement to move trucks the day the cabinet declared a national emergency. Kanellakos told the inquiry he had no warning cabinet would invoke the Emergencies Act. He confirmed that no city of Ottawa bylaw officers or tow-truck drivers were ever assaulted by the protesters. In a phone call, Keith Wilson told me Steve Kanellakos was shocked at "how reasonable and intelligent" the Freedom Convoy protest leaders were to negotiate with.[80]

Specific testimony was provided by city of Ottawa staff, and protesters Tom Marazzo and Tamara Lich, and lawyer Keith Wilson regarding removal of 102 protest vehicles from a four-by-five block area in downtown Ottawa. According to their collective testimony, these vehicles left downtown Ottawa by noon on February 14, 2022. Commissioner Paul Rouleau and his legal team heard this testimony firsthand during the public hearings. They also had transcripts of these testimonies to refer to while the POEC Report was being written. Nonetheless, they couldn't summon the diligence to align the removal of the 102 protest vehicles with the chronologies provided by witnesses taking oath. Inexplicably, the POEC Report claims that the first protest vehicles only began to be removed at 1 p.m. on February 14, 2022, and that the last of these were removed around 5 p.m., a half hour *after* the invocation of the Emergencies Act.

Testimony at the inquiry from city of Ottawa officials and some of the protest leaders made clear an agreement to remove many of the protest vehicles had been reached. And that plan was proceeding. However, what most Canadians trusted as authoritative were comments by Public Safety Minister Marco Mendicino that the plan to remove protest vehicles had fallen apart.

CHAPTER SEVEN

EMERGENCIES ACT THRESHOLD FOR "THREAT TO NATIONAL SECURITY" NOT MET

It would be a stretch to say the trucks barricading the streets and the air horns blaring at whatever decibels for however many days constitute the 'use of force.'

~ RCMP

The Canadian government's justification for invoking the act was not based on any of the tests of the Emergencies Act being met. CSIS Director David Vigneault admitted the four criteria for declaring a public order emergency were not met. During cross-examination by Justice Centre for Constitutional Freedoms lawyer Mr. Hatim Kheir, Vigneault was walked through the triggers for invoking the Emergencies Act.

1. Was there espionage or sabotage? "No," said Vigneault.
2. Was there foreign interference? "We investigated foreign interference in relation to the event, including foreign funding, and we did not see these activities amounting to a threat to the security of Canada. No," said Vigneault.
3. Was there any serious violence associated with the protests against persons or property? "No actual serious violence," said Vigneault.
4. Was there a plot to overthrow the government? "No. Didn't even investigate. It was so nonexistent," said Vigneault.

During cross-examination of Vigneault, Commissioner Rouleau interjected saying to Kheir, "you could have skipped (a), (b), (c), (d) (Section 2 of the

Emergencies Act). It's been testified to many times that it wasn't met but go ahead." Hatim Kheir asked Vigneault ". . . this determination . . . that the *Emergencies Act* standard (that) the definition is broader under the *Emergencies Act* than with respect to under the *CSIS Act*, that was not the product of you reading the *Emergencies Act* and developing your own assessment." The CSIS Director replied, "that is correct." Vigneault understood the definition of the triggers for invoking the Emergencies Act as being contained by sections 2 (a), (b), (c), and (d).[81]

In the "Recommendation to Cabinet" section of Vigneault's interview summary to Commission staff, it states Vigneault "felt an obligation to clearly convey the Services (CSIS) position that there did not exist a threat to the security of Canada. . . ."

RCMP officer emails reflected a lack of urgency. "It would be a stretch to say the trucks barricading the streets and the air horns blaring at whatever decibels for however many days constitute the 'use of force.'"[82] When protesters arrived in Ottawa, many of them honked horns all day long and into the evening. Understandably, this was maddening and wearing for all within earshot. Area residents, business owners, even protest leaders found the incessant honking hard to endure. But accounts from local residents and protesters show that by early February the honking was now ending by 6 p.m. each night, though this was not the case in late January. On February 7, 2022, Ontario justice, Hugh McLean, issued an injunction against the honking.

Protest leader Tom Marazzo and other protest leaders took the injunction against honking seriously. They wanted the honking to stop. It distracted from the purpose of the protests, which was a hoped-for meeting with some government officials to discuss the vaccine and travel mandates and infringements of the Charter of Rights and Freedoms. Marazzo told me that protest block captains had instructions. These were to tell any rogue truck drivers who honked their horns after February 7 that they'd have air horn wires cut if they didn't cease honking. Faced with this consequence, the holdouts stopped honking their horns.

Anyone who has had to put up with a car alarm or incessant horn honking knows how infuriating this can be. Nonetheless, as RCMP correspondence showed, noise violations do not rise to the threshold of triggering a national state of emergency. There are other existing tools that law enforcement draws on to deal with noise violations. Honking in Ottawa was not cited in either the Decision Note to Justin Trudeau at

3:41 p.m. on February 14 or in the Privy Council Office Comment. Both the horn-honking-free Decision Note and the Privy Council Office Comment paved the way for the prime minister to invoke the Emergencies Act.

Former CBSA President John Ossowski testified that the Situational Report classed all border points at 8:30 a.m. ET on February 14 as "the threat is low." He confirmed that the threat level for the CBSA throughout the protests remained "low." A Situation Report, at 4:00 p.m. ET, again judged "overall threat is low." Half an hour later, the prime minister invoked the Emergencies Act. Asked about CBSA officers having the capacity to preemptively turn American protesters away from Detroit and Sarnia to support the protests, Ossowski said, "Well, it wasn't an unlawful protest at that point in time before the *Emergencies Act*, right?."[83] Ossowski testified that he did not advise anyone in the federal cabinet to invoke the Emergencies Act.

In a February 23, 2022, speech against supporting invocation of the Emergencies Act, Senator Denise Batters reminded the Senate that the Emergencies Act wasn't invoked even "during the October 2014 Parliament Hill shooting. And I remember that well, because I was locked in a caucus room for ten hours with my colleagues throughout." She underscored, "Both houses of Parliament were able to meet for weeks, mere steps away from the protesters. Prime Minister Trudeau and his senior cabinet ministers attended several question periods in House of Commons sittings in person. If there were a true public order emergency, surely none of that would have been allowed to have occurred."[84]

On February 4, 2022, Bill McCrimmon, Deputy Director of Diplomatic Security and Outreach Programs with Global Affairs Canada, wrote an email providing an assessment of the impact of the protests on the diplomatic community. McCrimmon wrote, "The Office of Protocol has not been made aware officially of any significant concerns by the diplomatic community in the National Capital Region linked to current ongoing demonstrations in downtown Ottawa. The RCMP Protective Operations Assessment Unit advised that there is no particular concern at this time for the diplomatic community."[85]

CHAPTER EIGHT

EXPANDING THE DEFINITION OF THREAT

A Public Order Emergency is broader as defined in the CSIS Act.
~ Jody Thomas, National Security Advisor to the Prime Minister

Jody Thomas, the National Security Advisor to the Prime Minister, was appointed on January 11, 2022. A month later she advised Justin Trudeau to declare a national emergency. Canadian Civil Liberties Association lawyer Cara Zwibel asked Thomas at the POEC, ". . . you understand that currently the definition of a Public Order Emergency in the *Emergencies Act* is tied exclusively and exhaustively to the definition in the *CSIS Act*?" Thomas testified "The Federal Government legal opinion is different, and there will be legal arguments to that end."[86] Lawyer for the Justice Centre for Constitutional Freedoms, Rob Kittredge took Jody Thomas through the CSIS Act tests for declaring an emergency. She confirmed there was no espionage, no sabotage, no foreign interference.

But what about serious violence? Thomas replied by swapping the word "serious" for "continual." Said Thomas, "There was continual violence in the streets of Ottawa. . . ." Kittredge asked her to be specific about what she meant by "continual violence." Thomas identified "harassment, people being followed, people being intimidated, the noise, the pollution. . . ." Yet, incidents of harassment, stalking, and physical intimidation are matters police address every day across the nation upon receiving a complaint.

In a phone call with protester Tom Marazzo, he told me he was continually in contact with the OPS Police Liaison Teams (PLTs). The PLTs would alert him if there was anyone blocking an emergency lane. Both protest leaders, police, and City of Ottawa officials agreed these needed to be cleared. Yet, on one occasion, it turned out an emergency lane in downtown Ottawa was being blocked by the City of Ottawa's own equipment vehicles. Marazzo confirmed that any protesters intimidating or harassing Ottawa citizens would be counterproductive to the aims of the protest. But the PLTs never brought to Marazzo or any protest leaders' attention a single case of a protester intimidating or harassing Ottawa residents. The disconnect between the rhetoric of protesters being violent and what was happening on the ground was problematic.

While several Ottawa residents testified to the irritation of the horn honking, no testimony emerged that pointed to any actual physical violence. Instead, "phantom honking" that was emotionally traumatic was brought up. Councillor Mathieu Fleury could only point to nonspecific "microaggressions" and "the noise, the smell, the fumes." Though he alleged a protester bear sprayed a homeless person who was a client of the Shepherds of Good Hope shelter, the allegation was hearsay evidence and could not be substantiated.[87] Eventually, Jody Thomas conceded, "No, not serious violence." In a February 21, 2022, email, RCMP Deputy Commissioner Brian Brennan wrote, "There was no serious violence in Ottawa, the main reason for the *Emergencies Act*."[88]

Jody Thomas cited "pollution" as one of the elements of "continual violence" during the Ottawa protests. And yet, the federal government continues to be ineffective in addressing unsafe, contaminated water in indigenous communities across Canada. In November 2020, Neskantaga First Nation held signs that read "Water is a Human Right: Lives Matter" as they protested twenty-five years of boil water advisories. In November 2020, the CBC reported, "In an audit report tabled in Parliament, Auditor General Karen Hogan said many First Nations will continue to live without access to clean water without long-term solutions to address deficiencies in their water systems. . . . some communities won't be able to get clean water out of their taps for many years." And so, boil water advisories remain the norm. But, apparently, this ongoing lack of access to safe drinking water for many indigenous communities across the nation is not the kind of pollution that results in invoking the Emergencies Act. Some indigenous communities might want to reflect on the lack of a federal response to the continual pollution for decades. Does the lack of access to safe drinking water in their communities represent a level of negligence manifesting in "continual violence" on the part of the federal government toward indigenous peoples?[89]

Considering the lack of serious violence, Jody Thomas quickly reframed matters. She stated, "A Public Order Emergency is broader as defined in the *CSIS Act*." She elaborated, "There's a range of threats that need to be considered when you're talking about this country, economic security; The threat of IMVE; The rhetoric of threats against public figures; The inability to conduct a livelihood in the City of Ottawa—as an example, the Coutts border blockade. . . . The threat to public institutions and the undermining of the confidence in public institutions."[90]

Thomas identified "economic security" as a national security threat. Yet, in contrast with the border point blockades in February 2022, the Liberal government dealt with the 2020 protests differently. From January to mid-March 2020, mostly indigenous protesters variously blocked construction of a BC pipeline, disrupted BC Ferry sailings, shut down CN Rail freight and VIA Rail passenger service for over a month, blockaded an Ontario highway, and more. Through eleven weeks of economic disruptions, Prime Minister Trudeau maintained the importance of engaging in dialogue with protesters to resolve matters.[91]

Deputy Minister of Transport Michael Keenan and Chief Economist for Transport Canada Christian Dea spoke at the inquiry about economic harms to Canada as a result of border blockades. However, Statistics Canada reported in April that "Cross-border trade between Ontario, Alberta and the U.S. was up for all major types of goods in February, with the notable exception of Ontario's largest commodity: vehicles and vehicle parts."[92]

On February 11, 2022, in an email to his colleagues, Dea concluded, "The current net cumulative effect (of the blockades) is relatively small." Julie Turcotte, the finance department's director general of economic analysis, dismissed a *Bloomberg* figure in a February 10 staff email. "Seems large to me!" wrote Turcotte, adding the numbers were "of course too cute to be really backed by analysis and most likely overstated to make up for nice media attention."[93]

As well, concerns about the wisdom of the vaccine mandate restrictions placed on truck drivers were conveyed to the Liberal government by several provincial premiers and sixteen state governors in the United States. They wanted the restrictions removed.[94]

The Coutts, Alberta, border blockade, and arrests were handled by the RCMP under existing Canadian law. Weapons and conspiracy charges are serious. But those arrested were now behind bars *before* the Emergencies Act was invoked. Convoy protester and veteran Jeremy MacKenzie was arrested on charges of "assault, pointing a firearm, mischief and use of a restricted weapon." But this was related to charges in Viscount, SK, in

November 2021 and not at the Ottawa protest.[95] However, the "threat to national security" was becoming fungible. "Threat to national security" was becoming an elastic term the government could shape for its own purposes in order to invoke the Emergencies Act.

The Liberals, on a legal opinion to expand the definition of threat, invoked the Emergencies Act. Asked about the basis for the legal opinion, Justice Minister David Lametti testified, "For reasons of solicitor-client privilege (he) could not describe the various kinds of legal analysis relied upon by cabinet." Justice Rouleau told Lametti that by taking this position the government is asking Canadians to "just assume (it) acted in good faith," to just "trust us." Asked if he agreed "that Section 2 of the *CSIS Act* has a different meaning . . . a different scope based in its reference in the *Emergencies Act*," Lametti responded, "I will neither confirm nor deny that."[96]

In addition to David Lametti and Jody Thomas, another person who recommended the prime minister invoke the Emergencies Act was Janice Charette. Named Interim Clerk of the Privy Council in March 2021, Charette was confirmed in her role in May 2022, three months after the Ottawa protests. She had a BA in commerce and served in a number of capacities as deputy minister (DM) of human resources, DM for immigration, and DM of Health Canada. Charette had no background in national security. She said under oath, "I'm not an expert in any of these domains. My assessment from a layman's point of view was it (the protest) was not legal." Charette's assertion contradicted Ontario court rulings that the protest was legal.

CHAPTER NINE

"A MEANING CAN HAVE DIFFERENT MEANINGS AT THE END"

Humpty Dumpty: "When I use a word, it means just what I choose it to mean—neither more nor less"
Alice: "The question is, whether you can make words mean so many different things"
Humpty Dumpty: "The question is, which is to be master, that's all"
~ Lewis Carroll, Through the Looking Glass

Janice Charette fretted that the government "didn't really have a full 360-degree view" of the protest. She urged her Incident Response Group to "really think outside the box." Yet, this didn't include meetings with some of the protest leaders. Since early February, protest leaders have wanted a meeting with senior Public Health Agency of Canada staff and politicians. Still, the government declined to meet with protest leaders. Even though this would have helped them gain a 360-degree view of the facts on the ground.[97]

As authorities scrambled to get a grip on the protest, consultants were hired to help the Ottawa Police Service get a handle on who the protesters were. Advanced Symbolics Inc. provided a report to the OPS that mused, "Are the protesters actually right-wing Christians, protesting vaccine mandates only as a ruse to get more disciples?" Consultant Erin Kelly offered, "Given that today is the Lord's Day, we are starting to see some of the real agenda here. . . . More evidence this isn't really about vaccine mandates. It's a movement by right wing Christians who used mandates as a pretense to gain a following. . . ." Police Chief Peter Sloly viewed this line of thinking as providing "really important insights."[98]

Deputy Clerk of the Privy Council and Associate Secretary to the Cabinet, Nathalie Drouin, explained one of the reasons the prime minister was advised to invoke the Emergencies Act. We "couldn't wait to invoke the Emergencies Act because then it would have been a national security threat." By waiting any longer, Drouin explained, "We would have been in a situation where the threat would have materialized." By underscoring her panicked reasoning, Drouin made clear no threat to national security had actually materialized. Asked about the definition of "threat" in the Emergencies Act, Drouin stated a "meaning can have different meanings at the end."[99]

Drouin took part in Justin Trudeau's February 14, 2022, phone calls with the First Ministers of the Canadian provinces and territories. It was clear to her that a majority of provincial premiers opposed the looming federal government decision. Drouin summed up that viewpoint: "that there is a risk that invoking the *Emergencies Act* can inflamate [*sic*] the situation."

Janice Charette was shown a memo where she commented on the legal advice the government was relying on as a basis to invoke the Emergencies Act. She stated in a Privy Council Office (PCO) Comment to the Prime Minister on February 14, 2022, "While there is no current evidence of significant implications by extremist groups or international sponsors, PCO notes that the disturbance and public unrest is being felt across the country and beyond Canadian borders, which may provide further momentum to the movement and lead to irremediable harms—including to social cohesion, national unity, and Canada's international reputation. In PCO's view, this fits within the statutory parameters of the Emergencies Act, but this conclusion may be vulnerable to challenge."[100] The Emergencies Act states that it is to be a measure "of last resort" when all other options under the laws of the land are exhausted.

Yet, not all other options had been exhausted. By February 14, OPS, OPP, and RCMP didn't view the protest as unlawful. Had it been deemed unlawful, the Riot Act could have been used to declare the protest a riot. As well, the OPS had signed off on a detailed seventy-three-page plan with the RCMP and Ontario Provincial Police to de-escalate the protest. Under testimony, Prime Minister Trudeau referred to it as a "so-called plan." When shown the plan during his testimony, Trudeau stated he had never seen the plan. Nonetheless, he asserted he had "no confidence" in the plan.[101] Short of invoking the Emergencies Act as a "last resort," the federal government also had the option to solicit the Canadian Armed Forces to intervene in an unlawful assembly. This option was not reached for. Both internal police memos and Ontario court rulings judged the Ottawa protests to be legal.

Charette was cross-examined by Canadian Constitution Foundation lawyer Sujit Choudry. Charette confirmed that CSIS Director David Vigneault was not asked to speak during the February 13 Liberal cabinet meeting regarding the need to invoke the Emergencies Act. Choudry said to Charette, "I would like to put this point to you . . . in a constitutional democracy, to prevent the abuse of executive powers by an elected government, it is imperative that the views of a professional non-partisan and expert security services be front and centre and that they not just be a factor, but that they be at the core of whether a government decides to invoke emergency powers."[102]

Nathalie Drouin jumped in, responding to Choudry's point by stressing other threats to the nation: "We saw kids, you know, being used as (human) shields." Children were sitting with their parents in their trucks to keep warm. Children were making snow sculptures, playing in bouncy castles, and playing hockey.

When pressed under cross-examination to substantiate allegations of rape committed by Ottawa protesters, Public Safety Minister Marco Mendicino said, "The absence of a criminal charge doesn't mean it doesn't happen."

Freedom Convoy lawyer Eva Chipiuk contrasted the Ottawa protests to a riot in Vancouver on June 15, 2011, after the Vancouver Canucks lost to the Boston Bruins. In a tweet she wrote, "Compare one night of Stanley Cup rioting where 268 people were charged with a total of 814 charges to three weeks of Freedom Convoy and eleven charges, ZERO hate crimes, and we don't know how many of those were protesters because @OttawaPolice did not provide those details."[103]

The *National Post* in an editorial wrote, "The Ottawa Mayor, if requested by the chief of police, could invoke (municipal) Section 4 to prohibit public assemblies, or perhaps more simply just impose an overnight curfew in the downtown area, so police could fine and even detain anyone not in their residence. Emergency management, whether for public welfare or public order, starts at the lowest level of government before it—if necessary—escalates upwards. The prime minister shouldn't be declaring a national emergency if the only result will be to prohibit assemblies or impose curfews. Having declared a municipal emergency, the mayor of Ottawa can do so, and the question is, why hasn't he?" As the police were not indicating the protest was an unlawful assembly, this may have been a factor in the City of Ottawa not reaching for this option. In any event, the municipal tools for responding to the protest at Parliament Hill should have been employed before Trudeau reached for the Emergencies Act to resolve matters.[104]

Before the Liberal cabinet retreat on January 24, 2022, Department of Public Safety Director of Communications staff, Alexander Cohen, and the Prime Minister's Office Issues and Policy Advisor Mary-Liz Power were sending texts to each other. Their text messages discussed the best ways to exploit a narrative to frame the protesters travelling to Ottawa as a "January 6 style insurrection" and as "extremists."[105]

Cohen and Power texted that they had friends at Global News who could push this narrative. Right on schedule, Global News ran a headline on January 25, 2022, warning readers, "Far-right groups hope trucker protest will be Canada's 'January 6th.'" Anonymous posters on a chat had made incendiary comments about their intentions for protests in Ottawa. Cohen texted that he was going to get Marie Woolf with Global to write a story in synch with the government narrative, which Woolf did on January 26.[106]

Yet, the experience on the ground as the convoy headed east indicated the protesters were peaceful. Global News had reported earlier that week that "Salmon Arm RCMP are expressing their appreciation to protesters who were peaceful Sunday (January 23) during a demonstration in support of the 'Freedom Convoy.'"[107]

When anonymous posters can make inflammatory statements, could this include CSIS or other government staff helping to create the appearance of a threat? After all, the McDonald Commission found the RCMP burned down a barn in Quebec in 1970 and blamed it on the FLQ. In 2007, at a North American leaders' summit in Montebello, Quebec, some of the protesters turned out to be undercover police. The *Toronto Star* ran this headline, "Quebec police admit agents posed as protesters: With the proof caught on video, Quebec provincial police were forced to admit Thursday that three undercover agents were playing the part of protesters at this week's international summit in Montebello, Que." The *Toronto Star* described how:

> The three officers, sporting bandannas, showed up on the front lines of a peaceful protest at the Security and Prosperity Partnership summit earlier this week.

One carried a large rock, and protesters allege the officers were trying to incite a riot so that police could move on the crowd.

The event was captured on video and shows one of the mystery men talking to police officers before being brought to the ground, handcuffed and quietly led away along with his friends.

The men were never charged, and photos show them wearing combat boots with identical markings to the ones worn by police at the scene.

"It's just too coincidental that these guys attack a (police) line with a boulder and they're not charged," (union leader David) Coles said.[108]

In his testimony before the Commission, Keith Wilson was asked about those in the protest group trying to bring a Memorandum of Understanding to the Governor General to sign and abolish Parliament. Wilson said:

[A] Memorandum of Understanding, in its simplest legal concept, requires all parties to it to sign. And it was evident that the signature lines on the last page were not going to be signed by the Governor General, nor someone from the Senate; and in any event I would explain—when I was asked by the Board, to brief them on it, I explained that . . . there's only two ways that governments change under our Parliamentary system. The first is when the Prime Minister contacts the government, the Governor General, and dissolves Parliament and asks that the writ be dropped. The second, through Parliamentary tradition, is where a bill is identified as a confidence vote and Parliament votes to defeat the bill. In that second instance, the Prime Minister would similarly contact the Governor General.

This idea that a certain number of people could sign a document, and that would somehow compel, or incentivize, and lead to a changing government, I explained (to the Freedom Convoy board), consistently and repeatedly, is legal nonsense." Wilson added, "this is not the first time I've run into this; I've had to litigate opposite the Sovereign Citizen folks, and quoting Admiralty law and think that if they present a flag in a certain way in a court, the Judge loses jurisdiction. I've had to encounter this many, many times in my career, so I was just like, here's another one.[109]

As the MOU became a talking point against the protesters in media coverage, James Bauder was convinced to retract his MOU.

On January 27, 2022, at 4:21 p.m., Caroline Williams, Director of Parliamentary Affairs at the Office of the Queen's Privy Council and Minister of Emergency Preparedness, emailed Zita Astrava, Chief of Staff to the Minister of Emergency Preparedness Bill Blair, and Annie Cullinan, Director of Communications, Office of the President of the King's Privy Council for Canada and Minister of Emergency Preparedness. Williams told her colleagues, ". . . I feel like we as Emergency Preparedness are a well-positioned office to provide more of the high-level messaging going forward. . . . These are lines we worked up earlier today. Any thoughts on if this is a helpful approach?" Williams offered as a trial balloon for the governments' outrage toward the Ottawa protesters: "Threatening acts of violence and inciting hatred, as we have seen from a select few in recent days, is unacceptable and does not reflect the views of a majority of Canadians."

But on January 27, 2022, no protest vehicle had arrived in Ottawa. Staff in senior government positions were preemptively rehearsing the language for their sound bites of outrage toward the protesters. Later on, January 27, Prime Minister's Office staff Samantha Khali celebrated the "good job" the "Ministers" were doing with the media and "I think our narrative is getting through." At the end of January 27, at 23:05 p.m., Caroline Williams confirmed to her colleagues that "we've been spending the last 24-48+ hours . . . to compile the messaging." She offered this rehearsed line that would be a talking point once the protesters arrived, "We condemn all such hateful and violent rhetoric in the strongest terms." Government of Canada staff had a narrative they cooked up between January 25 and 27 to frame the protesters in Ottawa as violent and hateful.[110] The first protesters arrived in Ottawa on January 28, 2022.

In their Final Submission to the POEC on December 9, 2022, Freedom Corp. lawyers Brendan Miller, Bath-Sheba van den Berg, Keith Wilson, and Eva Chipiuk concluded, "In using the Emergencies Act, which gifts the government with extraordinary powers, including infringing on s.92 of the *Constitution Act*, 1867, the Government of Canada ('GOC') chose the use of force, that is, state violence over peaceful negotiation and democratic engagement with the Canadians. The sad irony is that the protest in Ottawa was fundamentally about government overreach." Moreover, they asserted, "the invocation of the Emergencies Act by the GOC on February 14, 2022, and the measures that followed, were entirely unlawful, violated s.92 of the *Constitution Act*, 1982, violated s.7 and s.8 of the *Charter*, were politically motivated, based on misinformation created and spread by the GOC and the Liberal Party of Canada . . . hurt Canadians, and hurt Canada's reputation internationally."[111] Since invoking the Emergencies Act on February 14, 2022, the Government of Canada is the subject of a court case brought by the Canadian Civil Liberties Association that it acted unlawfully.[112] This resulted in a Judicial Review of the invocation of the Emergencies Act by Justice Richard Mosley, discussed in chapter fifteen.

CHAPTER TEN

VACCINE MANDATES AND CANADIAN CHARTER OF RIGHTS AND FREEDOMS

We have a robust, functioning democracy and public protests are an important part of making sure . . . Canadians are getting messages out there and highlighting how they feel about various issues. But using protests to demand changes to public policy is something that I think is worrisome.
                                        ~ Prime Minister Justin Trudeau

Justice Rouleau was petitioned to have the Honourable Brian Peckford testify at the POEC. Peckford was one of the speakers at the Freedom Convoy in Ottawa. He is the last living First Minister to sign the Patriation Agreement, later to be called the Constitution Act 1982, containing the Canadian Charter of Rights and Freedoms. The protesters were not only challenging the rationale for the vaccine mandates in Canada but the infringements on the Canadian charter as well. This included the right of all Canadian citizens to mobility. Quoting Section 6 of the Charter, Peckford said to the protesters, "Every citizen of Canada has the right to enter, remain in and leave Canada." As stated in all Canadian passports, "The Minister of Foreign Affairs requests . . . all those whom it may concern to allow the bearer (of the passport) to pass freely, without delay or hindrance, and to afford the bearer such assistance and protection as may be necessary." But the inquiry was not interested in having such an eminent person involved with the protest give testimony. It would have put Rouleau in a tough political spot to argue for a certain interpretation of the Charter of Rights and Freedoms with one of its authors.[113]

Several sergeants with the Police Liaison Teams of the OPS, Sgt. Phong Li and Sgt. Andrew Wisbecki, were also declined by the POEC to testify.

They worked closely with protester Tom Marazzo and Freedom Corp. lawyer Eva Chipiuk. Dean French, who helped establish contact between the City of Ottawa and protest leaders, was also not selected by the inquiry to testify. Others recommended to the POEC as witnesses to testify included indigenous women. Noeline Villebrun, a clan mother from Yellowknife (NWT), stood beside protest organizer Tamara Lich on the main stage on January 30. Villebrun emphasized that the Freedom Convoy protest was about peace, freedom, and love. Sandra MacKenzie, a clan mother from Sucker Creek Treaty 8 in Alberta, was another First Nations protester on Parliament Hill. Another was Candice Sero, the Mohawk woman with a walker who was trampled by police horses.

Though the Commission declined to let Sero speak, she was present at the public hearing to listen to Prime Minister Justin Trudeau testify. The Commission allowed lawyers for the Union of British Columbia Indian Chiefs to be among the groups to conduct cross-examinations of witnesses. However, the inquiry chose not to call to the stand any indigenous protester. It would only make sense that a government that had declared a national holiday each year on September 30—the National Day for Truth and Reconciliation—would welcome testimony from indigenous protesters. The Prime Minister, Liberal cabinet ministers, and the media depicted the protesters as racists. Was the decision not to have these indigenous women protesters appear at the public hearings made because their testimony would have undermined the talking point about the protesters being white and racist?[114]

Testifying before the POEC, Prime Minister Justin Trudeau stated, "We have a robust, functioning democracy and public protests are an important part of making sure . . . Canadians are getting messages out there and highlighting how they feel about various issues. But using protests to demand changes to public policy is something that I think is worrisome."[115] As someone who previously voted for Justin Trudeau in a federal election, I find his apprehension of the right to public assembly and free speech worrisome.

Trudeau is saying Canadians have the right to protest. But if those protests are used to demand changes in government policy, the current Canadian government will tell those protesters that they've crossed a line. It seems the prime minister thinks of democracy as something that citizens engage in by keeping their heads down, watching what they say, and not publicly questioning government action.

Several MPs with the Liberal Party disagreed publicly with the prime minister, advising the need for Trudeau to listen to citizens' "legitimate concerns." Liberal MP Joel Lightbound said on February 8, 2022, "It is time to stop dividing people, to stop pitting one part of the population against another."[116] Liberal MPs Nathaniel Erskine-Smith and Yves Robillard agreed with Lightbound.[117]

The invocation of the Emergencies Act by Justin Trudeau on February 14, 2022, was political theatre. It was not a last resort. It was a choice made by a government that wouldn't countenance public debate about the basis for its continued pandemic measures at a time when Canada was now an outlier. Where dialogue was the solution to address eleven weeks of national protest in early 2020, Trudeau closed the door to any possibility of discussion with protesters in January 2022 before they arrived. Documents entered as evidence before the POEC suggest the Liberals were restless to invoke the Emergencies Act many days prior to February 14, 2022.

Ms. Shantona Chaudhury, the Commission's co-lead council, was the first to examine Prime Minister Justin Trudeau under oath. She asked him, "when did the *Emergencies Act* come into play as a possibility?" Trudeau replied, "from the very beginning."[118]

Contrast Justin Trudeau's response from the outset to the Freedom Convoy and his response to the Boston Marathon bombing. In 2013, Trudeau appealed to classic liberal values of tolerance and inclusion to frame a discussion of an event that resulted in the deaths of Americans. The CBC's Peter Mansbridge asked Trudeau for his response to the April 15, 2013, Boston Marathon attacks that killed three people and left 265 injured. Trudeau said he would offer the Americans material support "and . . . we have to look at the root causes . . . there is no question that this happened because there is someone who feels completely excluded. . . . At war with a society. And our approach has to be, where do those tensions come from?. . . . But we also need to make sure that as we go forward, that we don't emphasize a culture of fear and mistrust. Because that ends up marginalizing even further those who already are feeling like they are enemies of society." In response to Trudeau's statement, Prime Minister Stephen Harper slammed Trudeau, saying, "Don't sit around trying to rationalize it."[119]

Reflecting on the support of the convoy, protester Tom Marazzo told me during a phone call, "What we do know is that there were over 175,000 people who donated in this country. And the ones that were out-of-country, their IP addresses were overwhelmingly Canadian. . . . In 2021, 26.3 million (was raised by) the Conservatives and 18.1 (raised in donations by) the Liberals. While the convoy raised over 24 million in under a month." Was the Trudeau Liberal response to the protest one of alarm at the level of support for the Freedom Convoy across the country?

Another indicator of the trajectory Canada is on is the matter of Dr. Jordan Peterson. Back in mid-February 2022, on social media, Peterson questioned the wisdom of interim Ottawa Police Chief Steve Bell. At the time, Bell was threatening protesting parents in Ottawa with having their children removed. Peterson commented, "Children removed? How exactly? Why, exactly? By whom, exactly? Sent to where, exactly? And for how long, exactly? Think this through, Canadians. This is a bad decision." For this, and a handful of other political opinions unrelated to his work, it was announced on January 3, 2023, that Dr. Jordan Peterson faces a mandatory six-month re-education by the Ontario College of Psychologists. Otherwise, he will lose his license to practice.[120] In January 2024, Peterson lost his appeal of the decision. No reasons were given.[121] The message to all Canadians, when exercising free speech, is stifle your dissenting political opinions.

CHAPTER ELEVEN

DID THE LIBERAL CABINET BREAK THE LAW?

Evidence of the cabinet proceedings that led to the decision to invoke the Emergencies Act was not disclosed despite repeated requests.

~ Justice Richard Mosley

In early February 2023, Attorney General David Lametti lost a key Federal Court ruling on his use of emergency powers against the *Freedom Convoy*. Justice Richard Mosley ordered internal emails, contradicting Liberal cabinet claims of a national crisis, must be admitted as evidence in a court case with the Canadian Civil Liberties Association. Mosley found that "Evidence of the cabinet proceedings that led to the decision to invoke the Emergencies Act was not disclosed despite repeated requests." He concluded the internal emails were "essential to the just and proper determination" of whether cabinet broke the law.[122]

Over the decades, progressive and "classic Liberal" voters in Canada—like myself—have looked over our shoulders nervously at attempts by conservative governments to reign in democratic freedoms. Decades after the Canadian Charter of Rights and Freedoms was adopted into the Canadian Constitution, Justin Trudeau warned citizens to "listen very carefully to those who choose to divide, or play up fears and insecurities as a way of advancing a political agenda."[123]

Ironically, Trudeau's present Liberal government in Ottawa offers us a sobering lesson. An autocratic trajectory can also be instigated by political parties in the middle of the political spectrum, as well as on the "left." This is no time for Canadians to be complacent. Is Canadian democracy healthy enough to have a fair and balanced public debate about what unfolded at the Freedom Convoy protests? Why can't our mainstream media engage in a robust discussion about what testimony at the Public Order Emergency Commission revealed and the shortcomings of its report? Is our democracy so fragile that we can't discuss the disconnect between the allegations against the protesters, advanced by the media and government leaders, and the livestream footage of the protests and live reports from independent reporters?

Speaking on the Emergencies Act vote before the Canadian Senate on February 22, Senator Denise Batters cited her firsthand experience of the protest.

> My office faces right onto Wellington Street, and I had a front row seat to this convoy for the past weeks. What I witnessed of protesters was peaceful, organized and non-threatening. I do not tolerate harassment, intimidation or destruction, ever. But I did not see any of that behaviour exhibited by the protesters. I have been here in Ottawa during all three weeks of the protest. I can say that in the last two years, I never felt safer walking home from my office at night. The protesters I met . . . reminded me of the people I know in Saskatchewan: friendly, hard-working, patriotic Canadians. . . . These truckers are our constituents and it is our job as parliamentarians to hear them out. . . . They drove all the way to Ottawa from those Saskatchewan towns. Birch Hills is almost 3,000 kilometres, a thirty-two-hour drive away. To simply have a conversation. . . . What is the national emergency this time? Dance parties and loud horns? Horns that, by the way, had long stopped honking by the time this act was invoked, due to a court injunction that the truckers complied with.[124]

In his testimony before the Commission on November 2, 2022, lawyer Keith Wilson stated, "The truckers had agreed amongst themselves— and (in) an affidavit . . . before the Superior Court . . . (February 5, 2022) injunction application that they put in this informal protocol of being silent between 8:00 p.m. and 8:00 a.m." Days before Justice Hugh McLean issued an injunction to stop the honking of horns, the protesters agreed that both they and Ottawa residents needed to be able to sleep.

There was also a disconnect between the promised fairness of the inquiry proceedings and their dysfunction. The inquiry failed, or refused, to fulfil its obligation to garner unredacted records where the redactions had no legal basis in law. The Government of Canada legal team repeatedly dumped hundreds of documents, often heavily redacted, during the testimony of witnesses on the stand. It was raised in the Parliamentary Committee of Inquiry that these redactions were not justified. On November 22, 2022, Freedom Corp. lawyer Brendan Miller was ejected from the proceedings by Rouleau for requesting that the commissioner at last rule on the matter of redacted documents.

After Brendan Miller was ejected from the public hearing, Keith Wilson addressed the matter of redacted documents with the commissioner. He said to Paul Rouleau:

> The federal government disclosed over a week ago an extensive volume of documents that are highly redacted. It is obvious from the face of the documents that they don't meet the criteria for lawful redactions. A motion was made last week for those redactions to be lifted. The submissions closed on Thursday evening (November 17, 2022). We still have no ruling. A number of days have passed. For the cross examination and the discovery of truth process to be valid and effective, the parties require access to the documents. We don't have that. So, we would appreciate some indication as to when the commission is actually going to rule on that and hopefully compel the proper disclosure of the records, so that cross-examination can be effective. I emphasize that these documents are not related to future witnesses, but present witnesses; making the process inefficient, with all due respect, by not allowing the parties to have access to unredacted documents.[125]

On January 23, 2024, Justice Mosley ruled that the invocation of the Emergencies Act was unconstitutional. It breached several sections of the Charter of Rights and Freedoms, and legislation in the Emergencies Act itself.

CHAPTER TWELVE

SAFE AND EFFECTIVE

Science . . . is a way of skeptically interrogating the universe with a fine understanding of human fallibility. If we are not able to ask skeptical questions to interrogate those who tell us something is true, to be skeptical of those in authority; Then we're up for grabs for the next charlatan, political or religious, who comes ambling along.

~ Carl Sagan

Throughout the pandemic, our prime minister claimed that every measure and regulation imposed was done with the sole purpose of keeping Canadians safe. It was asserted that the only way out of the pandemic was to get every single Canadian vaccinated. One hundred percent. However, given the recent revelations of former UK Health Secretary Matt Hancock, it appears that some Western democracies have other things in mind besides keeping their citizens safe. A BBC headline in March 2023 read, "Matt Hancock: Leaked messages suggest plan to frighten public." In messages with an aide on December 13, 2020, Hancock suggested, "We frighten the pants of [sic] everyone with the new strain." His aide responds: "Yep, that's what will get proper behaviour change." Hancock asks: "When do we deploy the new variant."[126] He announced the new variant the following day.

Canadian citizens are right to wonder if the Trudeau government hasn't had equivalent objectives to "frighten the pants off of everyone" with announcements of new variants. The *Ottawa Citizen* reported in September 2021 that "Military leaders saw pandemic as unique opportunity to test propaganda techniques on Canadians, Forces report says. A plan devised by the Canadian Joint Operations Command relied on propaganda techniques similar to those employed during the Afghanistan war."[127] Citizens were right to wonder about the new normal and the constant focus on alarm, panic, and fear. Governments in the past had sought to reassure citizens during a pandemic they had matters in hand. But were we now being gaslit, nudged to feel insecure, impotent, and apprehensive? In May 2023, a *Toronto Sun* headline announced 'Propaganda Program's Documents Vanished: DND can't find papers on public manipulation.' The Canadian military conceded that its "detailed course curriculum, progress reports and a live case study conducted by Canadian Forces personnel using the behaviour modification techniques can't be found." Apparently, our military lost track of how it has been nudging citizens to influence behaviour and learn how best to achieve compliance.[128]

The *New York Times* reported on February 21, 2023, that the mask mandates did nothing to protect people from the virus. Reporting on a rigorous and extensive study, Oxford epidemiologist Tom Jefferson said, "There is just no evidence that they [masks] make any difference. Full stop." Jefferson said that even if one were to don an N-95 mask that it "makes no difference—none of it." The microscopic hole in an N-95 mask was 35 microns. The much smaller droplet from the C-19 virus was 0.15 microns and could easily float through the N-19 mask hole. And the holes in cloth masks were much larger than N-95 masks.[129]

In his book *The New Abnormal: The Rise of the Biomedical Security State*, Dr. Aaron Kheriaty wrote:

> The science on masks was clear from the outset. Prior to Covid, there was not a single rigorous study showing that cloth or surgical masks, or indeed masks outside a hospital setting, are useful for slowing the spread of respiratory virus. The CDC initially acknowledged this, then flipped its recommendations in favor of masks. A few sloppy backfilled studies, using abstract models or highly contrived situations like mannequins wearing masks, were published to justify that recommendation. These half-hearted attempts to reinforce mask policies lacked clinical outcomes, control groups, and rigorous study methodology. Every one of the fifteen randomized control trials—the gold standard of medical research—done prior to the pandemic for masks and respiratory viruses found no benefit; but somehow, we pretended these rigorous studies no longer mattered.

Wearing a mask, as Dr. Anthony Fauci remarked, provided "psychological comfort." And though the regulators surely understood the lack of benefit, the mask became a "talisman of security, a charmed amulet to ward off infection." Psychologically, it helped frightened people feel less helpless. It gave them a sense of agency by taking some action which could ease their anxiety.[130]

Still, studies showed that in the long run, mask-wearing amplified fears of those who wore them. Wearing a mask reminded the wearer of how vulnerable they felt. Free-floating anxiety was fused with mask-wearing and led to feelings of impotence.[131]

On February 26, 2023, the *Wall Street Journal* reported, "The Lancet medical journal this month published a review of sixty-five studies that concluded prior infection with Covid—i.e., natural immunity—is at least as protective as two doses of mRNA vaccines."[132] So, how necessary was it to insist everyone get the mRNA vaccine when it turns out unvaccinated people who got COVID-19 were protected by their own natural immunity? Recall that a few years prior to the pandemic, Dr. Anthony Fauci had regarded "natural immunity as the mother of all vaccines." That is, until the pandemic, and all historic scientific data were thrown out the window. Drawing on a basic principle of immunology, Fauci had previously stated before the pandemic that people who had recovered from influenza didn't need the flu vaccine "because the most potent vaccination is getting infected yourself."[133]

Perhaps worst of all, the World Health Organization (WHO) published a medical article in October 2020 showing that the *overall* infection fatality rate (IFR) of COVID-19 was 0.23 percent—which is twenty-three deaths in 10,000 infected people. For people under age seventy, the IFR was 0.05 percent—five deaths in 10,000 infected people.

Why did WHO publish these astonishingly low figures near the end of the first year of the virus? Because its author is one of the most-cited epidemiologists in the world. Stanford's Dr. John Ioannidis[134], whose article in the *WHO Bulletin* on October 14, 2020—*before the vaccines arrived in December 2020*—showed that actual blood serum testing (as opposed to PCR testing) was the best evidence of the low death rate of the COVID-19 virus.[135]

There is little doubt that Canada's Chief Public Health Officer Dr. Theresa Tam[136] would have been well familiar with these vitally important *seroprevalence figures* long before February 2022. There is even less doubt that she would have informed the prime minister long before he imposed the punishing vaccine mandates on the truckers; long before he declined to talk to them; and, certainly, before he embroiled Canada in the unprecedented use of its Emergencies Act—and the travesty of its farcical justification.

In America, Dr. Anthony Fauci was alleging the spread of Covid was due to a "pandemic of the unvaccinated." The claim was repeated in Canada. Yet Peter Doshi, a senior editor of the prestigious *British Medical Journal*, concluded, "We are not in a "pandemic of the unvaccinated." Doshi said, "It saddens me that we as a society are oversaturated with the attitude of 'everybody knows,' which limits intellectual curiosity and leads to self-censorship." If hospitalizations and deaths occur almost exclusively in unvaccinated people, "why would booster shots be necessary?" asked Doshi. "And why would the statistics be so different in the United Kingdom, where most hospitalizations and deaths from COVID occur among the fully vaccinated? There's a correlation there that you should be curious about," Doshi said. "Something's not right."[137]

As well, it was Dr. Fauci who told the press on January 28, 2020, "The one thing historically people need to realize, even if there is some asymptomatic transmission, in all the history of respiratory-borne viruses of any type, asymptomatic transmission has never been the driver of outbreaks. The driver of outbreaks is always a symptomatic person. Even if there's a rare asymptomatic person that might transmit, an epidemic is not driven by asymptomatic carriers."[138] Nonetheless, health authorities in America and Canada continued to blur the distinction between symptomatic carriers who had a measurable amount of the virus and those who had no symptoms—though many "asymptomatic" carriers often tested positive due to having a false positive test.

Lockdowns were employed as a strategy across Canada. However, this was never a strategy recommended in any of the provincial emergency management protocols for responding to a pandemic. A Johns Hopkins report in early 2022 found that lockdowns had little impact on preventing deaths from the virus. A *National Post* headline on February 2, 2022, explained, "Lockdowns only reduced COVID deaths by 0.2 percent, Johns Hopkins study finds: 'We find no evidence that lockdowns, school closures, border closures, and limiting gatherings have had a noticeable effect on COVID-19 mortality.'"[139]

Some might argue that the cottage industry of self-appointed "fact-checkers" validated government claims over and over. They did, indeed. But, the "fact-checkers" were hatched by the pharmaceutical industry and its financial backers. Most prominent among the "fact-checkers" who aligned 99.99 percent of the time with the pharmaceutical companies was Reuters. But there was a conflict of interest. The CEO of Thompson-Reuters, Jim C.

Smith, has been a director on the board of Pfizer since 2014.[140] Reuters is also part of the Trusted News Initiative, which, along with CBC, BBC, and numerous media outlets, was in lockstep with pandemic reporting, where seldom was a discouraging word heard.

There were many Canadians who wanted a discussion with their government about how and why we think we know what we think we know. But those in charge kept citing their irrefutable data that could not be questioned. In a final interview on May 27, 1996, astronomer Carl Sagan told Charlie Rose about the challenge we face in our Western society. He warned:

> We've arranged a society based on science and technology in which nobody understands anything about science and technology. And this combustible mixture of ignorance and power . . . is going to blow up in our face. Who is running the science and technology in a democracy, if the people don't know anything about it? . . . Science is more than a body of knowledge. It's a way of thinking, a way of skeptically interrogating the universe with a fine understanding of human fallibility. If we are not able to ask skeptical questions to interrogate those who tell us that something is true—to be skeptical of those in authority—then we're up for grabs for the next charlatan, political or religious, who comes ambling along. It's a thing Jefferson laid great stress on. It wasn't enough, he said, to enshrine some rights in a constitution or Bill of Rights. The people had to be educated and they had to practice their skepticism. . . . Otherwise, we don't run the government, the government runs us.[141]

During the 2023 National Citizens Inquiry (NCI), witnesses who testified demonstrated their skepticism toward the government's mantra of "Safe and Effective." In September 2023, the NCI issued a paper titled "In the Public Interest: An Interim Report on the COVID-19 Vaccine Authorization Process." It described how the conventional process for evaluating and recommending vaccines was jettisoned in the case of the COVID-19 vaccine. Instead, Health Canada "authorized" the COVID-19 vaccine under an Interim Order. The Interim Order was issued on September 16, 2020, just weeks ahead of the authorization applications filed by AstraZeneca and Pfizer.[142] By taking these alternate steps, the government bypassed the need to establish the safety and effectiveness of this vaccine. The COVID-19 vaccine was not approved after being approved by Health Canada for use in humans. Instead, "the Interim Order allowed unapproved and unauthorized COVID-19 vaccines to be imported into Canada as long as the Canadian Government was the purchaser. This was called pre-positioning in the Interim Order. . . ."[143]

On September 16, 2021, Minister of Health Jean-Yves Duclos "made an Interim Order exempting all COVID-19 drugs (including COVID-19 vaccines) from the normal review and approval process. The Interim Order was made under section 30.1 of the Food and Drugs Act, R.S.C., 1985, c. F-27, which permits the Minister of Health to make an interim order that overrides normal regulations."[144] The NCI points out that "rather than requiring significant evidence of safety and efficacy of the COVID-19 vaccines as mandatory requirements for approval, only required the vaccine manufacturers to provide:

3(1) . . . sufficient information and material to enable the Minister to determine whether to issue the authorization, including . . .

(o) the known information in relation to the quality, safety and effectiveness of the drug.

By letting the Minister make a decision based on 'known information' about safety and effectiveness, this allowed the COVID-19 vaccines to be authorized in advance of actual knowledge about their safety or effectiveness."[145]

Advertising campaigns have used this slogan before. In the 1940s and 1950s, a Black Flag ad campaign told consumers, "No flies on me, thanks to DDT." It was accompanied with a photo of a smiling baby. The ad continued, "Black Flag, long preferred by housewives everywhere for quickly killing flies and mosquitoes on contact, now does *double duty*. The amazing DDT ingredient now in Black Flag stays on walls, floors, doorways to keep on killing flies for weeks! To use wonderful DDT *safely* and *effectively* in your home . . . ask for Black Flag."[146]

Camel cigarettes once boasted that "4 out of 5 doctors smoke Camels." These doctors came from "every branch of medicine." L&M assured consumers in their "Just what the doctor ordered!" campaign that their product was "entirely harmless." L&M filters "effectively filtered the smoke."[147]

For many decades in the 20th century, big tobacco insisted there was no connection between smoking cigarettes and cancer. Tobacco companies paid scientists who delivered research that instilled doubt among the general public that cigarette smoking could possibly cause cancer. The public was persuaded to possibly consider that it was stress, asphalt dust from newly tarred roads, or air pollution that caused cancer. Big tobacco hired an army of scientists who published reports, each concluding it was only "the 'junk' science that found harms associated with smoking." The American Medical Association and its journal endorsed Kent cigarettes filters with asbestos. Ads with the AMA backing stated these Kent filters were made of "completely harmless material that is not only *effective*, but *so safe* that it actually is used to help filter the air in operating rooms in leading hospitals."[148] Twenty-first century moderns tell themselves they'd never fall for something like that today.

In October 2023, the Manufacturing and Supply Agreement between Canada and Pfizer of October 26, 2020, was made public in November 2023. Representing Canada in the agreement was the Minister of Public Works and Government Services Canada. Oddly, that ministry had been renamed in 2015 with the new title Minister of Public Services and Procurement. In any event, the minister representing Canada in the agreement with Pfizer was Anita Anand. She oversaw the procurement of vaccines during the pandemic. The Purchaser Agreement on page 18 stated, "Purchaser acknowledges that the vaccine and materials related to the Vaccine . . . are being rapidly developed due to the emergency circumstances of the COVID-19 pandemic and will continue to be studied after provision of the Vaccine to Purchaser under this Agreement. Purchaser further acknowledges that the long-term effects and efficacy of the Vaccine are not currently known and that there may be adverse effects of the Vaccine that are currently not known."[149]

Canada's contract with Pfizer was exposed after an Access to Information Request made public a highly redacted 59-page document. It confirms that by October 26, 2020, the government of Canada, and Health Canada, knew that the Pfizer vaccines' efficacy and safety were not known. Despite this, Health Canada aggressively marketed the vaccines as "proven safe and effective." They were joined by a chorus of provincial and territorial health officers and ministers of health. None of them, actually, had any idea if the vaccines were safe and effective. They made a bet that by their constant, endless, insistence they vaccines were "safe and effective," most citizens wouldn't call their bluff. Turns out they were right. One takeaway from the pandemic is that most of us will fold are cards and refrain from exercising further scrutiny when public officials double down on their claims during a declared 'emergency.' The Counter Signal media outlet broke the story on November 15, 2023.[150]

After Pfizer released its mRNA vaccine to the public, it sought to have the documents for its clinical trials sealed for seventy-five years. Pfizer was immune from legal action under United States Emergency Use Authorization, unless they were guilty of fraud. So, why did Pfizer and the FDA want to have the Pfizer documents sealed for seventy-five years? In 2022, all of the 55,000 Pfizer documents, many thousands of pages in length, were released in a court order in the United States. This was as a result of a Freedom of Information Act lawsuit launched by attorney Aaron Siri. Dr. Naomi Wolf was following this story closely. She worked with podcaster Steve K. Bannon to issue a call for medical experts to volunteer to examine the Pfizer documents. A team of 3,500 specialists was divided into teams by Amy Kelly, who was the project manager for the investigation.

They discovered that the mRNA vaccines are unstable. Consequently, it would be essential to monitor the integrity of the full molecule. Amy Kelly's team concluded, "The failure to set up routine quality assurance standards in the huge number of facilities administering the vaccine precludes an assessment of the appropriate handling of the vaccine to ensure stability. Therefore, it is not correct to state that the vaccines are safe, as this aspect is not monitored." They also discovered that "During the Pfizer safety evaluation, no pregnancy evaluation is done. It was impossible to declare the vaccine safe for pregnant women."[151]

As well, while Pfizer was making public statements about how safe and effective its COVID-19 vaccine was, they were recruiting new staff. This was because in the initial twelve-week rollout, there were 158,000 separate adverse events reported to Pfizer. The pharmaceutical company "had to hire a small army of 2,400 *additional* full-time staff to manage the case load."[152]

In 2022, Edward Dowd published his book *Cause Unknown: The Epidemic of Sudden Deaths in 2021 and 2022*. In addition to the astonishing rise in deaths among athletes, he documents changes in the health in the Civilian Labor Force by the US Bureau of Labor Statistics. From 2008 to April 2021, there was average fluctuation between 29 and 30 million disabled Americans of working age. But since May 2021, when working-age Americans began to get the mRNA vaccine, the number increased to over 33 million. Dowd summarized, "nearly 3.5 million more Americans of working age are now too disabled to work."[153] There was no increase in disability rates of working-age Americans during the outbreak of COVID-19 in 2020 up to April 2021. It was only when the mass vaccination campaign began to impact working-age people that disabilities simultaneously shot up. Dowd noted that the greatest increase in disability is among the "healthier employed folks," at 22.6 percent increase, while the general US population has experienced an overall increase of just 6.6 percent.

Dowd said, "Obvious question of the day: Why are healthier folks seeing a bigger increase in the rate of their disabilities starting around May of 2021? What else was increasing at a substantial rate in mid-2021?."[154] In June 2023, the number of disabled working age Americans rose to 34.15 million.[155] But the public health agencies remain silent in the face of this alarming trend, which Dowd notes is occurring in other nations. They seem incurious that healthy young people are dying and becoming disabled in astonishing numbers. Perhaps they don't want the public to look at the elephant in the room: the vaccination campaign.

The "safe and effective" campaign by Health Canada and the Government of Canada is a case study in deception. The boast by Health Canada that "All COVID-19 vaccines authorized in Canada are proven safe, effective and of high quality" was untrue.

CHAPTER THIRTEEN

FREEZING BANK ACCOUNTS

There was a phone call to the PMO from Wall Street which cautioned, 'We are going to publicly distance ourselves from your actions. We are going to criticize your actions. You have 24 hours to reverse them.'
~ *Keith Wilson*

On February 17, 2022, Deputy Prime Minister and Minister of Finance Chrystia Freeland decreed bank accounts and assets of all convoy protesters, and those who donated to their cause, would be frozen.[156] The message was clear: if Canadians wanted to protest government policies, they might not be able to have access to their bank accounts, to pay mortgages or rent. This caused a run on the banks, according to Martha Durdin, CEO of the Canadian Credit Unions Association. She testified before a parliamentary committee in early March.[157] There was also a run on precious metals, which largely were unavailable as an alternative to store wealth.

Convoy lawyer, Keith Wilson, told Viva Frei:

I have it from a very high source, that a) the banks realized what had happened when they saw how their customers reacted. Having people who don't trust your institution . . . is bad for your business model. There were some people withdrawing millions of dollars from their accounts. As well, big financial players in the investment community in the USA weighed in. They were asking if investing in Canada was now like investing in Venezuela or Cuba. *"What just happened to Canada? I thought it had the rule of law. I thought it had checks and balances."* There was a phone call to the PMO from Wall Street which cautioned, *"We are going to publicly distance ourselves from your actions. We are going to criticize your actions. You have 24 hours to reverse them."* So, Justin Trudeau held a press conference and said *'circumstances have changed and now it's time for Canada. . . .*[158]

The freezing of bank accounts sent a chill across the nation. Citizens were second-guessing whether making a donation to this or that organization would be frowned upon by the government. Freezing bank accounts and sending police to violently break up a peaceful protest on Parliament Hill eroded trust in democracy. This created charitable donation hesitancy. Going forward, would more people worry more about "not saying the wrong thing" and "not getting into trouble," rather than challenging the status quo?

Christine Van Geyn of the Canadian Constitution Foundation observed that even when the Emergencies Act was withdrawn on February 23, the chill remained. On the plain text of the regulations to freeze bank accounts, "even a $20 donation could result in accounts being frozen. At the House finance committee, Isabelle Jacques, an assistant deputy minister in the Department of Finance, was asked why the federal government felt the need to declare an emergency when existing laws could also be used to freeze illegal donations, as they were in Ontario under Sec. 490.8 of the Criminal Code. Her answer: to 'make an impression upon those considering offering financial support.'"[159]

In his testimony before the POEC November 2, 2022, Keith Wilson said protesters who have had their "accounts were frozen have been denied credit applications, and I have explained to my clients and others who contacted me that the Canadian Bankers Association representative who testified before the House (of Commons) Committee said that each of these persons will have their accounts—their names marked—flagged for life."[160] The message to the rest of society is that peaceful protests can be framed by the government and the media as hostile, deplorable, insurrectionist. The facts on the ground need not matter since most people are watching newscasts and not at the protests in person to verify the incendiary rhetoric. So, if you are thinking of protesting a policy in the future that the government doesn't want criticized, think twice. Otherwise, you can have your assets frozen and be stained for the rest of your life with the label of being a "bad citizen."

In an inquiry document, "Interview Summary: Deputy Prime Minister Chrystia Freeland," the deputy prime minister discussed her thinking about the reasons for freezing protesters bank accounts. "DPM Freeland also pointed out that if Canada's capital had still been occupied when Russia invaded Ukraine, in her view, such a situation would have completely discredited Canada as an ally in support of Ukraine. Russian media would have been focused 24/7 on what was occurring in Canada, which would have made Canada appear very weak at a time it needed to be strong."[161]

Freezing protesters' bank accounts to demonstrate strength to Russian President Vladimir Putin! This is a shocking political motivation for Canadian politicians to crack down on citizens who question their policies. That optics ahead of the looming war in Ukraine—and not an unmanageable national security crisis—guided the deputy prime minister in her decision-making is deeply troubling.

In addition, Chrystia Freeland, in a confidential videoconference with bankers, said she "couldn't agree more" with a recommendation that cabinet deploy armed soldiers against the Freedom Convoy. "It is a threat to our democracy," she said in a discussion that also considered framing protesters as terrorists. Her remarks to bankers followed disclosures at the inquiry that on February 2, 2022, David Lametti texted Marco Mendicino regarding the use of troops against protesters. "You need to get the police to move and the Canadian Armed Forces, if necessary," texted Lametti. "How many tanks are you asking for?" asked Public Safety Minister Marco Mendicino. "I reckon one will do!!" replied Lametti. Freeland told the bankers, "We have to ensure Canada doesn't enter a post-COVID, January 6th spiral."[162]

On February 14, 2024, a 35-million-dollar lawsuit was launched by twenty protesters, including Canadian Armed Forces veteran Edward Cornell and retired police officer Vincent Gircys. The defendants include Justin Trudeau, Chrystia Freeland, David Lametti, Bill Blair, Marco Mendicino, Brenda Lucki, six major banks, four credit unions and the Canadian Anti-Hate Network.[163] Concurrently, Tamara Lich, Chris Barber, Tom Marazzo, Daniel Bulford and others, each filed a $2 million lawsuits against the government. In both cases, claimants argue their section 8 and 24 rights were breached. Section 24 states "Anyone whose rights or freedoms, as guaranteed by this Charter, have been infringed or denied may apply to a court of competent jurisdiction to obtain such remedy as the court considers appropriate and just in the circumstances." Keith Wilson stated, "Sec. 24 of our Charter of Rights and Freedoms gives Canadians the right to sue their government for damages when Charter rights are violated. Doing so affirms the seriousness of respecting Charter rights and is intended to deter future governments from breaching Canadians' fundamental rights."[164]

CHAPTER FOURTEEN

THE REPORT

I do not come to this conclusion easily as I do not consider the factual basis for it to be overwhelming. Reasonable and informed people could reach a different conclusion than the one I arrived at.

~ Justice Paul Rouleau

Justice Paul Rouleau, a former executive assistant to Liberal Prime Minister John Turner, released his Report on February 17, 2023. He concluded, "reluctantly," that the Trudeau government was correct in its decision to invoke the Emergencies Act. Rouleau explained, "I do not come to this conclusion easily as I do not consider the factual basis for it to be overwhelming. Reasonable and informed people could reach a different conclusion than the one I arrived at." Rouleau recommended the tests named in the existing Emergencies Act for declaring a state of emergency—espionage, sabotage, serious acts of violence, plots to overthrow the government, foreign influence—be omitted. He states in the Report, "The incorporation by reference into the Emergencies Act of the definition of 'threats to the security of Canada' from the *CSIS Act* should be removed." Rouleau recommends that perceived threats be the measure for invoking the Emergencies Act in the future. His report will be considered by the Trudeau cabinet, as they craft revisions to existing legislation.

The POEC Report was written at a lightning pace. Final submissions by lawyers' teams cross-examining witnesses before the Commission were made by December 9, 2022. The over two-thousand-page Report was finished—writing, copyediting, proofreading, typesetting and printing—in time for its February 17, 2023, publication. This is quite a feat given over six weeks of transcripts to review and many thousands of documents to cross-reference. There can be no doubt that the authors of the Report include numbers of uncredited staff who helped draft different chapters.

The Report affirms, "The right to protest is protected under the *Charter of Rights and Freedoms* primarily by three provisions: freedom of expression under section 2(b); freedom of peaceful assembly under section 2(c); and freedom of association under section 2(d). Expression is inherent in the very idea of protest, since protests are, by definition, attempts to express grievance, disagreement, or resistance. The guarantee of freedom of expression in section 2(b) protects a person's right to communicate a message, as long as the method and location of that expression is compatible with the values of truth, democracy, and self-realization." However, on the other hand, the Report cautions that "violence and threats of violence are not protected . . ." under the Charter.[165]

While laying out this parameter, the Report fails over and over to point to any actual serious acts of violence. As noted in a previous chapter, testimony of Interim Ottawa Police Chief Steve Bell conceded that the only "violence" at the Ottawa protests was "felt violence." Bell conceded that nothing any of the protesters did in Ottawa constituted acts of violence as described in the Criminal Code.

The Report frets that "Open fires were used by protesters to stay warm, despite the nearby storage of diesel, propane, and fireworks."[166] Yet it omits mention that protester storage of diesel and propane was inspected and approved by the Ottawa Fire Department, as Tom Marazzo explained.

The Report comments on the application to request an injunction against honking granted on Justice Hugh McLean on February 7. McLean ruled that the protesters had the right to proceed with their legal right to assembly and protest a public policy they disagreed with. But Rouleau does not seem to be aware that there was a second injunction granted by McLean on February 16. The latter injunction was given in light of the earlier conditions of the cessation of horn honking being—in the judges' view—satisfied. Oddly, the Report gets the timeline wrong on February 14, when 102 vehicles had been moved from downtown Ottawa by noon. Instead, the Report incorrectly states these vehicles only began moving at 1 p.m. and vacated the downtown by 5 p.m., a half hour after the Emergencies Act was invoked.[167]

When discussing why no one from the federal government met to have discussions with the protesters, the Report states, "Minister Mendicino explained that this was because there were unanswered questions about which protesters were in charge and whether they had the ability to get other protesters to leave."[168] The Incident Response Group could not identify who it might contact to have any dialogue with. This confusion persisted despite both city of Ottawa officials and PLTs meeting with key protest leaders and getting results. City of Ottawa officials worked with key convoy volunteers to remove protest vehicles out of the downtown on the morning of February 14. PLTs worked with Tom Marazzo and others to ensure emergency lanes were clear and other matters. Federal authorities had no problem identifying who the key protest leaders were that they wanted to arrest after the Emergencies Act was declared.

In one of a number of instances, when raising the matter of violence during the protests, the nuance of what is happening on the ground is lost. Rouleau comments, "For his part, Mr. Wilson testified about a concern the organizers had regarding what he described as 'Antifa' vandalizing property and harassing people in order to discredit the protests. Mr. Wilson heard that the group had come in at night and cut air lines and tires in trucks. Assuming that this actually occurred, it reflects knowledge among protest organizers that certain actors had and were intent on engaging in unlawful conduct."[169]

The Report ignores that the individuals Keith Wilson identified as engaging in unlawful conduct were not connected to the protest, but Antifa. The damage in question was being done *to* protester vehicles.

The Report contends that because of government mismanagement and incompetence, the Emergencies Act had to be invoked. "Existing legal tools were seen to be inadequate, and provincial and municipal governments were thought to lack the plans or power to end the protests. Cabinet concluded that there was only one option left: invoking the *Emergencies Act*. . . . The additional protests that government officials feared would erupt either did not arise."[170] This is not encouraging. All a government needs to do is mismanage its response to a protest and its failure to do so triggers a national emergency?

The preponderance of evidence in the Report, and presented in testimony before the Commission, did not support a conclusion that the government was justified in invoking the Emergencies Act. Nonetheless, oblivious to all the information he listened to in person for six weeks of public hearings, Paul Rouleau released a Report exonerating the government.

The Report correctly observes, "Canadians who disagreed with COVID-19 policies had the right to engage in lawful protest against what they saw as government overreach. In part, the scale of the early 2022 protests was the culmination of more than two years of COVID-19 restrictions. The spark itself was the Federal Government's decision in November 2021 to require commercial truck drivers to be vaccinated in order to enter Canada."[171]

The Report cites the blockage of an emergency lane on Kent Street as an indication that the protest was unsafe.[172] Here, it fails to mention that, as Tom Marazzo's testimony shows, the specific blockage of Kent Street was due to city of Ottawa vehicles blocking the lane.

The Report states, "Several parties at the Commission relied heavily on the testimony of OPP Superintendent Morris, whose unit was responsible for the Hendon reports. He described the absence of credible threats that protesters intended to engage in violence or other unlawful activity, and, in fact, commented on there being no instances of serious violence despite the size and length of the protests. I disagree with his assessment and accept the evidence from several witnesses that there was violence."[173]

Oddly, when presented with evidence by the senior intelligence officer for the OPP that their reports revealed no actual serious violence, the Commission rejects the evidence. Despite Supt. Morris stating there was "no credible threat" to the government of Canada, Rouleau appeals to evidence from other witnesses as proof of actual serious violence. Despite that, *evidence* consisted only of "phantom honking," "felt violence," "microaggressions," the persistence of honking which had ceased by February 7, and diesel fumes.

In the Executive Summary of the Commission Report, Rouleau discusses the Diagolon group. "Another controversial group associated with the protests was Diagolon, and its founder, Jeremy MacKenzie. Diagolon may have started as a joke on Mr. MacKenzie's podcast, but it has grown into a larger community. The Royal Canadian Mounted Police (RCMP) has described Diagolon as a militia-like network with members who are armed and prepared for violence. In his testimony, the head of the Ontario Provincial Police (OPP) Intelligence Bureau described Diagolon as an extremist group. Mr. MacKenzie strongly rejected these characterizations when he testified, asserting that they are a product of certain individuals and groups—including the RCMP—with ulterior motives. I do not accept Mr. MacKenzie's evidence in that regard. I am satisfied that law enforcement's concern about Diagolon is genuine and well founded. The fact that a ballistic vest was seized by the RCMP during the protests in Coutts—along with numerous guns—bore a Diagolon patch suggest as much."[174]

After reading the Report, Tom Marazzo commented, "They didn't hear my testimony? A cocaine addicted, time travelling, plastic goat figurine is a threat to the very survival of the Government of Canada!" In his testimony before the Commission, Marazzo stated:

> Diagolon being a time-travelling cocaine addicted goat. That is just an internet meme that has no meaning at all . . . I spoke to Jeremy . . . when the Liberal government was debating whether or not they should use the *Emergency Act*, and they were citing this fictitious goat that time travels as a domestic terrorist group and justification for invoking the Emergency Act. And I saw a video that Jeremy and his friends were doing, and they were laughing hysterically, showing clips of the government actually talking about Diagolon as being a real thing. Everybody knew it was a joke. When I saw the video, I contacted Jeremy and I said, "*Tell me everything there is to know about Diagolon.*" He said, "*If you draw a diagonal line from Alaska through Alberta to Texas it makes a diagonal line. And that's why it's called Diagolon. They're the only states and provinces that don't have mask mandates.*" And he used it as a joke. He made the symbol for Diagolon in a second on his cell phone because it's a joke. And it is meaningless.[175]

The POEC would have had at its disposal the RCMP investigation into Diagolon. An RCMP officer was tasked to produce a key briefing on Diagolon for senior government and federal cabinet ministers to help government decision-making. This was accomplished in only fifteen minutes. RCMP officer Lisa Ducharme, staff with the Ideologically Motivated Criminal Intelligence Team, effused in an email about how quickly the research on Diagolon was completed for senior government officials. With the subject heading "Kudos to Ashley," Ducharme wrote to Ashley Chen, "Well Done Ashley! Talk about amazing 'pull it together in 15 minutes' assessment! Thank you so much. Your work has been shared at the highest level over at PCO."[176]

On July 21, 2021, RCMP officer Kristen Little emailed her colleague, Ashley Chen, regarding Diagolon. She wrote that Diagolon was "Conspiracy theorist in nature but not accelerationist and you're right no incitement of violence. Some of the usernames have racists references/photos in them but no criminality"[177]

Simon Pollay, an inspector with the Office of Information Commissioner, Federal Policing National Security, wrote that "despite how 'Diagolon' is being portrayed in the media and the House of Commons," it was not consistent with the "source material and evidence I have personally viewed." Pollay advised his counterparts, "our direction to investigators is to be evidence focused and not caught up in the hype of the media surrounding this matter."[178]

The Ideologically Motivated Criminal Intelligence Team submitted a report on Diagolon that was approved by the Director of Federal Policing National Intelligence on May 19, 2022. They concluded, "Although DIAGOLON is based on a set of satirical ideas, the community does not appear to have any coherent ideologically purpose, objective or cause. . . . It appears that DIAGOLON as a distinct entity does not pose a criminal or national security threat. . . ."[179]

On March 16, 2022, RCMP officer Matthew Desjardins concluded, "DIAGOLON does not meet the dictionary definitions of a group."[180] Not only did Diagolon not pose a threat to the government of Canada, the RCMP was not satisfied that Jeremy MacKenzie's creation even constituted a group. The RCMP's own "Diagolon Profile" stated:

> Based on available open-source information it is exceedingly difficult to ascertain the extent to which Diagolon is a distinct group, with common ideology, a political agenda, and the cohesion necessary to advance such an agenda. DIAGOLON as a distinct entity does not pose a criminal of national security threat at this time. The Canadian Anti-Hate Network (CAHN) is cited as the main authority on the group by all mainstream media outlets; due to the fact that all information traces back to one source, triangulation and the verification of facts is almost impossible at the current time. Based on the information that is publicly available, it is difficult to understand how CAHN can confidently assert that Diagolon is an 'accelerationist movement that believes a revolution is inevitable and necessary to collapse the current government system' . . . Due to a lack of substantive open-source material, operational information would be needed to supplement the profile."[181]

Open-source material is information coming from media reports. The RCMP file on Diagolon relied on media reports, as the RCMP didn't have an active investigation into what Jeremy MacKenzie had invented in an online podcast.

Rouleau suggests that when the RCMP produces evidence of criminal activity, is must always be trusted. He has no concern that arrests made by the RCMP can ever be politicized. Were the arrests in Coutts good timing by the RCMP? Or was this the product of the RCMP manufacturing threats to serve a political agenda?

On July 1, 2013, there were reports that a plot to bomb the British Columbia legislature had been averted by the RCMP. Offices acting undercover, with the support of over 200 staff working to prevent the plot, saved the day and caught the plotters red-handed. Or so the public was led to believe. When the case went to court, it turned out that the RCMP was in the spotlight and uncomfortably so. The CBC reported, "RCMP entrapment of B.C. couple in legislature bomb plot was 'travesty of justice,' court rules: John Nuttall-Amanda Korody's convictions had been stayed due to entrapment, abuse of process."[182]

In her verdict, Justice Catherine Bruce wrote, "Simply put, the world has enough terrorists. We do not need the police to create more out of marginalized people who have neither the capacity nor the sufficient motivation to do it themselves." Bruce made clear that the RCMP had not foiled a pre-existing plan. The couple in the RCMP's crosshairs were not terrorists. They were not people with capacities that terrorists might want to recruit. Said Bruce, "This is truly a case where the RCMP manufactured the crime."[183]

Writing for *The Tyee*, Bill Tieleman asked:

Why did the RCMP create the July 1, 2013 B.C. Legislature bomb plot and train and equip a hapless, methadone-addicted, developmentally challenged couple to undertake terrorist actions? And why did the RCMP also break Canada's laws in doing so? Money. Lots and lots of money. John Nuttall and Amanda Korody were freed Friday after three years in jail thanks to a stunning decision that saw a respected judge condemn the RCMP in the strongest terms possible, while overturning a jury's guilty verdict on terrorism changes because the Surrey couple were 'entrapped' by police, who also committed an 'abuse of process.' So why did the RCMP take such obviously reprehensible actions? What was their motivation in turning two sad, naïve recovering heroin addicts who barely left their basement apartment into Canada's most famous terrorists? To get government money for its huge operations. The RCMP has a $2.8 billion annual budget and more than 29,000 employees. It depends on the federal government for its funding—and counterterrorism dollars depend on results, as I wrote in *The Tyee* in

2013 after covering the first court appearances of Nuttall and Korody. The RCMP is also competing with the Canadian Security Intelligence Service for financial support, so it is highly motivated to show public success. And in the RCMP's Departmental Performance Report, one of the major 'expected results' is 'Terrorist criminal activity is prevented, detected, responded to and denied.'

In the absence of real terrorist plots to foil, the case of Nuttall and Korody indicated the RCMP's work can include manufacturing plots in order to foil them. From the success of these sting operations, the RCMP gets favorable media coverage and a subsequent boost in future yearly budgets. As long as they don't get caught.[184]

In the past, the RCMP engaged in policing to advance political agendas of the federal government. The *Halifax Examiner* ran this headline in June 2022: "RCMP Commissioner Brenda Lucki tried to 'jeopardize' mass murder investigation to advance Trudeau's gun control efforts." The paper reported:

> RCMP Commissioner Brenda Lucki "made a promise" to Public Safety Minister Bill Blair and the Prime Minister's Office to leverage the mass murders of April 18/19, 2020 to get a gun control law passed." RCMP in Nova Scotia were left out of the loop regarding numbers of victims and release of information. The article detailed how "Contravening the agreed protocol, throughout the early hours of Sunday evening, RCMP Commissioner Brenda Lucki agreed to a number of one-on-one interviews with reporters. At 7:36 pm, CBC News quoted Lucki as stating there were 13 victims; at 7:40 pm, CTV reported Lucki had said 14 victims; and at 7:56 pm, the Canadian Press quoted Lucki as having confirmed 17 dead, including the gunman. The public and the press corps were both confused and alarmed.
>
> 'So how does it happen that Commissioner Lucki. . . .?' Mass Casualty Commission lawyer Krista Smith started to ask Communications director Lia Scanlan during an interview last February. 'I don't know, ask National Headquarters,' retorted Scanlan. 'The commissioner (Lucki) releases a body count that we (Communications) don't even have. She went out and did that. It was all political pressure. That is 100% Minister Blair and the Prime Minister. And we have a commissioner that does not push back.'[185]

During the FLQ Crisis in the fall of 1970, the RCMP was found to have engaged in illegal activities. As the McDonald Commission Report of 1981 found, the RCMP forged documents and was involved in the theft of the membership list of the Parti Quebecois, several break-ins, illegal opening of mail, and the burning a barn in Quebec.[186] The McDonald Commission recommended revisions to the War Measures Act. These were tabled by Perrin Beatty in Parliament in July 1988 as the Emergencies Act.

The case of the Coutts Four charged with weapons possession is before the court. Those accused are innocent until proven guilty. But in the court of public opinion, aided by the media, politicians, and now the POEC Report, those charged already have been found guilty. Anthony Hall, a writer in Lethbridge, Alberta, has attended the bail hearings for the accused. Hall writes:

> From the bail hearings in the Lethbridge courthouse, a vague picture is emerging of what the Crown is trying to prove. It seems that special units of the heavily politicized Royal Canadian Mounted Police developed some facets of their accusations on the basis of recorded private phone conversations as well as on the claims of infiltrators hired by police to pretend to be protesters. Local hearsay is that these infiltrators were largely attractive young women who may have been encouraged to entrap their targets. . . .

Hall describes how the Crown's case against the Coutts protesters materialized only *after* police failed in their concerted efforts to find weapons in the possession of the Ottawa Truckers and their supporters. . . . The arrest of the Coutts Four dovetailed with the Feb. 14 invocation. Deputy Prime Minister Freeland highlighted Canada's Terrorism Financing Act in publicly explaining the seizure without court order of Trucker-related bank accounts and donations. The resort by Trudeau and Freeland to terrorist laws required some indication that a terrorist plot had been discovered and apprehended.

How convenient that the RCMP provided "the government with these bombshell arrests just prior to (when) Trudeau and Freeland appeared in front of the cameras."[187]

Elsewhere, Rouleau explains that the Emergencies Act needed to be invoked despite a variety of police powers available to use according to the laws of the land. "It is clear that legal tools and authorities existed; the problem was that these powers, such as the power to arrest, were not being used because doing so was not thought to be an effective way to bring the unlawful protests to a safe and timely end."[188] And yet, after the Emergencies Act was invoked, the police went ahead and arrested protesters. Making arrests is something they knew how to do before the *Act* was invoked.

The Report states that "The Government of Canada has confirmed that, in invoking the *Emergencies Act*, the Governor in Council relied on paragraph (c)" of the Emergencies Act legislation: "activities within or relating to Canada directed toward or in support of the threat or use of acts of serious violence against persons or property for the purpose of achieving a political, religious or ideological objective within Canada or a foreign state. . . ."[189] This is the same definition—acts of serious violence—which eluded the Commission throughout the inquiry. When pressed under cross examination, those suggesting "violence" had occurred conceded no actual violence had taken place.

The Report affirms that the Cabinet was correct to support invocation of the Emergencies Act as it was exercising its "power based on reasonable grounds to believe" as long as they "must believe in the probability that certain facts or a certain situation exists. However, the existence of the facts or situation need not ultimately be proven on a balance of probabilities."[190] Again, the threat to national security is in the eye of the beholder. Especially if the "reasonable ground to believe" advances a political agenda that can shield a government from citizen protest of its policies. Indeed, it was advantageous to believe such a threat to national security existed. Notes from PMO staffer Sarah Jackson indicate that by early February the strategy for dealing with the protests by the Minister of Emergency Management and Preparedness Bill Blair was to invoke the Emergencies Act.

The Report comments on the solicitor-client privilege that Attorney General David Lametti called upon to keep secret the legal advice given to justify invoking the Emergencies Act. "Some suggestion was made that in the absence of disclosure of the legal advice that Cabinet received, which is protected by solicitor—client privilege, it cannot be known whether its decision conformed to that opinion. I do not accept this argument. Numerous witnesses, including, but not limited to the Prime Minister, the Clerk of the Privy Council, and the minister of Justice . . . testified that they believed the legal thresholds for invoking the Emergencies Act were met . . . I do not need to see the legal advice itself in order to accept the evidence that they believed their conclusion to be justified in law."[191] If there was an instance that deserved further scrutiny, this would be the top contender. Instead, Rouleau shrugs. The Commission was supposed to inquire and scrutinize key decisions. Instead, the Report invites Canadians to engage in blind faith.

The catastrophizing tone of many cabinet ministers and senior government bureaucrats is a contagion among authors of the Report. "Children were present at many protest sites, placing them at risk, and there were suggestions that they were being used as human shields to prevent police enforcement."[192] Children sat in strollers with their parents. Children ate burgers, samosas and chicken noodle soup. Children played ball hockey, with giant Lego and in bouncy castles. They joined in conga lines to music. 'Be afraid, be very afraid' the Report advises citizens. It seems there is nothing that cannot be construed as dangerous given enough political spin. No parent who brought their child to the protests in Ottawa in did this to use them as a human shield. CSIS observed the protests including thousands of children were "family-oriented." The government and its Report mistook the Freedom Convoy protests in Ottawa for the Syrian Civil War.

The Report takes Transport Canada's "assessments" based on modelling projections as definitive. But Rouleau does not rely on actual Statistics Canada data that show the protests had a negligible impact on trade and commerce because trucks were re-routing to other nearby bridges to cross the Canada–US border.[193] The Decision Note to the Prime Minister at 3:41 p.m. on February 14, 2022, was based on economic impact. "The economic impact to date is estimated at approximately 0.1 percent of Canada's gross domestic product (GDP) per week, however the impact on important trade corridors and the risk to the reputation of Canada as a stable, predictable and reliable location for investment may be jeopardized if this continues."[194]

Commenting on the impact of the protests on the Canadian economy, Rouleau states, "I recognize that the Emergencies Act was not intended to apply to 'economic emergencies.' Financial costs and trade impacts are not sufficient in themselves, and I have not considered them to be so. What is relevant, however, is the human health and public safety consequences that may flow from a serious, sudden, prolonged, and deliberate disruption to economic security and the ability to earn a living."[195]

As he makes these observations, Rouleau seems oblivious to the harsh economic impact of the lockdowns that went on for months. It resulted in mental health issues, a spike in suicides, bankruptcies, domestic abuse, alcoholism, and more. The ability to earn a living is in the eye of the beholder. When the Government of Canada creates mass economic dislocation as a result of its policies, those disruptions don't merit inspection. The Report reimagines "serious violence" that can threaten the security of Canada as "interference with someone's . . . psychological integrity, health, or wellbeing."[196] However, when discussing the freezing of bank accounts and other assets, the Report attests, "The asset freezing regime, while highly impactful on protesters, did not involve physical force or violence."[197] The psychological integrity, health, or well-being of protesters whose financial assets were frozen is not of concern.

Rouleau makes clear that ". . . peaceful, lawful protest that seeks to achieve a change in government policy" is not "in any way a threat to the security of Canada. To the contrary, it is a fundamental and cherished part of a healthy democracy. Indeed, the right to protest helps ensure the security of Canada. But the situation that Canada experienced in February 2022 was not peaceful, lawful protest."[198] This on-the-one-hand-on-the-other-hand approach to writing permeates the Report. It is long on generalizations and short on specifics. Rouleau infers much without pointing to specific evidence to justify his conclusions. What the protesters did that specifically was "not peaceful" and not "lawful" the Report does not say. In this way, the Report is a fraud. It fails to accurately report the testimony presented and distinguish between hearsay evidence and solid evidence.

As mentioned in the opening of this chapter, Rouleau gives the government the benefit of the doubt that it was in the right to invoke the Emergencies Act. He concedes, "I do not come to this conclusion easily, as I do not consider the factual basis for it to be overwhelming and I acknowledge that there is significant strength to the arguments against reaching it. . . . The standard of reasonable grounds to believe does not require certainty."[199]

Recall the Royal Commission on the Status of Women and its Report in 1970. It concluded that two-thirds of people on welfare were women. Imagine if it had stated, "We do not come to this conclusion easily, as we do not consider the factual basis for it to be overwhelming and we acknowledge that there is significant strength to the arguments against reaching it. . . ."

In 1976 the Royal Commission on the Health and Safety of Workers in Mines released their Report. What confidence would Canadians have had if that Commission didn't consider the factual basis to be overwhelming in order to recommend "that government make rules to measure dust exposure in mines, or that workers get compensated for injury from workplace hazards?" Or if the 1996 Royal Commission on Aboriginal Peoples felt that reasonable people could disagree and come to a different conclusion regarding the recommendation to recognize Métis rights to hunt and fish on Crown land. In this way the Public Order Emergency Commission Report is both a whitewash and a cop-out.

Invoking the Emergencies Act is supposed to be a last resort. The Report considered one of the options within the legal framework of existing law: deploying the Canadian Armed Forces. Rouleau writes, though this option "continued to exist, I agree with the Federal Government's view that it was not an appropriate solution in these circumstances. In saying this, I recognize that when the Emergencies Act was adopted, use of the military against civilians to quell protests was considered not only a viable option, but preferable to using emergency powers. The white paper proposes that '[l]ess serious emergencies arising from the breakdown of public order would continue to be dealt with under the *Criminal Code* or Part XI of the *National Defence Act* (which covers aid to the Civil Power [. . .])'. . . . Much has changed since then."[200] What specifically changed, given this option remains on the books, Rouleau doesn't say. What hasn't changed since the 1988 passage of the Emergencies Act is that the Canadian Armed Forces remain ready to respond to a crisis when asked to intervene.

The Report stands shoulder to shoulder with the Liberal government actions, lauding ". . . the ban on causing minors to travel to or participate in prohibited assemblies was also appropriate."[201] Regarding the freezing of bank accounts and insurance policies, Rouleau adds, "even the taking of property by government action would not, in itself, constitute a 'seizure' for the purpose of s. 8 of the Charter of Rights and Freedoms."[202] Perhaps the surprise after invoking the Emergencies Act is that in addition to freezing bank accounts, the Liberal government didn't proceed to seize the property and possessions of protesters and auction these off. Why not seize houses, vacation properties, small businesses, boats, vehicles, and auction them off? Rouleau's nonchalant view of seizing property forgets a whole chapter in Canadian history that led to Prime Minister Mulroney's 1988 apology to Japanese-Canadians for the government seizure of their properties during World War II.

In discussing the specifics of joint accounts, the Report sides again with the Government's action: "It is not difficult to imagine a scenario where an individual would participate in the protests without the involvement of their spouse (or, indeed, against the spouse's wishes). It is clearly unjust for individuals with no connection to the protests to have their accounts frozen. The difficulty, however, is that this appears to have been unavoidable."[203] What was avoidable was to conflate peaceful protesters with terrorists, and to freeze their bank accounts on that frenzied, baseless presumption. The proper response for the government should have been to simmer down.

Though he wants the "high threshold" for invoking the Emergencies Act to remain, Rouleau paves the way for the federal government to make it much easier to trigger a national emergency in the future. "The incorporation by reference into the Emergencies Act of the definition of 'threats to the security of Canada' from the *CSIS Act* should be removed."[204]

After the Report was released, independent journalist Trish Wood commented, "Never forget, the protests were over vaccine mandates and began when both the efficacy and safety were seriously in doubt. Surely, that is the issue that should have been weighed against the *jackboot of the state*. The medical merits of the convoy's actions were not the purview of the commission—part of a C-19 public policy bait and switch. Because it burnished Trudeau's personal brand, the Liberal government and woke public health took a different stance over the (May-June 2020) George Floyd protests in which protesters actually did commit arson and people were killed. Not to mention violating public health guidelines—citizens had been told to stay away from large groups.

> Canadian health officials are not suggesting people avoid protests, but they are stressing the importance of hand sanitizer and masks. With physical distance being nearly impossible in some of these settings, rally-goers may have to find other ways to try to keep themselves safe.

Legitimate protest is in the eye of the beholder. Trudeau took a knee for a movement becoming known for violence, property damage and threats but he lowered the boom on an event with none of those features."[205]

With the release of the Report, there is no appeal or judicial review of the inquiry. However, after the Emergencies Act was invoked the Justice Centre for Constitutional Freedoms, the Canadian Civil Liberties Association and the Canadian Constitution Foundation all initiated judicial reviews of the government's invocation. These applications to the court were made because the plaintiffs have reason to believe he Government of Canada made a decision that they didn't have the authority to do, was unreasonable or unlawful. Those three cases have been consolidated into one case to be heard in April 2023.

Asked to comment on the Report after its release Tom Marazzo said "It's a huge betrayal. Soldiers in Canada . . . undergo something called an unlimited liability. It means legally you could be ordered to your certain death in a combat situation. And in exchange for that you are willing to lay down your life so the people of Canada can be free. We justify all wars that we engage with for the freedom of people, the freedom of the citizens that you are there to fight for. And yet, we go to Ottawa to exercise our Charter rights to protest. . . . And in particular the veterans, if you remember on that day the police swept through (police) beat viciously Canadian military veterans wearing their berets, their medals. That was a very dark day in history. On a personal level, it's bad to see Canadians being beaten like that. And when your police are beating your veterans' wearing medals. And then we go a year later, and the Government of Canada who investigated themselves found no wrongdoing with themselves. . . . This is about accountability."[206]

Lawyer representing the protesters at the Commission, Brendan Miller, stated, "The report is a Parliamentary report and is immune from judicial review or appeal. The commission was an un-transparent process, riddled with unlawfully redacted Government of Canada records and suppressed evidence, with no remedy available to deal with these major shortcomings. The report may be good politics for certain parties, but it flies in the face of the rule of law and constitutionalism."

One of his colleagues at the Commission, Eva Chipiuk, added, "In other words, we were handcuffed and blindfolded, in an uphill battle, all while the federal government and the Commission threw stones down on us with their $800 million dollar Department of Justice budget."[207]

The author of the Emergencies Act, passed in Parliament in July 1988 to replace the *War Measures Act* was the Honourable Perrin Beatty. When Prime Minister Justin Trudeau announced there would be an inquiry, as required by law, Beatty resisted making any partisan comments. He said, "The only thing that I can say, as the author of the act, is that wherever you have extraordinary powers, there must be extraordinary accountability." *The War Measures Act* allowed for human rights abuses. This included the incarceration of Japanese Canadians during the Second World War, and seizure of their homes and possessions. Beatty said the goal of the Emergencies Act was to ensure future governments would protect the civil rights of Canadians even under the direst circumstances. "If you don't have (transparency), then people will always have their suspicions that something has been withheld. Trust us' is not enough if you want public confidence at the end of the day."[208]

In their editorial, "The failures of politics, and empathy, before the Emergencies Act," the *Globe and Mail* wrote:

> We disagree, for instance, with his conclusion that the invocation was justified. Justice Rouleau is prepared to give the Liberal government the benefit of the doubt for not establishing that existing policing plans and powers were not up to the task of ending the protests. That generosity stretches too far, in our view.
>
> Justice Rouleau does note that the factual basis for his conclusions "is not overwhelming" and that reasonable people could reach a different conclusion. And he points out that his opinion is not legally binding, and that it will be up to the courts to render a decisive verdict.
>
> Separate from that yet-to-be-decided legal issue is the more fundamental question of how this country became so badly divided that thousands of Canadians evidently felt their only recourse was to occupy the nation's capital, and that the federal cabinet evidently believed its only option was to curtail civil rights to oust them. . . .
>
> As the protesters made their way to Ottawa, Mr. Trudeau called them a "small fringe minority of people" that held "unacceptable views." That demonization was part of an unfortunate pattern from the Prime Minister, who during the 2021 election campaign had labelled anti-vaccine protesters as "very often misogynistic and racist." More broadly, Mr. Trudeau used vaccination as a wedge issue against his Conservative rivals in that campaign, a move that even one of his own MPs later criticized as a decision "to divide, and to stigmatize."
>
> Justice Rouleau is circumspect in his critique of Mr. Trudeau's comments, inferring that he was not referring to all Freedom Convoy participants. That is an overly optimistic assessment, and one that ignores the political motivations at work for the Liberals as they sought first to delegitimize the protest by painting it as a nest of neo-Nazism, and then to tie it to the Conservatives.[209]

The *National Post* commented,

> There was no threat to the Canadian state or a threat of mass violence, so based on what the law actually says, the convoy protests did not rise to the level of a national emergency. Yet, Rouleau accepted the government's argument that it is free to interpret the definition however it pleases.
>
> And even though the government refused to produce the legal advice it was given to justify its actions, here Rouleau shrugged again. "Each of them (witnesses) explained what they believed those thresholds to be. I do not need to see the legal advice itself in order to accept the evidence that they believed their conclusions to be justified in law," he said.
>
> What's the point of having your attorney general write up a legal justification if you're not going to dust it off when asked to . . . legally justify your actions?[210]

Writing for the *Toronto Sun*, Brian Lilley commented, "What the Emergencies Act does is use the CSIS Act to define what an emergency is to limit how and when the act can be invoked. It should be difficult for any government to declare a national emergency and suspend civil liberties. It should be difficult for any government to grant itself sweeping powers as the Emergencies Act does. The actions of the Trudeau government made it easier to seize those powers, which Rouleau admitted were not always handled well, such as the process of freezing bank accounts. In his report, Justice Rouleau calls for the government to remove the reference to the CSIS Act from the Emergencies Act, a move that I fear could weaken the law and allow future governments greater leeway in using extraordinary powers. . . . Trudeau can't be allowed to use this report to make it easier to grant himself special, sweeping powers in the future."[211]

Now, the Rouleau Report which smeared Freedom Convoy protesers as terrorists, is in the hands of this Liberal government. What will prevent the Trudeau government from revising legislation to lower the threshold for further use of the Emergencies Act?

Queens University law professor, Bruce Pardy, points out that the POEC was not a court of law. A lot of the *evidence* presented at the inquiry would not be admissible in a court proceeding. Pardy highlights the hearsay testimony about violence. After having watched countless hours of testimony, Pardy stated, "I did not see anybody on the stand relate a personal experience to violence. There were a lot of people who said there was violence . . . all around. But I didn't see anybody say 'somebody came up to me and hit me in the head.' Therefore, the evidence being relied upon by Rouleau that there was enough . . . a use of violence to justify the act essentially was hearsay."[212]

CHAPTER FIFTEEN

JUDICIAL REVIEW OF INVOCATION

On January 23, 2024, a federal court completed a judicial review of the legal and constitutional challenge to the first-time invocation of the Emergencies Act. Justice Richard Mosley wrote that the Liberal cabinet proclamation of the Emergencies Act was in contravention of Part 1 of the *Constitution Act of 1982*, several sections of the Emergencies Act, and Section 1 of the *Charter of Rights and Freedoms*. This resulted in multiple infringements of the civil rights of Canadian citizens. The invocation by the government was "not justified." Mosley wrote, "the decision to issue the Proclamation does not bear the hallmarks of reasonableness—justification, transparency and intelligibility—in relation to the relevant factual and legal constraints that were required to be taken into consideration. . . . there can be only one reasonable interpretation of the EA section 3 and 17 and paragraph 2 (c) of the *CSIS Act* and the Applicants have established that the legal constraints on the discretion of the GIC to declare a public order emergency were not satisfied."[213]

The government argued that the case should not be heard since the Emergencies Act was revoked on February 23, 2022. But Mosley concluded, "If the Court declines to hear these cases, a precedent may be established that so long as the government can revoke the declaration of an emergency before a judicial review application can be heard, the courts will have no role in reviewing the legality of such a decision."[214]

Originally, the 1984 Emergencies Act bill contained wording that allowed that Cabinet only needed to be "of the opinion" that an emergency existed to invoke the act. However, amendments were made to the bill in favour of the requirement that there be "reasonable grounds" for such a decision. As well, it is clear from the language in the 1984 bill, and its amendments, that Parliament envisioned ordinary citizens being able to challenge government proclamations in the courts.

He ruled that hearing the legal and constitutional challenges to the government's action were merited. Mosley wrote he was satisfied that "the Applicants have established that an adversarial context continues to exist and have built a record upon which meaningful judicial review of the decision to invoke the Act and issue the Proclamation . . . can occur".[215] The federal court ruled that the POEC inquiry was not a substitute for judicial review. The federal court observed "it is clear from the legislative history and language of the Act that the intent and purpose of the EA was to preserve and protect fundamental rights even in emergency situations where special temporary measures may be required."[216]

In his finding, Mosley pointed out that the Governor in Council was required by the Emergencies Act legislation to show that "the reasons for its decision" are "reasonable" and "demonstrate 'justification, transparency and intelligibility." However, the federal court declared that the Cabinet does not have untrammelled powers to act in any way it sees fit. Its powers are granted insofar as it acts in accordance with the constitution. Justice Mosley wrote "the determination of whether the objective legal thresholds were met is not (discretionary) and attracts no special deference . . ."[217]

The government also argued that because the Cabinet made the decision to invoke the Emergencies Act, that it deserves "an extraordinarily high degree of deference" from the courts. Moreover, the government contended that its GIC decisions should be "unconstrained and very difficult to set aside."[218] The court did not agree.

In his decision, the judge noted in section 16 of the Act, a public order emergency arises from threats to the security of Canada that are so serious as to be a national emergency. The court heard arguments that there was insufficient evidence to show that the lives, health and safety of Canadians were at risk beyond the capacity of federal and provincial jurisdictions to act in accordance with the laws of the land. As such, it was argued that the GIC actions were inconsistent with "Peace, Order and Good Government."

While the charges and arrests in Coutts were concerning, it was argued that the incident did not amount to a truly "national" threat. Furthermore, laws in the Criminal Code enabled the RCMP to make arrests before the federal proclamation. The court ruled that federal disagreement regarding a province or territory declining to exercise certain available powers is not an excuse to invoke the Emergencies Act. The Emergencies Act legislation requires a government to specify where a national emergency exists, if it does not include the whole of Canada. However, in the GIC proclamation the emergency was described vaguely as occurring at "various locations throughout Canada". In addition, the federal court observed "the Proclamation stated that it (the national emergency) "exists throughout Canada". This was, in my view, an overstatement of the situation known to the Government at that time."[219] As such, a national emergency did not exist as understood in the Emergencies Act legislation.

The Judicial Review found that the GIC did not reach for invocation of the Emergencies Act as a tool of last resort. Justice Mosley observed that the Cabinet cannot simply invoke the Act "because it is convenient."[220] This conclusion is consistent with numbers of those testifying before the POEC, including Ontario Deputy Solicitor General Mario Di Tommaso, stating that invoking the Act was not necessary.

In contrast with the opinions of National Security Advisor to the Prime Minister, Jody Thomas, the ruling of the federal court underscored the foundation of the *CSIS Act* and its relationship to the Emergencies Act. Mosley wrote, "the words 'threats to the security of Canada' do not stand alone in the Act and must be interpreted with reference to the meaning of that term as it is defined in section 2 of the *CSIS Act* and incorporated in section 16 of the EA." While the government argued that it should not be constrained by the investigative actions of CSIS as written in the *CSIS Act*, "the Court cannot rewrite the statute and has to take the definition as it reads."[221]

The federal court commented on the shaky basis for the Privy Council Office to advise the Prime Minister to invoke the Act. "The Clerk had cautioned the Prime Minister that PCO's conclusion that the criteria for declaring a public order emergency had been met was "vulnerable to challenge". Properly so, in my view, as the evidence in support of PCO's analysis was not abundant. It rested primarily on what was uncovered at Coutts, Alberta when the RCMP executed search warrants and discovered firearms, ammunition and the indicia of right-wing extremist elements."[222]

While the government has cited economic harms from the Freedom Convoy as a trigger for proclaiming the EA, the judge referred to the legislation citing no economic trigger for its invocation. The harm being caused to Canada's economy, trade and commerce, was very real and concerning but it did not constitute threats or the use of serious violence to persons or property."[223]

The proclamation of February 14, 2022, banned mere attendance at the protests and violated citizen rights to freedom of speech. Justice Mosley concluded the "scope of the Regulations was overbroad in so far as it captured people who simply wanted to join in the protest by standing on Parliament Hill and carrying a placard."[224]

The federal court reminded the government that "Political speech is granted the highest level of protection because of its essential role in democratic life." The proclamation of the EA extended from border to border within Canada. As a consequence, "the Regulations exposed everyone in the country to their reach: the fact that they were not enforced in particular areas is inconsequential because they still applied everywhere. The Regulations impaired the right to free expression more than was necessary. They captured bystanders who did not agree with the blockades, did not create them and protested in a non-disruptive way. The Regulations also criminalized travelling to a protest where there might have been a blockade, no matter the person's purpose for being there and whether an actual breach of the peace had occurred or not."[225] These infringements on citizen's rights were of great consequence and cast a chill on democratic discourse.

Evidence was presented to Justice Mosley that RCMP officers gathered names of citizens whose bank accounts were seized and frozen. They "did not apply a standard, such as reasonable grounds, before sharing information with the financial institutions." In fact, all that was required for a person's bank account to be frozen was "bare belief," not "reasonable suspicion" or "reasonable grounds to suspect."[226] As such, the regulations set in motion by the proclamation violated section 8 of the charter. Citizens have a right to be secure against unreasonable search and seizure. At least in a democracy.

As was brought to the attention of the POEC, Justice Mosley heard about the impacts of freezing bank accounts and credit cards. Canadian Armed Forces veteran Edward Cornell, and retired police officer Vincent Gircys, spoke about family members impacted by the freezing of joint bank accounts. Mosely wrote, "someone who had nothing to do with the protests could find themselves without means to access necessaries for household and other family purposes while the accounts were suspended." Testimony from RCMP before Mosley made clear the determination that this, that or the other citizen should have their assets frozen was entirely "ad hoc."[227]

The POEC was never intended to assess the legality and constitutionality of measures adopted by the Act, and it's a relief that a judicial review has proceeded despite the government's control of information and reluctance to disclose it. The government argued that the "likelihood of recurrence" of invocation of the Emergencies Act is "uncertain," and grounds for not proceeding with a judicial review. Justice Mosley disagreed, stating that the current political climate could not rule out the possibility of a recurrence of invocation of the Emergencies Act.

In his commentary, the judge pointed out the unprecedented nature of the legislation in the Emergencies Act. He wrote, "the Act vests extraordinary powers in the Executive, including the power to create new offences without recourse to Parliament, or public debate, and the power to act in core areas of provincial jurisdiction without provincial consultation or consent."[228]

Citing a 2012 Supreme Court of Canada decision, Mosley emphasized, "It is a fundamental principle of the rule of law that state power must be exercised in accordance with the law. The corollary of this constitutionally protected principle is that superior courts may be called upon to review whether particular exercises of state power fall outside the law. We call this function 'judicial review.'"[229]

Significantly, Justice Mosley declared that initially he was leaning in the direction of viewing the invocation of the EA as "reasonable." It was only after hearing arguments by the applicants for the judicial review that he reached the conclusion that the government had violated sections in the Charter of Rights and Freedoms, the Constitution Act of 1982, and sections within the Emergencies Act legislation itself. The legal arguments by the Canadian Constitution Foundation and the Canadian Civil Liberties Association were persuasive and comprehensive. And ordinary citizens speaking before a court likely would have not been able to make a convincing case.

He wrote of the CCF and CCLA, that the Judicial Review "demonstrated again the value of public interest litigants. Especially in presenting informed legal argument. This case may not have turned out the way it has without their involvement, as the private interest litigants were not as capable of marshalling the evidence and argument in support of their applications."[230]

The Emergencies Act itself is not illegal. But the February 2022 government proclamation of the Act, in response to the protests, has been deemed *ultra vires*. Unlike the POEC Report, the Judicial Review has the binding weight of precedent.

In response, mere hours after the release of the nearly 200-page ruling by Mosley, Deputy Prime Minister Chrystia Freeland gave a press conference. She told the press that she was "aware" of the decision, "however, we do not agree with this decision." Her comments were not made as a consequence at that time of having read the decision. She announced that the government would appeal the decision.[231]

Former Attorney-General, David Lametti, announced his resignation from Parliament within 48-hours of the federal court ruling. He also completely deleted his social media posts on his government's (X) account. Rebel News has accused Lametti of destroying official government records upon his departure as a federal member of Parliament. They asked a judge to order Lametti to cease deleting his records, especially those related to the Emergencies Act. Rebel News contends that by deleting his X (Twitter) account Lametti is "destroying evidence that may be used against him and the Trudeau government, just as lawsuits in light of the Court's decision on the use of the Emergencies Act are about to be launched." People like Edward Cornell and Vincent Gircys, who were harmed when their accounts were frozen, "now have the grounds to sue the government for what has been deemed an illegal action." In addition, Lametti's social media posts could have a bearing on the Liberal government's appeal to the Federal Court of Appeal.[232]

Five weeks after Justice Mosley's ruling, the new Attorney General, Arif Virani, maintains the Freedom Convoy posed a "risk of serious violence." Virani has refused to disclose to a parliamentary committee reviewing the invocation of the Emergencies Act what legal advice was provided to justify the government's action. He is refusing based on solicitor-client privilege. In this case the government, of which Virani is a cabinet minister, is the "solicitor." While Virani and his Attorney-General staff are the "client." As a result, Arif Virani is both a "solicitor" and "client." Technically, the solicitor-client privilege Virani wishes to protect is his relationship with himself.[233]

CHAPTER SIXTEEN

THE FATE OF DEMOCRACY

After a certain point in a fascist shift, it doesn't matter whether most people believe the faked news or not—eventually they simply don't have access to enough good information to assess what is real and what is not.
~ *Dr. Naomi Wolf*

When the CTV, Global News, and the CBC covered the police action against the remaining protesters on February 18–19, 2022, choices were made about what, and what not, to show their viewers. Canadian mainstream media reports aligned with Bill Blair's depiction of the police response as 'textbook police action' and 'peaceful.' This made Blair 'proud' of his 'profession' as a former police officer. Numbers of my friends glued to the CBC over the weekend of February 18–20, 2022, expressed relief at how peacefully they thought the protest ended.

In her testimony before the Commission, Margaret Hope-Braun recalled placing a copy of the Canadian Charter of Rights and Freedoms on the snowy pavement in front of riot police. When she looked up, she was looking into the barrel of a gun. Truck driver Csaba Vizi emigrated from Romania to Canada twenty years before the Freedom Convoy protests. On February 18, 2022, he was violently beaten and repeatedly kneed in the belly by at least three police on top of him.[234]

Christopher Deering, a decorated Afghan War veteran in the Canadian Armed Forces, testified before the inquiry that he was wounded in Afghanistan. He came to Ottawa to protest because he felt it was his duty. "I couldn't grieve my comrades in Nova Scotia because I wasn't allowed to cross the border in my own vehicle, by myself, to a cemetery where no one was living, and lay my flowers for my mental health. And I was denied that for two years." Next, Deering described his February 18 arrest. He said ". . . as the police took me down, again . . . he kneed me in my side, kicked me in my back. I was laying down. I was in the fetal position on my back. He kicked me in my ankle and my foot. As I was laying down, I had my hands completely up. I'm saying, *'I'm very peaceful. I'm peaceful. I'm not resisting.'* I was then punched four or five times in my head . . . a knee on my back to keep myself down . . . it was the worst pain I had been in since I'd been blown up."[235]

Freedom Corp. lawyer Keith Wilson was asked at the inquiry, "Did you have a concern about the fact that if that (police action) was going to happen, that you were suggesting to people to come back into the Red Zone, and potentially be in danger when the enforcement action started?" Wilson replied, "No. Because I'm a Canadian. And I never imagined that our government, our federal government, would use that level of force against nonviolent, peaceful Canadians."[236]

Police text messages revealed some officers thought trampling Canadian citizens with mounted horses was "awesome." Others wanted to have a chance themselves to beat up the protesters. They didn't want the protest cleared until they got a chance to rough people up. Can we take comfort in the fact that police in Canada refrained from firing bullets into the unarmed crowd of protesters at Parliament Hill on February 18, 2022?

In Tiananmen Square on June 4, 1989, BBC reporter Kate Adie described Chinese military shooting at crowds in the streets of Beijing. "As troop lorries were seen moving down the road, there was gunfire from those lorries. The troops have been firing indiscriminately. But still there are thousands of people on the street who will not move back. . . . There was confusion and despair among those (residents) who could hardly credit that their own army was firing wildly at them. . . . We were in the line facing the troops. They were about 250 yards away. . . . A huge volley of shots just as I left the front line caused panic. The young man in front of me fell dead. I fell over him. Two others were killed yards away."[237] Kate Adie described the scene in Tiananmen Square in 1989, reporting from among the crowd. In contrast to the BBC's Kate Adie in Beijing in 1989, the mainstream media in Canada were content to demonize the protesters from the comfort of their home offices. This began before the protesters arrived in Ottawa. By the time some mainstream reporters eventually showed up to interview protesters on Parliament Hill, slanted media reports had sown distrust. Protesters had an aversion to being interviewed.

After the Emergencies Act was invoked, the *National Post* interviewed constitutional lawyer Ryan Alford. He explained that the Emergencies Act, "the law that replaced the War Measures Act is so powerful, it was essentially designed to be unusable." The author of *Permanent State of Emergency*, Alford discussed the alarming breadth of Emergencies Act powers. He warned it was incompatible with the constitution. He cautioned that the Act can be used to target political viewpoints, and opponents, that a government doesn't welcome. Alford warned that invoking the Emergencies Act on February 14, 2022, could foreshadow an even graver expansion of state authority.[238] He worried that most Canadians did not understand what bridge had been crossed with the invocation of the Emergencies Act in response to the Freedom Convoy protests.

Is there a bottom line for Canadian democracy? Will a future government seize property, as was done to Japanese-Canadians in 1942? Or not only quarantine, but place them in internment camps? Will Canadian troops fire indiscriminately at unarmed citizens in response to some future protest? During the pandemic, there was graffiti in some parts of Canada that read "gas the unvaccinated." Is there a line that cannot be crossed once a prime minister has wondered aloud if a category of citizens should be tolerated anymore by the rest of society?

Many Canadians expect democracy to be something that just rolls along. There is a premise that anything that might undermine our democracy will come from a populist uprising and not from elements within the government. There have been news headlines in Canada about foreign interference in recent Canadian elections by the Chinese government to keep the Trudeau Liberals in power. The Trudeau government has resisted having an inquiry to find out who in CSIS blew the whistle on these allegations. Any blame, according to the Liberals, lies with CSIS.[239]

A pillar of democracy is freedom of the press. Elizabeth Woodworth has reported on the Trusted News Initiative. Her investigative report reveals a compliant media in a host of nations were willing to parrot government talking points during the pandemic and have government pay them off. During the pandemic, Canadians have experienced a stunning sea-change in integrity in reporting in this country.[240] News stories in the BBC, *New York Times,* and *Wall Street Journal* reveal lies and half-truths have been peddled to the public as a result of incompetence, groupthink, and Matt Hancock-type agendas to frighten the public.

Most Canadians have experienced the end of long-standing friendships and fraying of family relations. People may agree on some things, but the sources they consult don't. In 2007 Dr. Naomi Wolf wrote in her book, *The End of America*, about warning signs to watch for when a democracy starts to close down and slide into an autocratic state. She discusses the importance of freedom of speech and freedom of the press. When the press is restricted or co-opted democracy suffers, ordinary citizens can no longer rely on the news they follow to be based on fact.

Wolf states, "After a certain point in a fascist shift, it doesn't matter whether most people believe the faked news or not—eventually they simply don't have access to enough good information to assess what is real and what is not. In accounts of the Chinese prodemocracy uprising in 1989, you can hear well-intentioned Chinese citizens struggling with this: The *Voice of America* radio station was reporting on the uprising accurately, describing the protesters as idealistic students—but the Politburo was accusing the VOA of spreading unpatriotic lies. Chinese state TV, print, and radio called the protesters counterrevolutionary 'criminals' and 'ruffians.' Citizens, frightened by this, were writing letters to their newspapers haplessly explaining that they had diligently compared the VOA reports and the Politburo reports—and they found the Politburo reports to be the more accurate. . . . At that point, the state had made truth fungible."[241]

In the final chapter of her book, Wolf discusses another warning sign indicative of a slide away from democracy: subversion of the rule of law. By making threats to the security of Canada fungible, and the expanding serious acts of violence to now include psychological harm, the POEC Report waters down checks and balances on the executive branch of government. Cabinet now only needs to *believe* a threat exists in order to declare a national emergency. For a second time, an Ontario court on February 16, 2022, granted Freedom Convoy protesters the right to assemble and protest after the invocation of the Emergencies Act. Yet, the Report described the protest as unlawful. "Violence" is cited by the Report as a reason to declare a national emergency. However, not one of the seventy-six witnesses who testified under oath could point to any actual instance of physical violence according to the Criminal Code.

Ironically, Zexi Li, an inquiry witness who is an Ottawa resident and employee of the Government of Canada, stated it was "correct" that she "noticed the honking generally stop after the (February 7, 2022) injunction was granted, though some trucks still honked intermittently for short periods of time." She confirmed that she never "saw any protesters or truckers physically harm anyone." Li testified she did not see any truck drivers set fire to any vehicles or trucks. She stated that "the majority of the threats were through the internet. . . ." The closest thing to physical violence Zexi Li described in her testimony is egg-throwing *at* the truck drivers *by* Ottawa residents who lived in her apartment building. The OPS investigated this act of aggression on the part of Li's apartment residents.[242]

Making accusations for political gain that turn out to be without foundation has historically been associated with dictatorships. On January 13, 1953, nine eminent doctors in Moscow were accused of taking part in a vast plot to poison members of the top Soviet political and military leadership. It was known as The Doctor's Plot. *Pravda* reported the accusations under the headline "Vicious Spies and Killers under the Mask of Academic Physicians":

Today the TASS news agency reported the arrest of a group of saboteur-doctors. This terrorist group, uncovered some time ago by organs of state security, had as their goal shortening the lives of leaders of the Soviet Union by means of medical sabotage.

Investigation established that participants in the terrorist group, exploiting their position as doctors and abusing the trust of their patients, deliberately and viciously undermined their patients' health by making incorrect diagnoses, and then killed them with bad and incorrect treatments. Covering themselves with the noble and merciful calling of physicians, men of science, these fiends and killers dishonored the holy banner of science. Having taken the path of monstrous crimes, they defiled the honor of scientists.

Among the victims of this band of inhuman beasts were Comrades (Andrei) Zhdanov and (Alexander) Shcherbakov. The criminals confessed that, taking advantage of the illness of Comrade Zhdanov, they intentionally concealed a myocardial infarction, prescribed inadvisable treatments for this serious illness and thus killed Comrade Zhdanov. Killer doctors, by incorrect use of very powerful medicines and prescription of harmful regimens, shortened the life of Comrade Shcherbakov, leading to his death. . . .

The Soviet people should not for a minute forget about the need to heighten their vigilance in all ways possible, to be alert for all schemes of warmongers and their agents, to constantly strengthen the Armed Forces and the intelligence organs of our government.[243]

Soviet citizens reading their newspapers and listening to their radios believed at once the story of The Doctor's Plot. TASS and *Pravda* issued reports about uncovering a doctors' plot to assassinate top Soviet leaders, including Stalin himself. These reports were issued in the press at Joseph Stalin's insistence.[244]

But three years later, in a speech in February 1956 to the 20th Congress of the Communist Party of the USSR, Nikita Khrushchev told the Communist leadership The Doctor's Plot was a fabrication:

> Let us also recall the "affair of the doctor-plotters." Actually, there was no "affair" outside of the declaration of the woman doctor (Lydia) Timashuk, who was probably influenced or ordered by someone . . . to write Stalin a letter in which she declared that doctors were applying supposedly improper methods of medical treatment. Such a letter was sufficient for Stalin to reach an immediate conclusion that there are doctor-plotters in the Soviet Union. He issued orders to arrest a group of eminent Soviet medical specialists. He personally issued advice on the conduct of the investigation and the method of interrogation of the arrested persons. . . . The former Minister of State Security, comrade (Semyon) Ignatiev, is present at this Congress as a delegate. Stalin told him curtly, "*If you do not obtain confessions from the doctors' we will shorten you by a head.*" Stalin personally called the investigative judge, gave him instructions, and advised him on which investigative methods should be used. These methods were simple—beat, beat and, beat again.
>
> Shortly after the doctors were arrested, we members of the Politbyuro [*sic*] received protocols with the doctors' confessions of guilt. After distributing these protocols, Stalin told us, "*You are blind like young kittens. What will happen without me? The country will perish because you do not know how to recognize enemies.*" The case was presented so that no one could verify the facts on which the investigation was based. There was no possibility of trying to verify facts by contacting those who had made the confessions of guilt.[245]

This episode in Joseph Stalin's USSR is a cautionary tale of what happens when the press and politicians act with impunity. In a dictatorship there are no checks and balances on those in power. Allegations can be made against individuals and groups in order to serve political agendas. Canadians need to remember democracy isn't something that is guaranteed. Those brimming with allegations who warn of terrorists, mercenaries and insurrectionists protesting on Parliament Hill deserve as much scrutiny by the media and citizenry, as scrutiny toward those protesting.

In April 2023, the Liberal government was setting in motion more restrictions on free speech. Blacklock's Reporter wrote that "Cabinet in a letter to MPs said it is 'committed' to appointing an internet censor board called a Digital Safety Commission to police legal content. Prime Minister Justin Trudeau described uncensored speech as 'destabilizing.'"[246] The current Liberal government in Ottawa bears little resemblance to the liberal American administration of President John F. Kennedy. He said in 1962, "We are not afraid to entrust the American people with unpleasant facts, foreign ideas, alien philosophies, and competitive values. A nation that is afraid to let its people judge the truth and falsehood in an open market is a nation that is afraid of its people."[247]

In September 2021, *Toronto Sun* columnist Lorne Gunter was in possession of a confidential draft document from the Immigration Refugee Board of Canada (IRB). The document authored by board chairman Richard Wex discussed removing barriers for refuges to come to Canada. In the document, refugees would no longer need to prove they faced torture or death if they went back to their country of origin. As well, the definition of refugee was being watered down and was expanded beyond the United Nations' legal definition of a refugee. Gunter published a column about the new thinking in the IRB. Editors at his newspaper received communication from the IRB asking the paper to pull or correct Gunter's column. The *Toronto Sun* refused. Subsequently, the IRB approached social media platforms to have the article taken down.

The IRB and the Liberal government considered the column to be dangerous "misinformation." Gunter wrote, "This is a story because I had the confidential email outlining Wex's proposal. And it must have been obvious to the government I had a copy from the portions I quoted. Nonetheless, they still tried to have it banned as misinformation because it was embarrassing to them. It revealed a policy change they didn't want revealed, which is precisely why it had to be revealed and why the social media platforms should not have banned it." Under the cover of concern for "misinformation," the Canadian government under Bill C-11 may opt to remove news stories—not because they misinform—but because they inform citizens about what their government is doing which the government doesn't want them to know about and finds embarrassing.[248] But with its optimistic view of government, the Rouleau Report recommends passage of more legislation in line with Bill C-11.

After six weeks of testimony, the inquiry held a policy roundtable on National Security and Public Order Emergencies. Carleton University Professor Leah West questioned the framing and direction of the discussion. "[T]he premise of this panel is seemingly that what occurred in Canada in January and February of this year was a national security threat, at least as we understand them in the law." She declared the presumption was inaccurate. She pointed to protests where actual violence occurred, as defined in the criminal code, citing protests at the 2001 Summit of the Americas in Quebec City, and the G8 and G20 summits in Toronto. Yet, these were not labelled national security or terrorist threats.

West observed, "we have never labelled blockades and other non-violent but illegal means of obstructing critical infrastructure as terrorism. This country has a long history of protests along rail corridors and ports. While certainly these activities threaten trade and Canada's economic interests, they do not fall within (the definition of a public order emergency) no matter how broadly one interprets it." In response to the inquiry deliberating about reforming the legal and legislative parameters for threats to national security, Professor West issued a warning. "I do not believe this Commission or the Freedom Convoy should form the factual basis for those reforms." West pointed out that even if a protest is peaceful and illegal, it does not reach the threshold of triggering a national emergency. A majority of protests close down streets and bridges, as happens in my hometown of Vancouver with some frequency.

She cautioned that watering down the definition of threats to national security was not what was needed to come from the public inquiry. "I urge restraint in broadening our understanding of national security, and . . . expanding the powers and authorities of our national security agencies like CSIS. . . . We should ask whether Cabinet should have the authority to use executive action" to end protests. Professor West concluded that legislation to declare a national emergency must "explicitly define the trigger for that type of emergency. . . ."[249] I agree.

Rouleau conjures that there might be "a lone wolf actor" within a crowd seeking to inspire violence, or be violent. He suggests this would be enough basis to invoke a national emergency. But what future protest could not be construed as posing a threat to the security of Canada? Of potentially having a lone wolf actor? The inquiry Report offers future governments the freedom to conjure threats to national security based on 'worst case' logic.

In an interview with former CBC journalist Trish Wood, veteran journalist Rodney Palmer discussed the problems with the Nazi flag story in the media beginning the weekend of January 29, 2022. Palmer had worked as a general assignment reporter for the *Globe and Mail*, and a daily news reporter for the *Vancouver Sun*. He had also been a producer and investigative reporter for CBC radio and television, and as a foreign TV and news correspondent in India, Israel and China for CTV. Palmer testified before the National Citizens Inquiry. Palmer has cited Health Canada data that the government agency posted on its website acknowledging 455 Canadians died after getting COVID vaccines.[250] When he was on her podcast, Palmer told Trish Wood about being in Ottawa at the time of the Freedom Convoy protests. He was asked to film what was going on and spent the first five days there interviewing people and filming the crowds.

I was taking the pictures. I was down there by coincidence. I didn't mean to be in Ottawa, I was just visiting friends. My first instinct was to get out of town because the traffic is going to be stupid. . . . I texted a friend and said. . . . 'This is like Canada Day where we'd come all the time in our 20s, except it's freezing out here.' And she writes back, that's not what I'm seeing on TV. And I turned on . . . CTV and there was a still shot of the flag full screen. Still shot of the Nazi flag. Instantly . . . as a broadcaster, I think why do they have a still shot?. . . . The only still shot you will ever see that's not a video is the face of the reporter who's somewhere they can't get a camera to, and they want Rodney Palmer or Trish Wood live in the middle of an earthquake zone and we got no electricity, but their face is up there and we can hear their voice. So why is there a still shot of a Nazi flag, and I knew it wasn't unfurled long enough for there to be video.

And then I'm thinking, how did CTV get the shot? Somebody sent it to them. Who sent it to them? Why have they got it up there for so long? When I was here on the ground from sunup to sundown into the night for five days straight, I didn't see it, and I was right there walking a half a kilometre thirty or forty times a day filming. So, I instantly suspected that flag shot.

Months later, there was something about the picture (of the flag) that bothered me. It was the angle. It was down low. And I didn't even understand it to myself, I hadn't determined it yet. Alexia Lavoie of Rebel News put it together. She said this is the western wall of the Chateau Laurier Hotel because there is an angled stone staircase that doesn't exist anywhere else, except there. And she says the angle (is) from low, so how did they get there? They (the photographer) would have had to go down to the pedestrian walkway along the Rideau Canal. Then she points out, here is a gate that's chained for winter safety. The steps have never been cleared from snow the whole winter, and she shows me it. And she says, I can't even get down there to get that angle (shot). So how was there a photographer down there?

And then they look into the technical examination of the photo, and found it was a very high pixel photo from a professional camera, 10 mg . . . And then they looked up, where can we find this photo? And they found you could buy it (on the Internet). And the money went to a photographer . . . and it was his personal copyright, so he took the photo. And then they look up the guy and they found he's Paul Martin's personal photographer, he worked for the Liberal party, he worked with Cabinet. Holy smokes. The Liberals unfurled the flag for the picture, got it in a spot where nobody else would see it, released it somehow to CTV.

So, then they backtracked on Twitter to find out who initially posted it. Justin Ling, freelance CBC reporter, hater of people who don't get vaccinated under coercion. He talks about anti-vaxxers, conspiracy theorists, right-wingers. . . . The second tweet, Amneet Singh, Broadbent Institute, longtime advisor to Jagmeet Singh, tweet number two. So now, they plausibly connect this photo of the Nazi flag, this still shot, one-second snapshot, in a sea of Canadian (flags), Fleur de Leis, Quebec flags, peace flags, veterans (wearing) poppies—they put this (Nazi flag) and only this on the news. Alexa Lavoie connected that photo to the Liberals, the CBC, and the NDP.[251]

Palmer may have assumed it was implicit in his commentary that in addition to the Liberals, CBC and the NDP, listeners would understand CTV was also clearly complicit in this propaganda. Our federal government and the media colluded in smearing ordinary citizens as Nazis.

Nearly six million Canadians chose not to take an experimental medical procedure issued under emergency use and released in record time with very short clinical trials. For this they were fired from their jobs. They were prevented from getting social assistance, banned from socializing with others, and with the rest of society locked down. The protesters, who Rupa Subramanya found were mostly vaccinated, were concerned about the othering of nearly six million of their fellow Canadians. They wanted the sitting government to explain and be held accountable for all the pandemic measures they insisted had to be imposed.

When a government will go to this length to defame its opponents, and the media lets them get away with it, we are not living in a healthy democracy. It's debatable what democratic safeguards in Canada cannot be overturned in our current political environment.

From the start, the Liberal government wanted to invoke the Emergencies Act. Prime Minister Trudeau said under oath at the POEC that invoking the Act was on the table "from the beginning." Bill Blair signaled that by early February invocation of the Emergencies Act was his plan for dealing with the Ottawa protesters. RCMP Commissioner Brenda Lucki texted OPP Commissioner Thomas Carrique on February 5th about the governments rush to invoke the Emergencies Act. She noted that either the RCMP or the OPP could be asked to lead the response "if they go to the Emergencies Act." Lucki was on a call with a number of federal "ministers" who she explained to Carrique she was trying to "calm down." In her text to Carrique, she described how it was "not easy" to dissuade cabinet ministers from rushing to invoke the act "when they see cranes, structures, horses, bouncing castles, in downtown Ottawa."[252]

This was not the first time the Prime Minister was eager to invoke the Emergencies Act. On March 11, 2020, Justin Trudeau spoke to Canadians about COVID-19. He said there were ninty-three cases.[253] But on March 23, 2020, the Prime Minister put the Emergencies Act on the table as a way to handle the pandemic. "The federal Emergencies Act is a last resort, but as I keep saying, all options are on the table. If people do not comply with expert advice and government guidelines, we will have to take additional steps."[254] Recall, at the time Dr. Theresa Tam was not even recommending people wear masks. Between March 14 and 22 all ten provinces had declared a provincial health emergency.[255] How would having an authoritarian federal government free from parliamentary oversight aid the provincial pandemic measures?

Provincial premiers were opposed to invoking the Emergencies Act early into the pandemic. On April 9, 2020, Trudeau sent a letter to the premiers of the provinces and territories to discover it they would support invoking the Emergencies Act. CBC cited one provincial source who said "the whole idea of the letter was pretty quickly shut down." None of the premiers or territorial leaders supported his idea. "B.C Premier John Horgan—whose province has shown progress in flattening the curve of its coronavirus outbreak—was so angry he used an expletive and called the ordeal a waste of time. On the call with the prime minister, Saskatchewan Premier Scott Moe, chair of the Council of the Federation, questioned why the federal government keeps raising the act, which the provinces consider a non-starter." So, Trudeau backed off at the time.[256]

Along with government, the media, public health, police, and even the judicial system were singing from the same song sheet. Lawyer Bruce Pardy of Rights Probe observed an increasing pattern of deference by judges in Canadian courts toward those in power. Pardy commented, "judges have given deference to governments and public health authorities rather than scrutinize the rationales for COVID measures and mandates. Some have gone as far as to take 'judicial notice' —finding facts without evidence—that the situation was as public health and government agencies represented it to be."[257] If courts abstain from scrutinizing government claims, another pillar of democracy to stem government overreach is removed. Coming to terms with the shifting political landscape will be a bitter pill for many Canadians to swallow. It is not a given that the trajectory we have been on these past three years will not be ramped up again in new forms as we live into the 'new normal.'

In his book, *The Psychology of Totalitarianism*, Mattias Desmet describes how with a totalitarian system, there is a basic belief that human intellect can create a utopian society. The hands and feet of that utopian society are the technocrats, the 'experts,' who possess elite knowledge to take us to utopia. Yet, technocratic thinking, while appealing to a new horizon, "imposes itself based on anxiety, as a necessity to solve problems. With every 'object of anxiety' that has emerged in our society in recent decades— terrorism, the climate problem, the coronavirus—this process has leapt forward. The threat of terrorism induces the necessity of a surveillance apparatus, and our privacy is now seen as an irresponsible luxury; to control climate problems, we need to move to lab-printed meat, electric cars, and an online society; to protect ourselves against COVID-19, we have to replace our natural immunity with the mRNA vaccine-induced artificial immunity."[258]

The Canadian government has at times spoken about the need to eradicate COVID-19 one hundred percent. But, how can you ensure a virus is eradicated by a mass vaccination rollout where the vaccine employed does not prevent transmission or prevent infection? A respiratory virus is not the same as smallpox or polio. We have a choice as a society to either live with uncertainty and accept that people will—from time to time—get infected. We can take some comfort knowing that from the best data available that about 99.75 percent of those infected will recover. Or, as Mattias Desmet warns, we can build a shrine to human intellect and the experts and "look for a solution in an even more (pseudo) scientific ideology, false rationality, false certainty, and technological control . . . (and) end up with even more anxiety, depression, and social isolation. . . ."[259]

Desmet outlines the need for society to shake off the rhetoric of the past few years and "resolutely turn to truth as a guiding principle." He describes how truth-telling includes "the courage to publicly express words that break through the fallacious discourse of society," which leads society to a wider reappraisal of what it has endured.[260]

An example of the courage Mattias Desmet saw the need for is the witness of Dr. Julie Ponesse. She was a professor of ethics at the University of Western Ontario in London, Ontario, hired in 2001. Ponesse chose not to get the mRNA vaccine, and was fired from her position on September 7, 2021. She posted a video that went viral about her threatened imminent termination. In it she described her conundrum: "My school employs me to be an authority on the subject of ethics. I hold a PhD in Ethics and Ancient Philosophy. And I'm here to tell you that it's ethically wrong to coerce someone to take a vaccine. . . . My job is to teach students how to think critically, to ask questions that might expose a false argument. . . . I'm a professor of ethics and I'm a Canadian. I'm entitled to make choices about what does and what doesn't enter my body, regardless of my reasons."[261]

Truth as a guiding principle needs to include scientific debate about what is meant by 'safe and effective.' In April 2023, American civil rights lawyer Aaron Siri tweeted about a Food and Drug Administration (FDA) statement. Representing clients who are physicians and scientists who've taken issue with the US government response to the "pandemic," on April 23, 2023, Aaron Siri tweeted, "World-renowned scientists ask FDA to amend C19-V labels to state they don't prevent infection/transmission. FDA response: 'FDA's authorization and licensure standards for vaccines do not require demonstration of the prevention of infection or transmission.'"[262] While the pandemic has been promoted using the slogan "safe and effective," the US Food and Drug Administration climbed down that hill. They now insist they don't have to license vaccines that are required to demonstrate a capacity either to prevent infection or stop transmission of the virus they are advertised to combat.

Former US Center for Disease Control (CDC) Director, Dr. Robert Redfield "stated explicitly . . . that vaccine mandates and passports were unnecessary and unjustified for COVID-19. He stepped down at the CDC shortly before these measures went into effect" in the United States.[263] But when someone like Redfield called into question the pandemic mandates being implemented in America, like those in Canada and elsewhere, it got little attention in the media. After all, if the conclusions Redfield expressed were widely reported it could cause "vaccine hesitancy." Nonetheless, when Dr. Redfield testified before the United States Congress, many were able to watch it on social media. There is a disconnect between what many in the general public are learning from testimonies like Dr. Redfield that call into question the public health mantra of 'safe and effective.'

David Redman, a twenty-seven-year veteran of the Canadian Armed Forces who rose to the rank of lieutenant-colonel, is a former executive director of Alberta's Emergency Management Agency. In late April 2023, he testified before the National Citizens Inquiry. Redman said governments across Canada "threw away" lessons learned during previous pandemics when responding to COVID-19. He concludes that this caused "massive collateral damage" while proving to be unsuccessful in stopping transmission of the virus. Redman said the existing emergence management pandemic plan in Alberta long predated COVID-19. The plan was similar to that of other provinces. It involved four pillars for reducing illness and death from disease: (1) "appropriate" prevention, care, and treatment; (2) mitigating societal disruption through the "continuity of government services"; (3) minimizing adverse economic impact; and (4) supporting an efficient and effective use of resources during response and recovery. Redman commented, "we failed at four out of four."

"The aim is to minimize the impact of the virus on all of society. Within days (of the COVID-19 pandemic), it switched to . . . minimize the impact on the health care system and medical system. It was the absolutely wrong aim, and the result is what you've lived through for three years. . . . And what did our medical officers of health do? They tried to convince us that everybody was at equal risk. Absolutely untrue. . . . Eighty-three percent of the people who've died in Canada were obese." Redman asked, "So what did we do? We closed all the gyms, we told them they couldn't go outside and use the walking trails, and we gave them absolutely no feedback on how to make themselves healthier in terms of diet and exercise."

Redman emphasized that in a pandemic, according to Emergency Management protocols across provinces and territories, the premier is the responsible person. Provincial health officers and other members of a provincial emergency management agency assist the premier. The elected officials in a democracy are always in charge of the pandemic response. Not an unelected bureaucrat like a public health officer. A key principle in emergency management response to a pandemic since World War II has been to mitigate societal disruption and to minimize adverse economic impact. But in 2020, governments in Canada (and elsewhere) threw out decades of wisdom, disrupting society and maximizing adverse economic impact.

During his testimony, David Redman discussed the Emergency Management Process Hazard Assessment. He pointed to a chart from Health Canada providing an epidemiological summary of COVID-19 cases in Canada up to March 27, 2023. That chart confirmed that in Canada 91.3 percent of deaths from (or with) COVID-19 were seniors over 60 with severe multiple comorbidities. Redman also stressed that a proper pandemic response is to control fear and not to use fear.[264] Confidence in government was undermined when all the provinces, territories and federal government tossed aside their emergency management protocols for dealing with a pandemic.

As David Redman testified, the country with the lowest rates of COVID-19 hospitalization and COVID-19 deaths turned out to be Sweden. During the pandemic, Sweden did not lockdown its citizens. There were no school closures, except for the first two weeks for senior high school. There were no work closures. Social distancing was optional and only recommended, and at one meter not two meters as in Canada. Unlike Canada, Sweden didn't require its citizens to wear masks. At the end of the pandemic Sweden, unlike Canada, didn't have an increase in mental health issues, societal health issues—spousal abuse, suicides, overdoses, child abuse—or severe illness or disease. Sweden is a country with a population two and one-third the size of the province of Alberta. At the end of 2022, for those age zero to sixty-nine, Sweden recorded 2,188 deaths due to COVID-19. Alberta had 2,585 official deaths due to COVID-19 in the same timeframe. Clearly, lockdowns did not stop COVID-19 deaths. Sweden did have more deaths due to COVID-19 for those over seventy. But it is useful to note that twenty percent of Sweden's population is over seventy. While in Alberta, only fourteen percent of the population is over seventy.

In addition, Redman cited the Organization for Economic Co-operation and Development's Cumulative Excess Mortality in OECD Nations (2020–2022) statistics for September 2022. Chile had the highest excess mortality at 22 percent, and the United States ranked second at 17 percent. Canada was ranked in ninth place with 12 percent excess mortality. And Sweden was ranked at the bottom in thirty-first position with about two-and-a-half percent excess mortality.[265]

It was not permitted to question any of the pandemic measures, to ask: Safe in what way? How is it effective? Aside from repeated assertions, what evidence supported claims made to enact the lockdowns, social distancing, masking, vaccine travel mandates, quarantines? Never mind the increasingly dubious claims of asymptomatic transmission or vaccine mandates ignoring infection induced natural immunity? Problems with these claims and assertions are explored extensively in Dr. Naomi Wolf's book *The Bodies of Others*.[266] The question 'Is it true?' was ignored at every turn. Instead of establishing dialogue between protesters, politicians and government health officials—as recommended by police—the government responded by invoking the Emergencies Act.

A scrutiny-free zone was wrapped around every pandemic measure and the mRNA vaccine enjoyed 'religious' veneration. Journalism 101 was discarded as reporters asked one softball question after the next. Reporters functioned as cheerleaders for public health officials, pharmaceutical CEOs and government ministers. Almost without exception, 'fact-checkers' throughout the pandemic have functioned like a promotional arm of Big Pharma. The conflicts of interest should have been made transparent. Former CBC investigative journalists like Trish Wood and Marianne Klowak have commented on how far their former employer has fallen, as one example of media missing in action.[267]

When the National Citizens Inquiry held 24 days of public hearings across Canada in 2023, the citizen-led inquiry was ignored by the mainstream media. Over 300 witnesses testified. There were plenty of human-interest stories. Alberta resident Drue Taylor testified about her vaccine injury. At age thirty-one, this former power yoga instructor went to a hospital emergency hours after receiving her Moderna shot. Her resting heart rate was 130 beats per minute. Drue received a diagnosis from one of the specialists as having postural orthostatic tachycardia syndrome. This is a condition characterized by an abnormally large increase in heart rate upon sitting up or standing. She was barely able to walk, and only briefly with a walker. Her doctors agreed that her condition was triggered by the vaccine. A doctor has told her there is no cure. He sees it as his job is to make Drue Taylor "comfortable." Shortly after her visit to emergency, Alberta Health Service phoned her multiple times, insisting her devastating change in health was not caused by her vaccination. She was strongly encouraged to get a second dose which she did. Subsequently, her health became very precarious. Her adverse reaction from the second dose was magnified.

She described how her relationship with her children has changed. Previously, she used to run beside them while they rode their bikes, and go out to parks multiple times a week. Drue detailed how, "now they know to leave me alone if my door is shut, because I can't handle talking to them in that moment, or I'll puke or pass out. They know that if I'm dizzy, and my head is down on the table they can't approach me. They have to go to Dad." Drue Taylor has applied for compensation from the Vaccine Injury Program.[268]

Drue Taylor's off-message story about being disabled promptly after vaccination was of no interest to our mainstream media. The media have been averse to reporting news stories that question government pandemic narratives. The media has a responsibility to report both sides of the story of the outcomes for citizens during the vaccine rollout. Yet they neglected to report with fairness and accuracy what was unfolding. They only reported stories of people who were vaccinated who suffered no side effects. Canada's mainstream media failed to provide Canadians with access to enough good information to help gain make judgements during the pandemic. Our slanted media environment impaired our ability to gain perspective and make informed decisions.

In Ottawa, Rodney Palmer interviewed three truck drivers parked right outside of the CBC. Each were persons of colour. They were upset at media and politicians smearing protesters as racist. One remarked, there "are people from all walks of life out here. I'm a man of colour . . . every few trucks . . . there's someone of colour. There are people in the street who are coloured." Another man of colour sitting in his truck cab said to Palmer,

"Do I look like a white supremacist to you?" An Afro-Canadian trucker with dreadlocks said he wanted to tell the politicians "You know you're lying."[269]

When media reports are distorted and dishonest, democracy suffers. Depicting truck drivers as white supremacist was propaganda. Rodney Palmer observed that his former employer, the CBC, is "standing on the shoulders of decades of excellent journalism to trick us into believing they're telling us the truth, and this is happening on the very next newscast you'll listen to an hour from now. They're collaborating with the Canadian government, which is causing confusion. Because we believe the CBC to be telling the truth, it creates confusion."[270]

CHAPTER SEVENTEEN

WOULD I LIE TO YOU

. . . lies, by their very nature, have to be changed, and a lying government has to constantly rewrite its own history.

~ Hannah Arendt, historian

After the protests, courageous citizens began raising their voices to challenge the fallacious discourse gripping Canadian society. In order for our democratic society to return to health, there needs to be a reckoning—a logical and factual discourse—to discuss what has happened. This will require dissenting voices being included as part of the discussion. A vigorous debate will surely embarrass the government, and highlight its mistakes. But the government will not want the public to examine how it colluded with powerful corporations and pitched lockdowns, masking, social distancing, and vaccines to the public by creating fear and panic. During a pandemic, the government must seek to control fear and instill confidence, not to use fear to scare citizens into compliance.

Canadians are in the midst of an information war. For the most part they are only hearing from one side, now anointed by the Commission Report. A nation that builds a story about what has unfolded based on lies and half-truths is a nation that has lost its way.

Historian Hannah Arendt, in an interview in 1974 commented on what happens when you do not have an independent media in a society.

What makes it possible for a totalitarian or any other dictatorship to rule is that people are not informed. How can you have an opinion if you are not informed? If everybody always lies to you, the consequence is not that you believe the lies, but rather that nobody believes anything any longer. This is because lies, by their very nature, have to be changed, and a lying government has to constantly rewrite its own history. On the receiving end you get not only one lie—a lie which you could go on for the rest of your days—but a great number of lies, depending on how the political wind blows. And a people that no longer can believe anything cannot make up its mind. It is deprived not only of its capacity to act but also of its capacity to think and to judge. And with such a people you can then do what you please.[271]

Independent journalism in robust democracies had prided itself with reporting what happens in a headline news story, and providing perspective and context. In 2021, a new vaccine was being rolled out. Initially, Prime Minister Justin Trudeau stressed that no one would be required to take the vaccine. But that changed as Canadians learned if they chose not to get the mRNA vaccine they would lose their job, and get no employment insurance benefits. Canadian history teachers have taught students about World War II. Canada, as one of the Allied forces, defeated Germany, Italy and Japan in 1945. After the war the Nuremberg Trials took place in 1946–1947. Nazi German physicians were held responsible, and sentenced, for conducting unethical medical procedures on humans during the war. It was not good enough for physicians to testify that they were "just following orders." The security of one's person emerged as a standard for medical practice and experiments. This concern became the catalyst for creating the Nuremberg Code of August 1947. The judges at Nuremberg rendered this verdict in relation to any medical procedure or treatment. The Code was viewed at the time as a win for individual rights in democracies. The Nuremberg Code includes these values in the following sections below:

1) The voluntary consent of the human subject is absolutely essential. This means that the person involved should have legal capacity to give consent; should be so situated as to be able to exercise free power of choice, without the intervention of any element of force, fraud, deceit, duress, overreaching, or other ulterior form of constraint or coercion; and should have sufficient knowledge and comprehension of the elements of the subject matter involved as to enable him to make an understanding and enlightened decision. This latter element requires that before the acceptance of an affirmative decision by the experimental subject there should be made known to him the nature, duration, and purpose of the experiment; the method and means by which it is to be conducted; all inconveniences and hazards reasonably

to be expected; and the effects upon his health or person which may possibly come from his participation in the experiment. . . .

4) The experiment should be so conducted as to avoid all unnecessary physical and mental suffering and injury.

5) No experiment should be conducted where there is an a priori reason to believe that death or disabling injury will occur; except, perhaps, in those experiments where the experimental physicians also serve as subjects.

6) The degree of risk to be taken should never exceed that determined by the humanitarian importance of the problem to be solved by the experiment.[272]

But as the mRNA vaccine was rolled out, the media wasn't mentioning the Nuremberg Code. Were the new COVID-19 vaccines causing harmful side-effects? Were there reasons to re-examine what was going on? Documents released in the fall of 2021 by court-order in the USA revealed Pfizer knew by February 28, 2021 that 1,223 people had died from taking their vaccine. The data confirming this was according to the pharmaceutical companies own internal Cumulative Analysis of Post authorization Adverse Event Reports.[273]

After Pfizer's Worldwide Safety branch published this data, there should have been a five-alarm fire within the pharmaceutical company. Where was the impetus to pause the vaccine rollout and wait to learn more about who the 1,223 people were who died by the end of February 2021? Did they have any medical conditions in common that should exempt people with particular health profiles from taking these new vaccines? Did the dosage need to be adjusted with consideration to age and weight? Did a forty-five-pound five-year-old girl need as much of the vaccine as a fifty-year-old 250-pound man? Instead of issuing a press release about the concerning data and pausing the vaccine rollout, Pfizer and the FDA sought to have the documents sealed for seventy-five years. A court in the USA disagreed. The data was made public in January 2022. However, mainstream media outlets in Canada ignored the bombshell story. As Hannah Arendt warned, when citizens are not informed a government can do what it wants. Democracy devolves as people can no longer determine what the truth is regarding what they are being told. Canadian media ignored the damning Pfizer data detailing vaccine injuries and deaths in the first months of the vaccine rollout. They failed in their duty to report the news.

Instead providing citizens with fairness and accuracy in reporting, the media repeated the talking points of politicians. On September 9, 2021, the CBC reported that Joe Biden told the press, "My message to unvaccinated Americans is this: what more is there to wait for? What more do you need to see? We've made vaccinations free, safe and convenient. The vaccine is FDA approval. Over two hundred million Americans have gotten at least one shot. We've been patient. But our patience is wearing thin. And your refusal has cost all of us. . . . Listen to the voices of unvaccinated Americans who are lying in hospital beds, taking their final breath, saying, 'If only I'd gotten vaccinated. If only.'"[274] Though the lead CBC story was from the United States, its message was aimed at unvaccinated Canadians. But was this true? Were these new vaccines a panacea? Were the unvaccinated plague spreaders? The media didn't question these premises. A season of stigmatization was upon us. And lots of citizens joined in the sport.

The Public Health Agency of Canada released an epidemiological report that Global News ran a story about in July 2021. PHAC asserted "Since the start of the vaccination campaign on December 14, 2020, the majority (89.8 per cent) of cases being reported to PHAC were among those who were unvaccinated." This was a statistical sleight of hand since the rollout of the vaccine was graduated. Many citizens were still waiting for their first dose in the summer of 2021.[275] In August 2021, British Columbia's Provincial Health Officer, Dr. Bonnie Henry, announced that the 25% of the population that were categorized as unvaccinated—1.45 million people—were responsible for 84% of new COVID-19 hospitalizations. Henry said, "The science is clear."[276] While in the United States, Dr. Anthony Fauci told Americans in July 2021 that 99.2% of COVID deaths were from people categorized as unvaccinated. The Center for Disease Control Director, Dr. Rochelle Walensky, said "There is a clear message that is coming through: This is becoming a pandemic of the unvaccinated." Public Health Agency of Canada senior staff made the same admission.[277]

On August 26, 2021, the *Toronto Star* ran a front-page story with the headline "When it comes to empathy for the unvaccinated, many of us aren't feeling it." The front page ran comments from those who weren't feeling any empathy: "If an unvaccinated person catches it from someone who is vaccinated, boohoo, too bad." "I have no empathy for the willfully unvaccinated. Let them die." "I honestly don't care if they die from COVID. Not even a little bit."[278] Whether it was the intention to incite antipathy toward the unvaccinated or not, the *Toronto Star* was paving the way to make 'the unvaccinated' fair game.

There were consumer goods one could purchase to make things clear to any unvaccinated person who stumbled into your home unannounced. That Gay Candle Guy Co. in Michigan sold a candle in a holder that read: "If you're not vaccinated get the fuck out of my house." It got promoted on TV talk shows, including *The View*.[279] Prime minister Trudeau was explicit about who was responsible for spreading Covid in Canada, and spelled out consequences for travelers. "Canadians know that the way to get through this pandemic is for everyone to get vaccinated. So unless people have a medical exception, they will not be able to board a plane or a train in Canada if they are unvaccinated. That is about protecting our young people. It's about protecting Canadians. We are absolutely unequivocal on that because this is how we get through this pandemic."[280]

But experts began to walk back their bullishness about the Covid-19 vaccines over the following year. Deborah Birx was the White House Covid-19 response coordinator under President Donald Trump. When the vaccine rollout began, she told ABC on December 15, 2020, "I understand the safety of the vaccine . . . I understand the depth of the efficacy of this vaccine. This is one of the most highly-effective vaccines we have in our infectious disease arsenal."[281] However, in July 2022, Birx clarified her thinking. "I knew these vaccines were not going to protect against infection. And I think we overplayed the vaccines . . ."[282]

By the summer of 2022 it was becoming clear that data from health authorities were no longer pointing to 'a pandemic of the unvaccinated.' New South Wales reported that during the week of July 10-16, 2022, they had 2,058 patients in hospital with Covid-19. Of those, 142 were categorized as having died with Covid-19 (*though not necessarily as the primary cause of death*). The vaccination status of 140 of 142 of the deceased was known. 118 of these—or 84.3 percent—were fully vaccinated. In fact, 69 percent were triple vaccinated, 15.3 percent were double-vaccinated, and 15.7 percent either had just one dose or had never been vaccinated.

Former United Nations Assistant Secretary-General, Ramesh Thakur, reported sobering news about how effective the vaccines were. In the period for the weeks ending May 28 to July 16, 2022, the number of people who died in hospital in New South Wales *with or from* Covid-19 in this seven-week period were as follows: Unvaccinated: 110 |1 dose: 13 | 2 doses: 132 | 3 doses: 415 | 4 doses: 115. The pandemic of the unvaccinated was being supplanted by a "pandemic of the triple vaccinated," wrote Thakur.[283] Those categorized as "unvaccinated" included anyone who had been vaccinated in the previous 14 days and had subsequently died. The practice was the same in Canada.

There were also reports of some odd decisions in public health in Canada regarding Covid-related classifications. There was a tragic incident where an individual jumped from an eight-story window in Toronto. Advanced Critical Care Paramedic, Scarlett Martyn, was later informed that the case was classified as a Covid-related death.

Martyn testified before the National Citizens Inquiry in April 2023. She recalled, "We did witness strange things with classifications of Covid deaths. We were doing shift change one morning. So, the night crew goes off, the day crew comes on. We take a report from the night crew. They had just come from a jumper, and we said 'we'll help you clean things up.' It was just around the corner. It was from an eight-story building, and they had told us about the call. There really wasn't anything left to transport. Later that day, my partner and I received a call from Public Health—that the patient early that morning from that address had been swabbed for Covid and tested positive. . . . and I said, oh, that was the night crew that had the jumper. And I said I don't understand. What would you swab? Did you bring a spatula? This doesn't make any sense. That patient wasn't in a condition to swab. But they (Public Health) assured me that (it) was a Covid positive case. You certainly don't have to have medical training to understand the cause of death from jumping out of an eight-story building."[284]

I spoke to Scarlett Martyn by phone. She explained that the night crew told her morning crew the jumper in this case "exploded everywhere." The jumper didn't have an intact head or face for anyone to take a swab. The paramedic night crew that responded to the jumper had to bring spatulas to get the remains of his body into bags. Scarlett told me she also witnessed patients being admitted who had been swabbed three times and tested negative for Covid. Nonetheless, the patient would be entered into the system as having "tested positive." It was explained to Martyn that this categorization was made "just to be safe."[285]

In Morden, Manitoba, Shelley Overwater's father died on December 19, 2020. Before he died, at age 89 Patrick Rice was the oldest active skydiver in Canada. He still passed drivers' exams and drove a car. He was getting ready to get his ski pass for the coming ski season. Before he died it was known he had an aneurysm, which was diagnosed in 2015. Rice was told by his physician that any health issue arising from the aneurysm would lead to a very quick death. He was advised he likely wouldn't have time to get to a hospital. Around December 1, 2020, both of Shelley's parents got rapid tests for Covid. Her mother tested negative, while her father tested positive. It was known that these rapid tests could result in false positives. Nonetheless, Patrick Rice was asymptomatic.

At 5 AM on December 19, 2020, Shelley Overwater got a phone call from her mother. She was told that her father had a fall and was mumbling. By 5:30 AM, Shelley was at her parents' home. Two police and an ambulance were already there. One of the police standing at the entrance to the house told Shelley, "you're dad's gone," meaning her father had died. He was dead before the paramedics arrived. Her father had walked out of a bathroom and fell onto the floor, where he still lay. She covered her father with a quilt, because he was lying on the ground uncovered. At some point early that morning she found her mother on the phone with a health official from the provincial medical examiner. The provincial health official must have been alerted that a death had occurred at the Rice's address, after the death was reported entered into the health system by the paramedics. The health official was insisting that Patrick Rice's death was a Covid death. Shelley Overwater testified that "at this point no one had seen him. He had not gone to a doctor. He had not had any outside people look at him. The police weren't taking pictures. Nobody had seen him," examined him. His body was taken to a local funeral home and was cremated within days without any examination or autopsy.

Still, the Chief Medical Examiner's office with Manitoba Public Health was insisting to Shelley's mother that Patrick Rice had died of Covid. They told her mother there would be no autopsy. This was out of concern about catching Covid. Without any more information, besides that her father had died, the Chief Medical Examiner's official insisted Patrick Rice's death would be classified as a Covid death. Shelley testified that from the time he tested positive with the rapid test on December 1, 2020, until his death, her father had no symptoms. She stressed in her testimony that "he died in twenty minutes. You don't die of a lung ailment in twenty minutes." For members of the public who learned about this official "Covid death," what would be the takeaway? That when you get symptoms from Covid, these can suddenly result in falling, mumbling and dying within twenty minutes of being perfectly well?

Shelley learned later that day that Pembina Valley Online media outlet reported on December 19, 2020, that one Morden resident age 89, male, had died of Covid. She recalled that the Chief Medical Examiner's Office kept calling her mother. This was multiple times throughout the week after becoming a widow, insisting that she agree that her husband had died of Covid. Shelley testified, "at that point, my mother just gave up arguing. Because what was she going to do about it, exactly."

Shelley Overwater is a lawyer. In the spring of 2021, she happened to come across an affidavit signed by a doctor who was testifying in provincial court cases related to pandemic restrictions. The Director of Epidemiology and Surveillance Unit for Manitoba Public Health, Dr. Carla Loeppky, had submitted an affidavit regarding Covid deaths in Manitoba. In the affidavit, listed as a Covid-19 death on December 19, 2020, was male age 89, Morden, Manitoba. He was the only death in Morden on that day. Patrick Rice's death, and others, were being relied upon to develop Covid-19 death statistics. In her testimony before the National Citizens Inquiry, Shelley Overwater said that Manitoba Public Health "was padding, to put it politely, their (Covid) statistics. To me, this was an out and out lie. And they had no evidence to support that. They didn't even try to get any."[286]

In the fog of Covid hysteria, it was underreported that in July 2020 Dr. Anthony Fauci conceded that with "a cycle threshold of thirty-five or more, that chances of it being replication competent (accurate) are miniscule." Nonetheless the CDC and FDA in the United States, and public health authorities in Canada, were recommending Covid PCR tests be taken at a threshold of at least forty cycles or more. In Australia the cycle threshold was at 45. Yet, the inventor of the PCR test, "Nobel laureate Cary Mullis (in chemistry), said in an interview" that PCR tests "were not able to accurately detect the indication of the presence of live disease" and were "notorious for their ability to generate false positives. With PCR, if you do it well you can find almost anything in anybody," by amplifying the cycle threshold.[287] But this was not a story the media chose to remind the public about. Instead, the media reported positive case counts with full blown hysteria. Anxiety levels among the general public shot up.

On June 30, 2022, the Ontario Ministry of Health reminded its employees that "Unvaccinated is defined as not having any dose, or between 0-13 days after administration of the first dose of a COVID-19 vaccine."[288] Should anyone get the Covid-19 vaccine and happen to have an adverse reaction in the first two weeks requiring hospitalization, they would be counted as unvaccinated for the purposes of hospital admissions.

The late Hannah Arendt would tell Canadians that these are examples of lies governments tell their citizens. Scarlett Martyn was told by Public Health in Ontario that a jumper with no intact head or face had been swabbed for Covid. Shelley Overwater learned that the head of the Epidemiology and Surveillance Unit for Manitoba Public Health submitted a sworn affidavit contending Overwater's father died of Covid.

These are examples of the government trying to deprive citizens of their capacity to think and to judge. Scarlett Martyn and Shelley Overwater did not accept what public health officials were contending. But many how many other citizens would have given up? How many would have accepted that the jumper with no intact head had been swabbed? How many would have agreed with the Chief Medical Examiner's office in Manitoba that the 89-year-old man with an aneurysm who had no Covid symptoms, and had died quite suddenly of Covid? Hannah Arendt would say of those who would surrender to the insistence of these public health officials, "with such a people you can then do what you please."

The media has deformed democracy by serving up slanted reports while trying to frame it as news.

Former CBC journalists, Marianne Klowak and Trish Wood, recalled the golden years working in the CBC. On her Trish Wood is Critical podcast, Wood remarked that there was a time when everyone at the CBC understood that one of its principal roles as a broadcaster was "to hold to account the institutions of democracy." But in recent years the CBC had lost its way. Working at the CBC in Winnipeg, Klowak quit her job over the way the broadcaster handled reporting during the pandemic. Before she handed in her resignation, she had multiple meetings with senior CBC staff. Klowak recalls, "we weren't telling the public both sides of what was happening during the pandemic, violating our own pillars of balance and fairness. (We were) presenting one side of a complex multi-sided issue, and effectively censoring, cancelling and silencing the other side, only giving voice to experts who reinforce and control the narrative. . . . For the most part, logic, common sense, and critical thinking are suspended, preventing deep dives on stories holding power to account."[289]

The media could have held power to account by covering a court challenge against the vaccine mandates launched by Karl Harrison and Shaun Rickard. The Freedom Convoy protests were sparked by the vaccine mandate for truck drivers. But protesters also wanted all travel mandates requiring vaccination to be lifted. Freedom Corp. lawyer Keith Wilson, and former Newfoundland and Labrador premier Brian Peckford, flew in a privately chartered plane to attend the Ottawa protests. Regular commercial flights were unavailable to these unvaccinated citizens.

Both Harrison and Rickard were unvaccinated expat Brits who had family in the UK they wanted to visit. This included Harrison's 88-year-old mother. Rickard's father in Britain is suffering from late-stage Alzheimer's. Rupa Subramanya ran a story on August 2, 2022, on the US media outlet *Common Sense.* The headline read: "Court Documents Reveal Canada's Travel Ban Had No Scientific Basis." Subramanya described how just days before the vaccine travel mandate was put in place "transportation officials were frantically looking for a rationale for it. Then came up short." The Canadian government had always insisted that its COVID policies were based on "the science" and the latest evidence. The director-general of COVID Recovery was Jennifer Little. Her government panel issued the vaccine travel mandate and called it "one of the strongest vaccination mandates for travelers in the world."

But during pre-trial discovery in the case there were a number of bombshells that should have been of interest to the Canadian public. Especially since it had only been five months since Freedom Convoy protesters were challenging the rationale for having the vaccine mandates. It was learned that none of the members of the COVID Recovery unit, "including Jennifer Little, the director-general, had any formal education in epidemiology, medicine or public health." It turned out that the vaccine travel mandate did not originate from the COVID Recovery unit. Her unit had "discussions" with "very senior" people in the government about the vaccine travel mandate. Little was asked under cross examination by Harrison and Rickard's lawyer who had given her unit the order to impose the travel mandate. She replied, "I'm not at liberty to disclose anything that is subject to cabinet confidence."

The term "cabinet confidence" was in reference to the Prime Minister's Liberal cabinet. It was comprised of cabinet ministers, one (or more?) of whom had given the directive to the COVID Recovery unit to announce. The COVID Recovery unit itself, issuing its consequential mandate to require vaccination to travel by air or rail, has no website.

It was learned during discovery that Associate Assistant Deputy Minister for Safety and Security for Transport Canada, Aaron McCrorie, was behind the eight ball. In late October 20021, he was emailing Dawn Lumley-Myllari with the Public Health Agency of Canada. McCrorie wrote in an email, "To the extent that updated data exist or that there is clearer evidence of the safety benefit of vaccination on the users or other stakeholders of the transportation system, it would be helpful to assist Transport Canada supporting its measures."

As late as October 28, 2021, Lumley-Myllari was ignoring the questions Aaron McCrorie was asking now in a series of bulleted points. All she wrote back was to assure him that the Public Health Agency of Canada would be updating its "Public health considerations." The vaccine travel mandates went into effect October 30, 2021.[290]

Subramanya's expose was picked up in the London, UK, newspaper the *Telegraph*. A mid-August 2022 headline read "Justin Trudeau's Tyranny has Finally been Exposed—by Two Brits!"[291] Less than five months after protesters gathered in Ottawa to demand the government furnish documentation to support the need for vaccine travel and cross-border mandates, senior public health officials testified under oath they didn't have data to support the mandates. They didn't even recommend them. But the Canadian media largely ignored the story.

An exception was the *Toronto Sun*. Brian Lilley reported that Dr. Celia Lourenco, the person who authorized the vaccines for use in Canada was not asked for her advice regarding the vaccine travel mandates. She is the director general of the Biologic and Radiopharmaceutical Drugs Directorate within Health Canada's Health Products and Food Branch. No one in the prime minister's office, the health minister's office or the transportation minister's office thought to contact her and ask for an opinion. No one thought to ask Dr. Lourenco if it would be useful to mandate vaccination for travel by air or rail. As the court challenge was a matter of public interest, a judge made pre-trial discovery testimony available. Brian Lilley's article provided a link to the court records.[292]

Keith Wilson cross examined eleven senior officials with the Public Health Agency of Canada. The cross examination lasted for six weeks through May and June, 2022. This resulted in over fifteen thousand pages of evidence and transcripts from the discovery phase of this case. On a Viva Frei podcast in September 2022, Wilson detailed that during cross examination, Dr. Celia Lourenco "confirmed in her testimony that the final phase that has been used for every other vaccine in Canada was not completed by the pharmaceutical companies for the Covid-19 vaccine.

(It) is going on now on the mass population. (Lourenco) was under oath, (stating) that the last phase is going on and Health Canada is collecting the data from the general population. And she admitted this."

Dr. Lourenco was also asked by Wilson if she was familiar with the National Institutes of Health in America: "NIH." This is the primary agency of the United States government that is responsible for biomedical and public health research. The NIH partnered with Moderna in 2020 to develop a COVID-19 mRNA vaccine. When she was asked on the stand if she was familiar with the NIH, Dr. Lourenco said "No." On June 6, 2022, she testified that she agreed both vaccinated and unvaccinated individuals could contract and spread Covid.

Another official under cross examination was epidemiologist Dr. Lisa Waddell of the Emerging Sciences Group at PHAC. Waddell and her group are responsible for reviewing all "COVID-19 scientific literature being published on a regular basis." She is responsible to ensure this literature is communicated in lay terms for use by interested government personnel. Waddell, whose team reviewed the scientific literature on the issue of in-flight transmission, confirmed during cross-examination on May 31 that the latest PHAC brief on that topic was produced on Nov. 25, 2021.

Wilson cited a Public Health Agency of Canada report titled "Recommendations from the Public Health Agency of Canada to Transport Canada on the Mitigation of COVID Spread in Air Travel." In the report, Wilson learned that PHAC recommended to Transport Canada several mitigation strategies for travel. The first strategy was wearing masks. The agency also recommended social distancing in the departure and arrival lounges, and if the plane wasn't full. Finally, PHAC also recommended to Transport Canada COVID-19 testing. Keith Wilson was surprised at what PHAC omitted. They didn't recommend vaccination to Transport Canada as one of the strategies to mitigate COVID spread for travel. So, he said to Dr. Lisa Waddell under cross examination, "I put it to you that the Public Health Agency of Canada did not recommend to Transport Canada the vaccination of air travelers. Right?" And incredibly, Dr. Waddell said "Yes."

He asked Waddell, "Do you agree with me that requiring Canadians to be vaccinated to fly is not one of the identified strategies, correct?" Dr. Waddell confirmed, "There wasn't a lot of evidence on that so, as a strategy as a whole, it has not been evaluated in the literature and therefore is not elaborated in the review." The evidence obtained by the Public Health

Agency of Canada did not support a requiring vaccination for all travelers as being epidemiologically sound advice.[293]

Waddell confirmed that she was author of a study for Public Health Agency of Canada which showed little transmission on airplanes. Wilson read from the PHAC report that "A meta-analysis of studies from January–June 2020 found the risk of being infected with SARS-CoV-2 in an airplane cabin was estimated to be 1 case for every 1.7 million travelers." Waddell confirmed that this was the conclusion of the agency report.[294]

At a July 13, 2022, Dr. Celia Lourenco appeared before a hearing of the Federal Public Sector Labour Relations and Employment Board. She told the board that the people at public health "expected there to be a lot of underreporting" of COVID-19 vaccine injuries. Dr. Lourenco described this underreporting as "a well-known fact," since health-care professionals don't always report serious adverse events. Patients don't always speak to their physician, even if they've gone to emergency. Others don't even have a doctor.[295]

In December 2023, the Auditor General for New Brunswick, Paul Martin, released the Report of the Auditor General. Volume II contains a chapter titled "COVID-19 Pandemic Response—Department of Health." The Table of Contents read like a case study in dysfunction. Sub-headings include "Lack of Useful Reporting," "Key Performance Indicators Established but Not Monitored or Reported," "Targets Were Not Adjusted as Situation Evolved," "Inconsistent Documentation Pertaining to Infection Prevention and Control," and "Incomplete Situation Reports." The summary of findings on page 33 state, "*Technology was lacking and data was not always used to support staffing-level decisions while various performance targets were established, outcomes were not consistently monitored, tracked or used for decision-making there was inconsistent record keeping and documentation pertaining to infection and prevention control decisions there was a lack of established criteria to support decision outcomes related to exemption requests escalated to the Chief Medical Officer of Health.*"[296]

Paul Martin scrutinized the New Brunswick Office of the Chief Medical Officer of Health and its recommendations. Martin asked "the Department to provide evidence-based documentation to substantiate the decisions." He found "The Department was unable to provide requested documentation, acknowledging that they 'did not create a compendium or a repository of all of the scientific articles, papers, publications and analyses it consulted during the pandemic and therefore we cannot provide a fulsome and detailed list of all of the evidence consulted and used when recommendations were being formulated.'" Martin was stunned by the lack of evidence for the pandemic measures that those responsible for their creation could provide to anchor their rationale.

The CBC reported that the Auditor General also learned that the Office of the Chief Medical Officer of Health was at the bottom of New Brunswick's COVID-19 pandemic decision-making hierarchy. However, Martin concluded there was no way to know if there was "political interference" on the Department of Health regarding New Brunswick's pandemic measures. "I have no evidence that there was, or wasn't," said the Auditor General.[297]

While in December 2023, the British Columbia Supreme Court ruled in that fired unvaccinated Purolator employees must be compensated for lost wages and benefits. Compensation will be given to each employee to reflect lost wages between January 1, 2022, to May 2023. Testimony during the arbitration hearing included that of a top immunologist. They verified that "the COVID-19 vaccines in use provided no reliable protection from infection" sixty days after the second shot. The decision calls into question the guidance of provincial health officer Dr. Bonnie Henry throughout the pandemic.[298]

In November 2023, the *Daily Telegraph* headline reported the COVID-19 vaccine maker AstraZeneca was being sued. Their headline read, "AZ to be sued over 'defective' vaccine: Landmark legal action will suggest claims over jabs efficacy were 'vastly overstated.'" Clearly, the legal threshold for suing at least one vaccine manufacturer over the safety and efficacy of its COVID-19 vaccine had been reached.[299]

Finally, Chief of Defence staff General Wayne Eyre, was given legal advice on February 2, 2021, from the Office of the Judge Advocate General (JAG). The JAG document stated "We have no supporting evidence at this time that there is a need for all CAF members to be inoculated. Therefore implying that it is required for compliance with U of S [Universality of Service] or a BFOR [bona fide occupational requirement], at this time, would be incorrect." The JAG explained "considerable scientific medical evidence" would be required "to substantiate a COVID-19 vaccination as a minimum operational standard." But they could find none.[300]

Emergency room doctor, Gregory Chan, worked at the hospital in Ponoka, Alberta. Testifying before the National Citizens Inquiry, Chan spoke about the difficulty reporting Covid-19 vaccine injuries. "With the rollout it wasn't clearly communicated how to submit adverse events. I was trying to submit adverse events . . . I was trying to submit the adverse events online, you'd click on the link and they would go back to another link and then it would return back to the original page, and you would just go into this endless loop of trying to click to find out how to submit the information (10 to 15 minutes). I eventually I just printed the forms . . . filled them out by hand. . . . But that's not feasible for a busy emergency department. . . . And you have to remember that this occurred in May, the vaccine had already rolled out since December 2020 . . . this (was) five months into the rollout, and at this point, the vaccines adverse event system was operating in this manner."[301] Other doctors testifying at the National Citizens Inquiry complained about the website pages for reporting adverse events "timing out."

Dr. Patrick Phillips testified at the National Citizens Inquiry. He saw patients in an emergency room. Dr. Phillips testified that medical doctors have a legal obligation to report adverse events to a public health officer. He stated, "I did complete 10 adverse event reports . . . nine of them were rejected. I was contacted by a public health officer. He sent me a letter after the first five. He told me that none of these met their criteria for an adverse event . . . I send a note back to him by fax asking for details of why each one of them were rejected . . . *"Do you need more information?"* I want(ed) to make sure they were not rejected for a clerical reason and I did not get a reply." The one report that was accepted was for a patient who had a rash. Rejected reports included patients with "weakness in the arm and a complete decrease of sensation in an entire half or her body;" another who "lost the ability to walk and talk," and another who had "nausea for 2 weeks, bloody vomiting."[302]

In an age where public figures warn about misinformation and fake news, during the pandemic public officials were engaging in hype, misleading or lying to Canadians.

1. The federal government insisted on implementing vaccine mandates for truck drivers entering Canada. But in January 2022, neither Dr. Theresa Tam or Minister of Health, Jean-Yves Duclos, could provide any data to a parliamentary health committee to support the need for vaccinating truck drivers entering Canada.
2. Throughout the pandemic, all statements from public health officials and politicians championed the vaccines as "proven safe and effective."

Yet, the October 26, 2020, Manufacturing and Supply Agreement between Canada and Pfizer made clear the company required our government to acknowledge the long-term safety and efficacy of the mRNA product was not known. An access to information request made the heavily redacted agreement available for the public to view in November 2023. It confirmed the vaccine rollout campaign was at best aspirational.

3. Publicly available documents made available in the summer of 2022, from discovery in the vaccine travel mandate court challenge, reveal that the Public Health Agency of Canada (PHAC) did not recommend to the federal government that it require vaccination for travelers on airplanes. This was because there was a lack of evidence such a mitigation strategy would be effective. Testimony from senior officials in Public Health and Transport Canada also reveal that PHAC failed to provide Transport Canada with any rationale to support the vaccine travel mandate.

4. Though the Public Health Agency of Canada maintained the COVID-19 vaccines were safe, they had reason to halt the vaccine rollout given Pfizer's Worldwide Safety Branch Cumulative Analysis of Post-authorization Adverse Event Report of April 30, 2021. Pfizer determined that by February 28, 2021, 1,223 recipients of its new vaccine had died. The report was made public by early 2022. At that time, PHAC should have adjusted its guidance to Canadians, and informed citizens that one of the possible side effects of taking the vaccine was death. On September 15, 2023, Health Canada stated on its website there were "488 reports with an outcome of death were reported following (mRNA) vaccination" in Canada. Given Dr. Celia Lourenco testified before the Federal Public Sector Labour Relations and Employment Board that it was a "well-known fact" that adverse events in relation to the current vaccine rollout were "underreported," official public health statistics for injury and death post-vaccination do not reflect the full detrimental impact of this campaign on the nations' citizens.

5. The Auditor General of New Brunswick's report of December 2023 found that the Department of Health and the Office of the Chief Medical Officer of Health were constantly unable to provide evidence and documentation to support the pandemic measures they had advocated and insisted upon from 2020 to 2023. This one report of a provincial auditor general raises the question if a lack of evidence-based

documentation to substantiate the decisions is also the case with other provincial, territorial and federal jurisdictions?

6. Testimony from witnesses at the National Citizens Inquiry, including Scarlett Martyn and Shelley Overwater, showed examples of how public health officials were padding the numbers of COVID-related deaths. In the case of Patrick Rice, his death being "counted as a Covid death" was being used by public health in court affidavits to justify pandemic measures such as the closure of businesses.

The unvaccinated were blamed by politicians and public health officials for spreading COVID. However, these statistics included counting everyone as unvaccinated before they were able to get vaccinated. Ninety-nine percent of hospitalizations in January 2021 were among the unvaccinated because hardly anyone was old enough yet to sign up for their first dose. Anyone who was vaccinated and went to hospital, or died, within 14 days of vaccination was counted as "unvaccinated." By 2022, data from Australia and elsewhere reveal a majority of those either admitted to hospital, or had died, were vaccinated. In June 2022 pre-trial discovery for the vaccine travel mandate court challenge, Public Health Agency of Canada's Dr. Celia Lourenco testified under oath that both vaccinated and unvaccinated can contract and spread COVID.

On February 29, 2024, a class action lawsuit was brought against the government of Alberta and the Attorney General of Canada by plaintiff Carrie Sakamoto, from Lethbridge, Alberta. She testified at the National Citizens Inquiry in 2023, two years after getting a Pfizer vaccine in June 2021. After vaccination, she spent 17 days in hospital, lost her ability to walk, and almost died. Now 47-years-old, she testified, "I still have . . . full facial paralysis, the paralysis on my throat, the entire side of my body. I have a hearing loss that requires a hearing aid now. I have vertigo on both sides. I have a lot of neurological problems." Nonetheless, Alberta Health Services called her twice to tell Carrie it was safe for her to take a booster. She recalls telling the woman at the health agency, "I am still injured from my first vaccine. How can you say that it is safe?" She simply replied, "It just is."[303]

In the Vaccine Class Action Statement of Claim, plaintiffs assert "Health Canada negligently approved the Covid Vaccines under an expedited process which allowed manufacturers to apply for authorization for the sale and distribution of Covid Vaccines without the completion of all long-term safety studies or commitment to review new evidence about the Covid Vaccine as it became available . . ." It further claims "the Defendants knew, or ought to have known, that Covid Vaccines were neither safe or effective. The Defendants knew of reports of injury and harms caused by the Covid Vaccines and had access to information from the vaccine manufacturers stating the Covid Vaccines were not warranted for safety."[304]

There were other safe options. Ivermectin, initially only used for livestock in 1981, began being used to treat humans for a variety of ailments around 1987. It won a Nobel Prize in 2015, and was on the World Health Organizations List of Essential Medicine for humans. In his book, *The War On Ivermectin*, Dr. Pierre Kory—who successfully treats Covid patients with ivermectin in the ICU—documents that there were "ninety-five studies from 1,023 scientists including 134,554 patients from twenty-seven countries that show(ed) ivermectin's efficacy" in treating Covid. Though at first ignored by American doctors, by July 2021 outpatient Ivermectin prescriptions dispensed from retail pharmacies in the United States were through the roof. Kory describes how "Big Pharma and their big health agencies saw that US doctors . . . were increasingly and effectively treating Covid with a generic, repurposed drug. . . . They needed to bring in the big guns—a clever catch phrase or jingle or meme that would spread like wildfire and shut down the whole ivermectin business for good. Cue Mr. Ed."

On August 21, 2021, the FDA tweeted "You're not a horse." Around the globe, within weeks citizens were schooled to believe ivermectin was a dangerous horse dewormer. A CDC health advisory on August 26, 2021, warned US physicians of "reports of severe illness associated with the use of . . . ivermectin to prevent or treat Covid-19." It turned out the advisory was based alone on data from Mississippi. And the number of calls to the state's poison control center related to the "'veterinary version of ivermectin was . . . four. Four calls. Not overdoses, deaths, or emergency requests; just (phone) calls" with questions for information. No mainstream reporter bothered to tell their audience that ivermectin—like insulin for diabetes—is prescribed in distinct doses for both animals and humans. In the face of false media hysteria over ivermectin, by September 2021, vaccines for Covid were peddled as our only salvation. As it happens, in early October 2021, a campaign was launched in the media by Merck to promote molnupiravir to treat Covid. Ironically, "it turns out molnupiravir is also used to treat *equine encephalitis*. In horses."[305]

In her book, *W llful Bl ndness: Why we ignore the obvious at our peril*, Margaret Heffernan recounts the story of the vermiculite mine in Libby, Montana. It was owned by W.R. Grace. The corporation knew the mine was riddled with asbestosis and mesothelioma. "First it killed some miners. Then it killed wives and children, slipping into their homes on the dusty clothing of hard-working men. . . . W.R. Grace knew, from the time it bought the mine in 1963, why the people in Libby were dying. But for the 30 years it owned the mine, the company did not stop it. Neither did the governments. Nor the town of Libby, not Lincoln County. Not the State of Montana, not federal mining, health and environmental agencies, not anyone else charged with protecting the public health." And the townsfolk? They all thought that if there was something wrong going on with the mine, the doctors would tell them. But the doctors didn't tell anyone either. They kept quiet. Gayla Svenson, whose miner father died from asbestosis recalls, "It divided the town. People didn't want to believe it. There was real hatred between those who liked the company and those who were sick."[306]

Is the pattern of willful blindness by mining company W.R. Grace, to the presence of health harms in the Libby mine, something from which we've evolved? The Vaccine Class Action Claim by Carrie Sakamoto signals this same pattern of willful blindness prevails in Canada in 2024 across public health agencies, pharmaceutical corporations, provincial and federal governments, regarding harms from the Covid vaccines.

CHAPTER EIGHTEEN

A VIEW OF THE PROTESTERS: KENT STREET, DOWNTOWN OTTAWA

There is no honking at night.
~ David Maybury, Ottawa resident, February 3, 2022

Below is an excerpt of a February 3, 2022 account from David Maybury, a Kent Street resident in downtown Ottawa. Protesters were camped right outside his home. He walked into the crowds of protesters who were temporarily his new neighbours. David wanted to see for himself if what the media was reporting about the Freedom Convoy was fair and accurate.

I live in downtown Ottawa, right in the middle of the trucker convoy protest. They are literally camped out below my bedroom window. . . . I have read a lot about what my new neighbours are supposedly like, mostly from reporters and columnists who write from distant vantage points somewhere in the media heartland of Canada. Apparently, the people who inhabit the patch of asphalt next to my bedroom are white supremacists, racists, hatemongers, pseudo-Trumpian grifters, and even QAnon-style nutters. . . . At night I see small groups huddled in quiet conversations . . . There is no honking at night. What I haven't noticed . . . are reporters from any of Canada's news agencies walking among the trucks to find out who these people are. So last night, I decided to do just that—I introduced myself to my new neighbours. . . .

I spotted a heavy-duty pickup truck. . . . A young man . . . in his mid 20s, rolled down the window. . . . His girlfriend was reclined against the passenger side door. . . . I asked how they felt and I told them I lived across the street. Immediate surprise washed over the young man's face. He said, "You must hate us. But no one honks past 6pm!" That's true. As someone who lives right on top of the convoy, there is no noise at night. I said, "No, I don't hate anyone, but I wanted to find out about you. . . ." They said that they didn't want a country that forced people to get medical treatments such as vaccines. There was no hint of conspiracy theories . . . hint of racist overtones or hateful demagoguery.

(In) a stretch van . . . I could see the shadow of a man leaning out from the back as he placed a small charcoal BBQ on the sidewalk next to his vehicle. He introduced himself and told me he was from one of the reservations on Manitoulin Island. Here I was in conversation with an Indigenous man who was fiercely proud to be part of the convoy. He showed me his medicine wheel and he pointed to its colours, red, black, white, and yellow. He said there is a message of healing in there for all the human races, that we can come together because we are all human. . . .

As I . . . made my way back home, after talking to dozens of truckers . . . I realized I met someone from every province except PEI. They all have a deep love for this country. . . . These are the people that Canada relies on to build its infrastructure, deliver its goods, and fill the ranks of its military in times of war. The overwhelming concern they have is that the vaccine mandates are creating an untouchable class of Canadians. They . . . see their government willing to push a class of people outside the boundaries of society, deny them a livelihood, and deny them full membership in the most welcoming country in the world; And they said enough. Last night I learned my new neighbours are not a monstrous faceless occupying mob. They are our moral conscience reminding us. . . . We are not a country that makes an untouchable class out of our citizens.[307]

~ *David Maybury, "A night with the untouchables,"*
The Reformed Physicist, *February 3, 2022.*

125

CHAPTER NINETEEN

GUILTY UNTIL PROVEN INNOCENT

To release the Coutts Four would be to admit not just to the fact that Canada imprisoned men unjustly and denied them bail, but to call into question Trudeau's every action since the beginning of the Freedom Convoy.

~ *Gord Magill,* Newsweek

Over two years ago, between the evening of February 13 and afternoon of February 14, 2022, four men were arrested for their participation in Freedom Convoy protests at the Alberta border town of Coutts. They were charged with conspiracy to commit murder of police officers in support of a plot to overthrow the Government of Canada. Nicknamed the 'Coutts Four,' they are landscaper and contractor, Chris Carbert, electrician Chris Lysak, lineman Jerry Morin, and construction company owner Anthony "Tony" Olienick. They were taking part in protests about the vaccine mandates, and the unique requirement that truck drivers entering Canada be vaccinated. After 723 days, on February 6, 2024, Lysak and Morin were released after plea deals to confess to firearms charges not included in the original indictment.

A quick online search makes it clear that even persons accused of murder are granted bail in Canada. In 2013, a case of double murder in the city of Mission in the Fraser Valley of British Columbia concerned the deaths of Lisa Dudley and her boyfriend Guthrie McKay. Accused of first-degree murder, Tom Holden was released on bail.[308] On September 2021, thirty-one-year-old Umar Zameer was released on bail after being charged with first-degree murder of Toronto Police Constable Jeffrey Northrup.[309] In April 2022, Marlena Isnardy was released on bail after while awaiting her trial for the charge of murdering twenty-seven-year-old Matthew Cholette in Kelowna, British Columbia.[310] And in March 2023, twenty-two-year-old Ali Mian was released on bail as he awaited trial to answer to charges of second-degree murder in the shooting death of an armed intruder, twenty-one-year-old Alexander Amoroso-Leacock.[311] But the Coutts Four are not granted bail. Meanwhile, others charged of first and second-degree murder are out on bail. What is going on here?

Does the RCMP have a case that proves the accused pose a danger, if released on bail, and plan to violently overthrow of the government? Or are their applications for bail denied part of political theatre within a larger government narrative to justify invocation of the Emergencies Act?

In 1166 the Assize of Clarendon ruling under England's King Henry II established the tradition of *habeas corpus* (in Latin: "that you have the body") which gave those charged with a crime a right to appear in court to defend yourself. The 1166 judgment declared, "No Freeman shall be taken or imprisoned, or be disseized of his Freehold, or Liberties, or free Customs, or be outlawed, or exiled, or any other wise destroyed; nor will We not pass upon him, nor condemn him, but by lawful judgment of his Peers, or by the Law of the land."[312] And in the Magna Carta, section 38, it states "No bailiff (legal officer) shall start proceedings against anyone [*not just freemen, this was even then a universal human right*] on his accusation alone (on his own mere say-so), without trustworthy witnesses having been brought for the purpose."[313] *Habeas corpus* rights are part of the British legal tradition inherited by Canada. The rights exist in the common law and have been enshrined in section 10(c) of the *Charter of Rights and Freedoms*, which states that "[e]veryone has the right on arrest or detention . . . to have the validity of the detention determined by way of *habeas corpus* and to be released if the detention is not lawful." While section 9(c) of the Charter states that a protected right of Canadian citizens is "freedom from arbitrary detention or imprisonment."[314] But, in Canada with the Coutts Four in custody for over 600 days, the government is making an exception. We have to ask why?

Donald Best, a former Toronto Police Sergeant Detective, took an interest in the case. He suggests the denial of bail after this period of time smacks of political interference in the justice system. Does the denial of bail mean the four must be guilty? Best says it appears the RCMP gathered evidence sloppily, even as they claimed other unknown persons were still at large and connected to a plot to overthrow the Canadian government. He says the RCMP didn't fingerprint and DNA test the firearms and other items that might have been connected with 'other unknown' suspects. Basic investigating practice mandates that you want to identify if there are others involved in a plot. So, if you discover weapons after being granted a search warrant, you want to obtain fingerprints and DNA evidence. This can lead you to the identify those still at large connected to the alleged conspiracy. But the RCMP didn't bag each item where it was found. They didn't protect each item for its secure transit to a forensic lab.

Best wrote on his website a commentary titled "Denying Bail to Coutts Four is a Political Decision and Act." In it he wrote:

> Failure of police officers to adhere to fundamentals of exhibits collection and protection doesn't just potentially weaken the prosecution's case, it can also deny exculpatory evidence to the defense. Many times, I have seen otherwise good officers get "tunnel vision" about a suspect or an investigation, and begin to pay attention only to evidence that supports their theory of the case and the crime. These officers become so focused that they will even deliberately exclude evidence that doesn't support their vision of events.[315]

On February 14, the RCMP had on display a table with a cache of weapons on, leaning against, and at the foot of the table. An RCMP vehicle was in the background, announcing to local Coutts Freedom Convoy protesters, and the media, who had courageously foiled the plot to overthrow the government. Best views the display table and photo-op as serving propaganda purposes and not a serious investigation.

> "Items have been arranged on the floor with five of the long-guns rather precariously leaning against the table for display. No (investigator) would normally position or story firearms in such a manner where a bump of the table might cause them to fall. . . ." A photo of the cache of weapons "had a national impact and was used by both the media and the government as justification for invoking the Emergencies Act, and the police operations to arrest and clear Freedom Convoy protesters in Ottawa."[316]

Comments made publicly by politicians and the media about the protests in Ottawa were described by police as "problematic," "being controlled," "one-sided." Was the same true in Coutts? On February 1, 2022 Alberta

Premier Jason Kenney spoke to the press and residents of the province. He stated that he'd "received reports in the last hour of people allied with the protesters assaulting RCMP officers, including in one instance trying to ram members of the RCMP, later leading to a collision with a civilian vehicle in the area. This kind of conduct is totally unacceptable. Assaulting law enforcement officers who are simply doing their job to maintain public safety and the rule of law is completely unacceptable. And without hesitation, I condemn those actions. . . ."[317]

However, Rebel News reporters Kiane Simone and Sydney Fizzard found Premier Kenney's statements were untrue. Simone recorded a phone call he had with RCMP Corporal Curtis Peters. The officer stated, "There were no physical altercation(s) between RCMP officers and protesters. Yesterday, when we had protesters go around and breach the road block set up on Highway 4 to the north, there was some public safety concerns and officer safety concerns that took place there. Vehicles travelled through, drove through fields to get around the road block and then onto Highway 4. They were travelling southbound on Highway 4 in the northbound lanes. And that was happening at the same time we had a few vehicles leaving the protest and travelling northbound in the northbound lanes. So, we had a traffic-meeting head-on on the double-lane highway there. And we did have a collision take place. A head-on collision occurred as a result of all this between a person trying to reach the blockade and a person who was just traveling north on the highway. And fortunately, it was a relatively minor collision. But a confrontation which led to an assault took place as a direct result of that collision."

Peters was asked, "Was that an assault on an RCMP officer?" He told Rebel News, "No. That was an assault between two civilians, between a protester and a civilian." Kian Simone pressed, "So, Jason Kenney's statement was not true at the press conference." RCMP Corporal Peters emphasized, "I can tell you what I just told you, sir. You can have my name. It's Corporal Curtis Peters. I'm the spokesperson here. My badge number is 5-2-9-5-7."[318]

The RCMP issued a press release on February 14, 2022 about arrests they had made in Coutts. It included a photo of an RCMP vehicle in the background and a table in the foreground. Leaning against, on and below the table were weapons the RCMP said it "discovered" in "three trailers associated to this criminal organization." The weapons displayed included 13 long guns, several handguns, multiple (three) sets of body armour, a machete, and high-capacity magazines. The press release did not name any of the individuals or the charges against them.[319] Alberta RCMP Supt. Roberta McHale told Global News, "There was a heavy stash of weapons and these weapons were brought by people who had the intent on causing harm." She explained that RCMP were looking into a number of charges. McHale added, "This was a very complex, layered investigation, and some people might ask why it took so long. These investigations aren't necessarily easy."[320]

On February 17, 2022 a *Toronto Star* headline read, "Father of accused in alleged Coutts blockade murder conspiracy says son was radicalized online, as others dispute RCMP narrative." Mike Lysak's son Chris is one of the four accused of conspiracy. He expressed exasperation to a reporter as he observed his son "fall further and further into an online world of COVID-19 misinformation." The father said Chris Lysak had become involved in Diagolon.[321]

Two days prior, Global News ran a story about tweets from the Canadian Anti-Hate Network. The tweets announced the RCMP had seized "a plate carrier with Diagolon patches." The tweets contended Diagolon was "an accelerationist movement that believes a revolution is inevitable and necessary to collapse the current government system." Deputy Director for Anti-Hate, Elizabeth Simmons, raised the alarm about Diagolon. "A lot of them claim to be ex-military and . . . have some kind of military training." She added, "this is a very anti-Semitic group. It's rife with neo-Nazis." She pointed to the February 3, 2022, arrest in Nova Scotia of Jeremy MacKenzie on firearms charges.[322]

On February 3, 2022, Global News depicted Jeremy MacKenzie as the "creator of Diagolon." An RCMP warrant to search MacKenzie's home in Pictou, Nova Scotia, on January 26, 2022, cited a video where MacKenzie spoke about "Diagolona" [*sic*]. RCMP alleged MacKenzie planned to create a new nation from Alaska to Florida, made up of two Western provinces and twenty-six states in the United States. A Canadian Armed Forces veteran of the Afghanistan War, MacKenzie attended Freedom Convoy protests in Ottawa. Yet his firearms charges are unrelated to the protests. MacKenzie had a firearms license. But he was charged with having an over-capacity magazine. The February 3 news story added to the narrative that the protesters in Ottawa were violent. "Man who attended Ottawa protest convoy arrested on firearms charges," ran the headline.[323] Most of his charges have now been stayed.[324]

On February 17, 2022, Radio-Canada added to the growing narrative. Chris Carbert and Chris Lysak were described as men who have "ties to Jeremy MacKenzie, of the "American-style militia movement" Diagolon. Radio-Canada added this was a "neo-fascist, white supremacist . . . violent insurrectionist movement." The news story echoed that it was the aim of Diagolon to "establish a white nationalist state . . . that would run diagonally from Alaska through westerns Canada's provinces, all the way south to Florida." Carbert, it was alleged, was "prepared to die in protest of government mandates." It was said he posted on Facebook, stating "I'll likely be dead soon and likely will be front page news. . . . I will die fighting for what I believe is right and I mean this." And, "I won't live long. I've come to terms with this." Radio-Canada stated that "Carbert has prior convictions for assault, drug trafficking and two drunk driving convictions." Jerry Morin, posted on February 13, 2022, "This is war. Your country needs (you) more than ever now."[325]

On April 25, 2022, the CBC reported that crown prosecutors Aaron Rankin and Matt Dalidowicz stated that the plan was to try all four men in one trial. Daldiowicz told the CBC that the cases for Carbert, Olienick, and Morin were "moving quickly." But there were complications with the Lysak case.[326] The *Lethbridge Herald* reported on June 10, 2022, that three of the Coutts Four had been denied bail, with Jerry Morin awaiting his bail hearing.[327]

In September 2022, some of the contents of the Information to Obtain search warrant by RCMP Constable Trevor Checkley were made public. An Alberta judge allowed RCMP officers to search properties in Coutts after Checkley's urgent request, swearing an oath that he believed a serious crime was about to be committed. In the ITO, Checkley swore before the judge, "I have reasonable grounds to believe that (Tony) Olienick, (Chris) Carbert and (Jerry) Morin were part of a group that participated in the Coutts blockade and brought firearms into the Coutts blockade area with the intention of using those firearms against police." The officer attested that "I believe (these protesters were) arming themselves for a standoff against police."[328]

On November 30, 2022, the *Calgary Herald* hollered, "Some Coutts protesters wanted to alter Canada's political system." Undercover officers reported Anthony Olienick bragged that Chris Lysak was "a hitman, sniper and gun-fighter." Checkley warned that Jerry "Morin said it was World War Three . . . and making everyone slaves was warfare."[329] The CBC also ran a story detailing how these men apparently made phone calls while in custody to bosses of their "extremist network . . . Diagolon." There were unnamed bosses outside of Coutts who were allegedly directing the Coutts accused to agitate for a new government.[330]

In *Newsweek*, commentator Gord Magill noted that after establishing the narrative about the four alleged conspirators, the media went dark. "Canada's media have been shamefully silent on the Coutts Four. Happy to report on the initial arrest and repeat the spurious allegations of the RCMP and the Crown, they have failed to ask deeper, fundamental questions about how this situation flies in the face of the rule of law and the presumption of innocence, or why in a country where it feels like almost everyone is granted bail, these men have been denied it."[331]

During the Public Order Emergency Commission in Ottawa in the fall of 2022, the protests at Coutts were on the A-list of events cited to justify the invocation of the Emergencies Act. The Clerk of the Privy Council is Janice Charette. In testimony, she warned about the protests in Coutts. "We were seeing the results of the law enforcement activity and what was happening at Coutts and we were seeing the size of the stash of firearms and ammunition that were found in Coutts amongst the protesters. So, this was new and I would say relevant information in terms of just the nature of the threat that we were worried about in terms of the risk for serious violence."[332]

Charette testified that "the situation at Coutts was more complex. . . . It looked like it was getting fixed, then it was not getting fixed; looked like it was getting fixed, then it was not getting fixed. . . . The quantity of weapons and ammunition that was discovered by the RCMP conducting that law enforcement activity was more than I would have expected. So that, to me, indicated a seriousness and a scale of the illegal activity that was either contemplated at Coutts or people were ready to engage in at Coutts . . . that was beyond . . . my prior expectations. . . ." When discussing the Freedom Convoy protests across Canada, including Coutts, Janice Charette warned of insurrectionist intentions. "There was talk of overthrowing the government and installing a different government with a governor general."[333]

Deputy Clerk of the Privy Council, Nathalie Drouin, was asked if she was aware that protesters in Coutts planned to leave the blockade. "Well, I was not aware of that. No, that's not true. I have heard about the potential breakthrough in Coutts . . . prior to the enforcement action, we didn't know about the cache."[334]

Public Safety Minister Marco Mendicino testified that Coutts was a trigger for cracking down on the Freedom Convoy protests. We did not know "exactly how . . . the operation in Coutts was going to play out at that time, and bearing in mind the sensitivities, the fact that the situation was combustible, that the individuals that were involved in Coutts were prepared to go down with a fight that could lead to the loss of life, . . . would (it) have triggered other events across the country . . . that's why I—in my mind, it was very much—it was a threshold moment."[335]

Trudeau's National Security Advisor, Jody Thomas, discussed the decision-making process regarding invocation of the Emergencies Act. She wondered, can "acts of serious violence" include "the violence that people . . . of Ottawa were experiencing on the streets, . . . the inability of the Town of Coutts to function, is that a line? . . . There is a spectrum of activity and behaviour and threat in there that we need to understand."[336]

In her testimony before the POEC, Deputy Prime Minister Chrystia Freeland spoke about the protests in Coutts as accelerating the sense that the government had to respond decisively to the Freedom Convoy. She recalled that on February 12, 2022, when "we heard from the RCMP Commissioner about concerns that there were serious weapons in Coutts . . . that really raised the stakes in terms of my degree of concern about what could be happening in this sort of whack-a-mole copycat situation across the country."[337]

Prime Minister Justin Trudeau explained that one of the reasons invoking the Emergencies Act was on the table "was (the) presence of weapons at Coutts . . ." Trudeau said once Premier Jason Kenney removed "a number of mandates" in Alberta, "the occupation at Coutts seemed to be emboldened. . . . 'Let's keep going.'" Trudeau, who had raised the idea with Canadian premiers of invoking the Emergencies Act in March 2020 in response to the pandemic, admitted under cross-examination that he thought of invoking the Emergencies Act in response to the vaccine mandate protests "from the very beginning"—possibly before the protesters arrived in Ottawa.[338]

Sometime before the arrests in Coutts, the mayor of Coutts, Jimmy Willett, sent a text to CTV reporter Bill Graveland. In it the mayor described the protesters in Coutts as "Domestic Terrorists." But he told Graveland in the text, "You need to find someone in a protected position to call these guys what they are, Domestic Terrorists. Won't be me. They are right outside my window. I would be strung up, literally. Just a thought." He stated that his wife saw some protesters "moving heavy hockey bags" and said, "it's guns." His text was entered as evidence during Willett's testimony before the POEC in Ottawa on November 9, 2022.[339] Why the mayor's wife presumed the hockey bags contained guns has not been followed up by any reporters.

On Tom Marazzo's Meet Me in the Middle podcast on June 20, 2023, Jeremy MacKenzie spoke about the lack of interest by the RCMP and the Canadian Security and Intelligence Service in asking him about Diagolon. He told Tom Marazzo on the podcast that sixteen months after the protests in the winter of 2022, "I still to this day have not been asked a single question by the RCMP or CSIS . . . regarding any of this (Diagolon)." MacKenzie asserted that the government of Canada needed a "punching bag" to scare citizens and invoke the Emergencies Act.[340]

At the POEC, MacKenzie testified from his prison cell in the Saskatchewan Correctional Centre. MacKenzie confirmed that in January 2021 he drew a diagonal line on his cell phone from Alaska, through Alberta and Saskatchewan, through the Dakotas, down to Texas, and across to Florida and named it Diagolon. It became a brand name for followers on his podcasts. He made a plastic goat figurine, named Philip, the vice-president of Diagolon. Philip, he explained to his viewers, was a demonic time-travelling, cocaine addict. He pointed out that the official narrative about Diagolon as "militia" and "extremist" has come from the largely government-funded Canadian Anti-Hate Network. MacKenzie observed how Anti-Hate posts scary articles about Diagolon, which both the media and the police take at face value.[341] While in Ottawa, Jeremy MacKenzie posted that he wanted any of his followers at the Freedom Convoy protests, "If there's a speed limit (go) slower than that. Don't even litter. Don't sit. Don't even throw a snowball. Don't give anyone any excuse to point at you and say, 'Look what you've done.'"[342]

MacKenzie testified he met Chris Lysak in person in Saskatchewan in the summer of 2021, including at a BBQ. As well, MacKenzie spoke to Lysak after charges for conspiracy to commit murder were laid. MacKenzie verified the patches on tactical vests on display by the RCMP on February 14, 2022, looked like Diagolon patches. "I really can't speak to their origins," stated MacKenzie.[343] During POEC testimony, it was recorded that the Afghan War veteran has no criminal record.

Should law enforcement take an organization with a plastic goat figurine as its vice-president seriously? How might the United States government view an attempt to trigger the secession of twenty-six states from Alaska and Idaho across to Florida and north to Virginia? Or, was this just a far-fetched story by the self-described "sarcastic" MacKenzie? Was it just what he said Diagolon was, "a joke" by a disillusioned decorated Afghan War veteran of the Canadian Armed Forces making fun of the Canadian intelligence community?

A Search Warrant was issued on February 13, 2022, to RCMP Constable Trevor Checkley. It was shown on a screen during the July 13, 2023, episode of the Good Morning with Jason podcast. Donald Best walked viewers through the document. The search was granted, effective 10 p.m. on February 13. This was due to Checkley's sworn oath that he had reasonable grounds to suspect "Mischief Over $5,000." The warrant was not issued on "weapons charges" or "conspiracy to commit murder." The search stated officers could search for "Documents and data related to planning organization and operations of the protest group's security for the Coutts blockade." A question the lawyers for the four accused need to determine is if it is legitimate to have a Search Warrant for a minimum charge; if the RCMP believes a far more serious crime is about to unfold but does not name it in the search. Best highlights that in order to get a Search Warrant, there are affidavits and likely photos presented to the judge to support the Information to Obtain a search.[344]

Chris Lysak got arrested in front of Smuggler's Saloon, in Coutts, in amongst all the protesters around 9 p.m. on February 13. Danielle Slettede, a friend of Tony Olienick, spoke on the Trish Wood is Critical podcast. She recalled, "Tony's last words while he was videotaping was 'I wish those cops would put those guns down and come and have coffee with us. He already knew about Chris Lysak's arrest. He didn't take any action, arm himself, or try to find his alleged co-conspirators. Instead, he kept videotaping." Olienick was arrested peacefully and unarmed about 9:50 p.m. among the protesters. Around 12:30 a.m. Chris Carbert was sleeping in his trailer when the RCMP did the raid on the property. . . . Carbert knew the other two had been arrested. Yet, Carbert chose to go to bed instead of trying to overthrow the government. Around noon on February 14, Jerry Morin was arrested by the RCMP. Morin knew the other three had been arrested.[345]

Retired police sergeant Donald Best flags several problems with the timeline of arrests. "This is all politically driven. They (several Liberal cabinet ministers) knew about it in Ottawa before the warrant went down. We saw that from the Commission (POEC) . . . that means the politicians on the political side of this were involved in the creation of, and the timeline, and the date and time of execution; And if all that is true, and

I believe it is . . . these men deserve to see their day in court. And they deserve to be out with an ankle bracelet, or whatever."[346]

Gord Magill reporting in *Newsweek* stated, "Undercover police officers at the Coutts protest alleged that Olienick and Carbert discussed the delivery of a heavy package, which officers said contained guns. But according to an application the RCMP filed for a search warrant, the men were discussing hockey equipment, an electric guitar, and toy trucks for the many kids at the protest—which the RCMP deemed was code for weapons."[347]

Commenting on the cache of weapons displayed by the RCMP on February 14, 2022, local gun owner Zach Schmidt spoke on a podcast hosted by independent reporter Jason Lavigne. Schmidt said, "This is not what I would be choosing if I were to hypothetically (try) to take down the RCMP. There were about fifty RCMP vehicles in the Coutts vicinity and so about a hundred officers. . . . This just looks like someone's basement was raided. Numbers of the guns are rifles that would be better for hunting deer. There are no sniper rifles, no precision riffles. They're just run-of-the-mill hunting guns." Donald Best added, "When the RCMP were investigating the multiple shooting in Nova Scotia (in 2022), the lead investigators refused to release the types and photos of the weapons involved. Why? Because they're in the middle of an investigation. They want to know where they came from. Contrast that with the RCMP action in Coutts."[348]

Donald Best commented on the Crown having offered some of the men a plea deal. If the Crown "had a really solid case after holding these guys for a year and a half . . . there'd be no deals. They would want to have these guys strung up in public."[349]

The POEC Report states "RCMP Commissioner Lucki called Minister Mendicino to update him on the situation in Coutts. The call was private because the RCMP has undercover personnel in the field . . . Commissioner Lucki told Minister Mendicino that Coutts involved "a hardened cell" of individuals, armed with firearms, who were willing to "go down" for their cause. Minister Mendicino testified that this was the most serious and urgent moment in the blockade so far. He told Commissioner Lucki that he could not keep the information entirely to himself; he had to at least inform the Prime Minister. After the call, he reached out to Katie Telford, Chief of Staff to the Prime Minister, and told her what he learned from Commissioner Lucki."[350]

Reading the POEC Report, Marco Van Huigenbos wondered, "How could Brenda Lucki inform Minister Mendicino on details stemming out of search warrants that would not be executed till the early morning hours of February 14th MST?"[351]

"Police later found firearms, 36,000 rounds of ammunition, and industrial explosives at Olienick's home—but according to friends and family, the guns were legally obtained, the ammunition is the kind commonly used in rural Alberta to shoot gophers, and Olienick's property sits on a gravel mine; he and his father used the explosives to mine gravel. The guns that police seized from Lysak's trailer were similarly legally obtained and registered."[352]

Though the RCMP alleged the Coutts accused of conspiracy to commit murder were taking direction from "unknown others," no one else since the initial arrests has been charged or named as being investigated in connection to the alleged conspiracy. No specific RCMP officer has been named as being a potential target of the accused. No specific time or event has been named to bolster allegations of conspiracy to commit murder. What would be the motive of these four men? Two were school mates. But the four only got acquainted for the first time during the Coutts blockade.

Jerry Morin was working on Vancouver Island the first two weeks of the protest in Coutts. He arrived in Milk River on February 11, and left for Calgary around 5 a.m. on February 13. He brought some groceries to Coutts to feed protesters and to bring a friend of his who was a country music singer to perform. In the noon hour on February 14, Jerry Morin was on his way to do an electrical job in a barn for a rancher in Priddis, Alberta. A police SWAT Team surrounded him and arrested him on the side of Highway 22X, while he was heading west of Calgary to his client's ranch. Trish Wood spoke with Jaclyne Martin, who was also arrested, about the guns displayed on the table by the RCMP. Wood asked Martin, "what is the table of guns, and what do they have to do with you guys?" Martin replied, "I have no idea. I was shown that table of guns during my interrogation on the night of the 14th. None of those guns belong to Jerry or I. No idea where they came from."[353]

Newsweek reported that Margaret "Granny" Mackay created a Facebook page and is in regular contact with the accused. "Mackay has highlighted the subpar treatment the men have received in remand, including being held in segregation, a polite term for the torture known as solitary confinement; having necessary medical treatment delayed."[354]

We are asked to believe that these four met in Coutts late during the protests. Upon making an acquaintance with each other, they came up with the idea of using some hunting rifles, and bear spray, to begin a standoff between the four of them and the hundred or more RCMP on the ground in Coutts. Moreover, this was to be a catalyst for overthrowing the government of Canada.

At the inquiry in Ottawa, evidence was entered related to Chrystia Freeland's note made prior to February 14, 2022. In her November 24, 2022, testimony, she was reminded of what she wrote. "We need to move faster. We need a new playbook. You need to designate this group as a terrorist group." Someone named "Dave" was the "you" in this instance. But under cross-examination, Freeland could not recall Dave's surname. Was it David Vigneault, the Director of CSIS, the Canadian Security and Intelligence Service? She stated that "one hundred percent" she did not meet with David Vigneault around this time. But, did she make a phone call? How many men named Dave does Chrystia Freeland know who are in a position to designate groups of Canadian citizens as terrorists? Were Freeland's notes indicative of a political agenda that led to the arrest of these Coutts protesters?[355]

A trial date is promised for late spring 2024. Chris Carbert has been leading a Bible study in the remand centre. Jerry Morin's partner, Jaclyne Martin, related on Jason Lavigne's podcast, that Jerry has been led inmates in yoga classes. "A guard told Jerry after he'd been in custody for a few weeks, *"This is weird. We were expecting a lot of different behavior from you. We thought that you were a white supremacist."*[356]

In their report, "The Hategate Affair: Unmasking Canada's Hate Industry," Caryma Sa'd and Eliza Hategan discuss documents released in a Freedom of Information and Protection of Privacy (FOIPOP) request to Federal Policing by Jeremy MacKenzie. Released on September 1, 2023, Sa'd and Hategan concluded after their review, that "the FOIPOP documents heavily suggest that RCMP intelligence takes their cues from the press, relying on second-hand information rather than presenting as the originating source of information distributed to the press. One wonders how much of their "intel" simply consists of scouring daily news and disseminating it through regular "MEDIA SCAN" emails."

Kristen Little, RCMP Intelligence Analyst with the Ideologically Motivated Criminal Intelligence Team (IMCIT) expressed concern in an email on February 14, 2022, about the stampede to jump to conclusions. In response to requests from senior government officials for an RCMP statement regarding threats to national security, she cautioned in relation to Diagolon and linking it to arrests in Coutts, "but before our unit's name is on something I want to be sure we are giving accurate historical context and a full picture."[357]

However, in the scramble to please the higher-ups, the RCMP threw caution to the wind. A fifteen-minute assessment was praised and apparently all that was needed for the RCMP to offer an opinion, based on open-source material from media reports. This, in turn, was seized upon by Public Safety Minister Marco Mendicino as sufficient to conjure a national threat to Canadian sovereignty was happening in real time.

If this pattern of RCMP intelligence gathering concerning Jeremy MacKenzie is typical, we should expect that the intelligence contributing to the charges against the Coutts Four may be just as dubious.

The Coutts Four have been denied bail. But this is not on the primary grounds where there is a concern that they might be a flight risk and fail to appear in court. They want to clear their names. They are not being denied bail on the secondary grounds where there is a concern that they would pose a danger to the public if they were released. Instead, they are being held on tertiary grounds to "maintain confidence in the administration of justice."

Guidance for denying bail on these grounds include "the apparent strength of the prosecution's case." But the Crown has failed so far to provide full disclosure so lawyers can know the case against their clients.

Speaking on Trish Wood is Critical, Jaclyne Martin discussed reasons a judge gave for denying Jerry Morin a bail hearing. The ruling to deny a bail hearing is "based on the public perceptions . . . That the public would lose faith in the judicial system because of the severity of the allegations."[358]

At the POEC it was argued that one basis for invoking the 1988 Emergencies Act was to restore "confidence in government institutions." The national security adviser to the prime minister, Jody Thomas, argued protesters questioning the legitimacy of pandemic measures constituted a threat to national security. She alleged the protests were "undermining of the confidence in public institutions. Those things . . . constitute a threat."[359] However, undermining confidence in public institutions is not identified as one of the triggers for declaring a national emergency under the Emergencies Act.

Similarly, denying bail to those facing serious charges on tertiary grounds out of concern that their release will undermine confidence in the justice system is a slippery slope. Autocratic governments throughout history have charged citizens of serious charges as a means to silence dissent, or to find a scapegoat to further a political agenda.

Writing for *Newsweek*, Gord Magill commented on the state of affairs in Canada in the fall of 2023. In September there was a visit from "a one-time member of a Ukrainian SS Waffen division into Canada's Parliament, and the former Nazi soldier, now ninety-eight-years-old, was given a thunderous standing ovation by a packed House of Parliament." Meanwhile, Canadian authorities have sought to conjure a national security threat on a case, based on what has been reported in the media, that is extremely thin. Magill concludes, "The four men arrested in Alberta represent the very best Canada has to offer: competent working-class guys that make our material world function. They are unjust prisoners of the very worst—the kind of people who see imaginary Nazis in the working class while giving thunderous applause to Nazis who are very real."[360]

On January 15, 2024, Chris Carbert was yet again denied bail. Speaking to reporter Mocha Bezrigan, Carbert's mother Betty said, "I'm hopeful that going forward more positive things will come out of all of this. Because, eventually the truth will come out."[361]

On January 24, 2024, Gord Magill had an interview with Tucker Carlson. This gave the story about the Coutts Four wide exposure. It added to the growing pressure to resolve the case.[362]

On February 6, 2024, Chris Lysak's new lawyer, Daniel Song, made a section 8 charter application regarding the wiretaps the Crown and the RCMP used to advance build its case against the accused. That day all charges in the initial indictment against Chris Lysak and Jerry Morrin were dropped by the Crown. This includes charges of conspiracy to commit murder. Song told a reporter, "To be clear, Mr. Lysak did not admit to possessing his handgun for a dangerous purpose. He did not attend the Coutts protests with the intent to harm anyone. He admits that his firearm was loaded with ammunition at the time of the police seizure, but denies having loaded and chambered the gun."[363] Jerry Morin spent 74 days in solitary confinement during his 723 days in custody. The Crown got plea deals from the two with Lysak pleading to possession of a loaded firearm. Morin pleaded guilty to possession of a weapon. Neither were armed while they were participating in the Coutts blockade. Both charges were brand new and not at all related to the initial February 2022 indictments.

As I write, Tony Olienick and Chris Carbert have remained in jail, and denied bail, for over 765 days. Since two of their co-accused have had all original charges dropped, what is the case against these two who remain behind bars?

Did the Crown have a case to begin with? Conspiracy to commit murder charges were cited in the POEC Report to justify invoking the Emergencies Act. There should be an inquiry into the whole case against the Coutts Four, and the conduct of the Crown.

From 1894 to 1906 France was consumed with the Dreyfus Affair. Jewish Captain Alfred Dreyfus was knowingly framed by French Army general staff of selling secrets about the new gun to the Prussians. After Dreyfus was court-marshalled, Parisian newspapers *La Libre Parole, L'Intransigeant, L'Echo de Paris, Le Jour, La Patrie*, and *Le Petit Journal* proclaimed Dreyfus was guilty of treason. It helped that these papers received subsidies, or assistance with their editorials, from the government. While he was being publicly degraded and deprived of his rank, Dreyfus cried out "Long live France. I am innocent. Gentlemen of the newspapers, proclaim to the world, I am innocent. I am innocent."

But Dreyfus was condemned in the court of public opinion as mobs carried torches and banners that read "Kill the Traitor Dreyfus." In 1894 Paris, who could question Dreyfus' guilt? General staff insisted that questioning the rightness of the verdict declaring Alfred Dreyfus guilty was outrageous. It would deprive the army and the public of confidence in its superior officers in the day of danger. But, as events unfolded, Dreyfus was brought back from Devil's Island in 1906. He was exonerated of all charges and reinstated to the rank of major in the French Army.[364]

The case of the Coutts Four and the Dreyfus Affair are not identical. Dreyfus was exonerated of all his charges. Two of the Coutts accused signed coerced confessions to minor charges after two years in custody. Yet, the Dreyfus Affair in France one example of what happens when democracy bends toward autocracy. In Canada in 2024, we are on a collision course with the Magna Carta. Is all that is required to deny bail for those accused of serious crimes to argue that their release will undermine confidence in the justice system? Is all that is required to make the Crown walk back charges of conspiracy to commit murder a smart lawyer who knows how to make a section 8 charter application?

Those who seek to protest public policies will think seriously about participating in any public protest at all. Recall that it was Justin Trudeau who cautioned in his testimony before the POEC in Ottawa, that citizens protesting to change public policy was "worrisome." Canadian justice must ensure that those charged with serious crimes have their day in court. Justice is not served if those presumed innocent until proven guilty are left in legal purgatory in order to protect the government's reputation.

An additional concern is placing those accused of crimes in solitary confinement. Tony Olienick has been in solitary confinement, on and off, for at least 80 days.[365] As well, about 90 percent of those accused of a crime in Canada never go to trial. If police and prosecutors bank on getting plea deals, they don't need to have solid evidence to convict. Especially when the Crown doesn't provide full disclosure to lawyers for the accused.

CHAPTER TWENTY

A NOTE ON TRIAL OF TAMARA LICH AND CHRIS BARBER

"the Crown's case is a case in search of a narrative"

~ Trish Wood, journalist

In September 2023, Freedom Convoy protesters Tamara Lich and Chris Barber were put on trial in Ottawa. They are charged with mischief, obstructing police, counselling others to commit mischief, and intimidation connected to their involvement in protests in Ottawa. They are not charged with treason, sedition, domestic terrorism, violence, or counselling violence. By all accounts, Justice Heather Perkins-McVey is running the trial in a fair and balanced way. She is sticking to the facts and making sure hearsay evidence is not admitted.

In September 2023, Crown witness Capt. Etienne Martel with Surete du Quebec took the stand for the prosecution. His Green Squad, made up of 45 officers, arrived in Ottawa on February 17, 2022. This was after Lich and Barber were already arrested and behind bars. There was body-cam video footage of the protesters chanting "love over fear."

During his testimony Martel discussed the major police clearing operations in the final days of putting down the protest. He admitted that during the climax of the protests, Martel's squad of officers took a one-hour lunch break at the Chateau Laurier Hotel. Protesters were chanting "love over fear." Such was the state of emergency as police dealt with protesters as things came to a conclusion.

Journalist Trish Wood was in the courtroom to witness Martel's testimony, and discussed her assessment of the case for the Crown on the

Andrew Lawton Show. Martel's testimony was one of many examples of Crown witnesses "not saying anything bad about the defendants." Wood summarized that after three weeks into the trial of Tamara Lich and Chris Barber, "the Crown's case is a case in search of a narrative."[366] Crown prosecutors are still trying to establish that Lich and Barber had 'control and influence' over protesters in downtown Ottawa.

Crown witnesses Zeki Li and other Ottawa residents have made claims of disruption and fear. However, Li and most of the other residents taking the stand for the Crown are plaintiffs in a lawsuit seeking a civil lawsuit asking for damages against the convoy in excess of three hundred million dollars. Li was repeatedly reminded by Justice Perkins-McVey to describe what happened and not exaggerate or embellish her testimony with demonizing rhetoric. Video and CCTV footage has shown nearly every complaint to be inaccurate or inflated. Under cross-examination, Li was constantly unable to substantiate her allegations. At the Lich-Barber trial, Zeki Li insisted that the honking of horns during the protest in Ottawa was "at least every other minute." But she was reminded that at the POEC she had stated that the honking had "stopped entirely." And elsewhere in her POEC testimony that there was "some intermittent honking for short periods of time." The Democracy Fund reported that on Day 17 of the Lich-Barber trial, "Li then agreed with this statement and admitted that her memory was likely better when she testified at (the) POEC."[367]

Of the eight civilian witnesses the Crown called to testify, over half have joined in the $300 million civil lawsuit against convoy protesters. Would there be a motive to embellish or exaggerate claims of harm from the convoy in their testimony? With all those hundreds of millions of dollars hanging in the balance?[368]

Ottawa Police Service officer Nicole Bach testified that she lost much of the content of her text messages, emails, and voicemail messages on her phone shortly after the Freedom Convoy ended. She was a key Police Liaison Team contact with Chris Barber. This was blamed on a tech upgrade to her phone. There were emails and text messages from superior officers to Bach and other PLT officers. The Ottawa Police Services legal department is claiming solicitor-client privilege to keep multiple emails redacted. Chris Barber's defence lawyer, Diane Magas, asked the Crown for disclosure. After an extended break, she "handed a 5-page document to Justice Perkins-McVey, which was 100 percent redacted." The Democracy Fund reported, "A second document was provided to defence—a heavily redacted email chain between Detective Benson, a number of crown attorneys and PLT officers. The subject line throughout the email chain was 'PLT Disclosure.' The Crown stated that the reasons for the redacted paragraphs were "solicitor-client privilege."[369]

Officer Isabelle Cyr "stated that she had an issue with her phone whereby all of her contacts and text messages were inexplicably 'wiped' from her phone between January 27 and February 9, 2022." It was PTL officer Cyr who was responsible for gathering information that included email, telephone, and signal chats during the protest. She communicated with protesters to gather information for the police liaison teams, which assisted in directing the protesters to downtown Ottawa.[370]

On October 23, 2023, the CBC reported that the Crown dropped bail violation charges against Tamara Lich. She had been arrested after she appeared at the George Jonas Freedom Award ceremony in Toronto in June 2022, where she was being honoured. The event was hosted by the Justice Centre for Constitutional Freedoms.[371] CBC reported, "She was not allowed to contact (Tom) Marazzo and others involved in the protest without lawyers present as part of the conditions attached to her original charges stemming from her role in organizing the convoy."[372] However, the CBC failed to mention that at the gala, her lawyers *were* present. This calls into question the charge of the bail violation in the first place. In early July 2022, Justice of the Peace Paul Harris said to Tamara Lich, "Your detention is necessary to maintain confidence in the administration of justice."[373]

The Crown took 27 days to present its case against Barber and Lich. No criminal behaviour on the part of the organizers was mentioned. On the 27th day, a number of messages from Officer Bach were made public. During cross examination, Bach stated she believed from the very start that the protest was going to last a long time. She also confirmed that the Ottawa Police directed all the protest vehicles into place in downtown Ottawa. She saw no problem with long-term parking of trucks and tractor-trailers on Wellington Street. She also admitted that in a duty book entry she recorded that she did not perceive any aggression from the protesters.[374]

On November 30 and December 1, 2023, I attended days 31 and 32 of the trial. The Crown cited January 9, 2022 texts by Chris Barber to support alleged mischief in Ottawa. But those texts concerned a January 2022 protest in Swift Current, Saskatchewan. Diane Magas cited testimony from Officer Bach that showed police gave Chris Barber permission to have a slow roll of trucks in Ottawa. On December 7, the Crown submitted a letter from Mayor Watson to some Freedom Convoy participants. Since this related to something lawful, an agreement with the mayor of Ottawa, the submission was exculpatory. The trial is scheduled to continue well into 2024. Mischief charges typically require a half day in court. This trial has lasted over 35 days and counting. Should the defendants be acquitted, the crown is likely to appeal.

As I write this chapter, the 40th to 47th days for the trial of Tamara Lich and Chris Barber are scheduled for late August, 2024. Should the defendants be acquitted, the crown is likely to appeal.

Concurrently, a class-action lawsuit brought forth by Ottawa residents including Zeki Li is proceeding. A motion to dismiss the lawsuit was dismissed by a judge on February 5, 2024. Freedom Convoy organizers named in the lawsuit include Tamara Lich, Chris Barber and Tom Marazzo. Lawyers for the protesters are arguing that the Ottawa Police Services Board should be responsible for paying potential damages. They have documentation to show that protestors were simply following police instructions. Police directed each protest vehicle into parking spots in downtown Ottawa.

Originally, Freedom Convoy protesters thought the Ottawa Police would direct them to park their vehicles on the Sir George Etienne Cartier Parkway, and the Sir John A. MacDonald Parkway. A defence filing asserts that these two parkways could have made room for 2,500 tractor-trailers. In contrast, Wellington Street in front of Parliament Hill was only able to accommodate "a small number of trucks."

Documents in the filing state Ottawa police created detailed maps and directions for where the trucks should park and how they should proceed to staging locations. All the protesters were "expecting to adhere to the police plan. None of the defendants . . . originally expected to park any vehicles on the streets of downtown Ottawa as part of the protest."[375]

CONCLUSION

You shall not bear false witness against your neighbour.

~ Exodus 20:16

With the invocation of the Emergencies Act in February 2022, a dangerous template for herding a panicked public to states of intolerance, fear, and contempt has been largely successful. Working hand in hand, the Government of Canada and the media are effective in manipulating public perception. Though ranked now in tenth place, how long will it take for the Democracy Index to reflect the fallout from the invocation of the Emergencies Act?

In the historic religions of Judaism, Christianity, and Islam, the Ten Commandments have been understood as essential guidance for creating a healthy community. Ancient societies understood the importance of telling the truth. Those who slandered anyone in their community with lies and half-truths undermined the health of their community. The ancient commandment "Thou shalt not bear false witness against thy neighbour" was one people lived by. In ancient societies, when people said, "I give you my word," it was a promise that they were telling the truth. It was common-sense wisdom. But in these times, for the powerful elite, truth is an impediment to accumulating and holding on to power. Any individual or group that challenges the status quo can be called names and demonized with impunity. Bearing false witness is just a political tool to fend off those who would challenge or question government policy. The collusion of politicians, media, corporations, and health authorities is creating a coercive society. Anything that impeded the agendas of those in charge—like the Canadian Charter of Rights and Freedoms or instructions to Canadian Customs officials about the bearer of a Canadian passport—is ignored.

The media, by exaggerating police incompetence where real progress was proceeding, fed a narrative of overwhelm. It shares part of the blame for stoking an emotional tone in which the government could rationalize its use of extraordinary measures. The media narrative, enmeshed as it was, helped the Liberals forcefully let those it governs know it cannot be pushed around.

The coverage of the Freedom Convoy protests by the media and statements by politicians is a case study in propaganda. Canadians are not the only citizens who have been manipulated or deceived when the government and media push a narrative. Soviet citizens were told doctors had plotted to poison Joseph Stalin in January 1953. It turned out that the story was false. In 1989, the media in China told citizens that protesters in Tiananmen Square were criminals, ruffians, anarchists, and foreign-influenced enemies of China. Though that remains the official story in China, the protesters were in fact peaceful, nonviolent students seeking a more open society. In 1990, Americans learned that Iraqi soldiers had ripped babies out of incubators, stabbed them with bayonets, and left them to die on Kuwaiti hospital floors. It turned out that the story wasn't true either. Neither was the 2002 allegation that Iraq had weapons of mass destruction (WMDs). Noisy horn-honking protesters started to arrive in Ottawa on January 28, 2022. The honking all but disappeared after an Ontario court placed an injunction on the honking on February 7 in order for the protest to continue. But the narrative that protesters in Ottawa were violent insurrectionists plotting to overthrow a democratically elected government was concocted. It was a story hatched by our government and the media. Add Canada to the list of nations that, from time to time, use propaganda to achieve political objectives.

One of the lessons of the Freedom Convoy protests is that Canadians can be manipulated to believe anything the government wants them to believe. This does not make us any more or less gullible than citizens in America, China, Russia, or elsewhere. But it should give us reason to reflect. How quickly do we attach ourselves to the emotional drama of a shocking breaking news story? When, if ever, do we question the narrative in headline stories when it seems the media are building a case against an individual or a group? While we may assume that our thoughts are our own, it seems the government and the media are quite capable of putting thoughts in our heads.

Before the Liberal cabinet went into a retreat on January 24, 2022, staff connected to the Prime Minister's Office and Minister of Public Safety Marco Mendicino were framing the protest as a "January 6th north." They knew people in the media they thought would amplify their message.

On the night of January 24, the first tweet by a CTV reporter echoed this talking point. Governments engage in propaganda to achieve political objectives. When they do, there is a playbook. It varies across time from nation to nation and government to government. Here are some elements on display in relation to the Ottawa protests in 2022:

1. *Feature headline news stories to create shock, confusion, and trauma*: Shocking news stories depicted the protesters in Ottawa in the most deplorable terms. Media and politicians suggested a "January 6th North" was unfolding in Ottawa. It was claimed there was an insurrection. The news was horrifying, confusing, and traumatic for the general public consuming these headline news stories. With feelings of heightened anxiety, many people found it hard to think critically. As a consequence, any smear against the protesters was accepted on its face.

2. *Identify villains, an enemy, a scapegoat*: Reporters and politicians called the Ottawa protesters names including "homophobic," "transphobic," "hillbillies," "mercenaries," "insurrectionists," "misogynists," "racists," "anti-vaxxers," "anti-Semites," "a feral mob," and "terrorists." Canadian truck drivers, nurses, and doctors fired from hospitals, federal employees in the Canadian Armed Forces, and different agencies were called "Trump supporters," "white supremacists," and "far-right." As negative descriptors piled up, the media and politicians drove this viscerally powerful message. The general public felt increasingly overwhelmed and threatened by what they saw and read.

3. *Repeat named scapegoat(s)*: Once the list of negative descriptors for the Ottawa protesters were introduced, the media repeated this over and over again nonstop, 24/7, fusing the protesters in the minds of the general public with a long list of deplorable qualities.

4. *Spread rumours about scapegoats*: Rumours about the Ottawa Protesters were many and varied. It was alleged they planned to ram trucks into Parliament buildings. It was claimed they planned to lynch politicians. Protesting parents were accused of using their children as human shields. It was alleged that the protesters in Ottawa were being violent. A children's hospital was going to be bombed.

5. *Push courtroom-worthy evidence aside*: In the case of the Public Order Emergency Commission, the Report ignored police and intelligence testimony that concluded that there was no credible threat to national security. Police testimony ran counter to justifying the need to invoke

the Emergencies Act. Instead, the Report relied on testimony about "phantom honking," "microaggressions," and "felt violence." The Report relied on hearsay evidence to justify the February 14, 2022, invocation, though no violence according to the definition of the Criminal Code occurred.

6. *Appeals to state authority*: The media ran stories with the underlining premise that the government must be relied upon in a time of crisis. Starting before the protesters arrived in Ottawa, a parade of politicians and senior government bureaucrats were interviewed in the media. They made repeated claims that the Ottawa protesters were violent, insurrectionists, rapists, unpatriotic, and more. The response of the media was to amplify these claims while failing to scrutinize them. If a government official or politician alleged that such and such was the case, it had to be true. The media failed in its obligation to ask tough questions.

7. *Cast dissent as treason*: The media didn't give dissenting voices any airtime. Canadian media ignored or buried off-message statements by police and intelligence officers regarding the lack of credible threats posed by protesters to the government. They largely declined to interview protest leaders and framed those interviews in incendiary ways.

8. *Present even more scary, gripping allegations*: Ottawa protesters on Parliament Hill were depicted as Nazis. It was asserted that thousands of protesters' children present on Parliament Hill were "being used as human shields." Children, babies, and harm are emotional triggers long utilized for purposes of propaganda. In World War I, Allied newspapers claimed German soldiers were bayoneting Belgian babies. The same was said of Iraqi soldiers falsely alleged to be bayoneting babies and leaving them to die on hospital floors in Kuwait in 1990.

9. *Invoke a threat that may be both external and internal*: It was alleged that crowdfunding for the Freedom Convoy was tied to international terrorism and/or Donald Trump. It was alleged that the Russians and/or US Republicans were behind the protests. Evidence was ignored, indicating that the IP addresses of many donors to Freedom Convoy from the United States were originating from vaccinated Canadian snowbirds on vacation.

10. *Subvert the rule of law*: The government froze the bank accounts of Canadian citizens who hadn't committed any crimes. This action

deprived citizens of their ability to pay rent, mortgages, utility bills, alimony and purchase medical prescriptions or groceries. The government ignored police evidence and intelligence reports confirming Ottawa protesters gathered peacefully—including reports on the early afternoon of February 14, 2022. Media reports and politicians avoided mentioning that no police or intelligence agency declared the protests to constitute an unlawful assembly. An Ontario court issued two rulings on February 7 and 16, giving protesters the green light to continue to protest peacefully. In the latter case, the protesters had satisfied the judge's February 7 horn-honking injunction. Nonetheless, politicians repeatedly referred to the protest as illegal.

When anxiety and emotion predominate in reaction to an individual or group that is scapegoated, it is hard to stem the hysteria, especially when those scapegoats have been plied with enough accusations. At that point, the political fever-pitch will decree that the scapegoat must be sacrificed in order for peace to return to society. Bank accounts must be frozen. Police are welcome to use brutal force to deal with nonviolent, peaceful protesters. It's here that we have crossed over to the world of ritual performed by the authorities—the state. But the fruits of this ritual only spawn fear. It gives permission for the state to create new scapegoats in the future.

The government, by its resorting to the Emergencies Act, appears disinterested in the messiness of democracy. It's strangely averse to the unpredictability of where dialogue might lead. Historically, Canada has often been a moderate society where political leaders sought a middle ground. The risk of open debate, novelty, and the search for common ground was worth the effort. When real violence appears, authorities have the legal tools under existing law to maintain law and order. This includes calling in the military. Political leaders are not obliged to have dialogue with protesters. Yet dialogue is a useful first step to calm things down. The police plan presented to Deputy Minister Rob Stewart on the weekend of February 13, 2022, included a recommendation that the government engage protest leaders in dialogue. The government had the names and contact information of the individuals they believed were the protest leaders. They wasted no time in arresting those they identified as Freedom Convoy leaders after the invocation of the Emergencies Act.

As a society, we must revisit our assumptions about what happened during the Freedom Convoy. We must ask some tough questions. Even if we have strong emotional reactions to what the media told us about the protesters, we must appeal to our better angels. We must look under some rocks we don't want to look under. A mostly working-class protest was thrown under the bus. It was reframed in the most defamatory way. We must not simply repeat the talking points of the official account because they are emotionally satisfying or advance short-term political goals. Watching old news clips of the coverage of the protests aired on the CBC, CTV, and Global won't get us any closer to understanding what happened around.

We must think about our vision for Canada. We must think beyond what is good for the political party we support. Given the Ontario Ford government's response to the pandemic, it's not a sure bet what a Conservative government under Erin O'Toole might have done *if* he had implemented vaccine mandates for truck drivers and been faced with the Freedom Convoy.

The Public Order Emergency Commission report illustrates that the government can't investigate itself. Canadians are still waiting for real accountability. This may come from challenges to the government's justification to invoke the Emergencies Act in the courts.

In this conclusion I highlight some of the details surrounding the Freedom Convoy protests and the government response. In the text that follows, I offer a series of recommendations to prompt a wider discussion of how to correct government overreach.

- **Recommendation #1:** that politicians pursue dialogue with protesters as a first strategy for resolving public protests

  PLT program analyst Leslie Jean pointed out that federal government officials had met with protesters during the rail blockades of 2020, providing an exit strategy for the majority of the rail and pipeline demonstrators. This should have been one of the first strategies the government employed. Citizens usually protest only when other avenues for seeking accountability have failed or been frustrated.

- **Recommendation #2:** that the freezing of bank accounts of citizens who are not engaged in money-laundering or terrorism be understood as an autocratic tool incompatible with democracy; and that the prime minister issue an apology in the House of Commons for the government's edict to freeze bank accounts that undermined confidence in both public institutions and Canadian financial institutions and harmed Canada's reputation internationally.

The freezing of bank accounts was employed by the government as a political tool. As Chrystia Freeland stated in an interview with Commission staff, the freezing of bank accounts was done to show Vladimir Putin and Canada's NATO allies that the Canadian government wasn't going to let anyone push them around. The government worried that having an ongoing protest in Ottawa would be embarrassing if it overlapped a Russian invasion of Ukraine. The run on the banks after the measure was put in place signalled that many Canadians viewed the action to freeze bank accounts as tyrannical. It also signalled to wealthy financial interests on Wall Street that banking in Canada had changed. It undermined confidence in the reliability of banking in Canada. It raised concerns that Canada was behaving like a banana republic. The protesters weren't engaged in money-laundering or terrorism.

- **Recommendation #3:** that any senior government bureaucrat or cabinet minister who is in a position to recommend the prime minister invoke the Emergencies Act must have a background in intelligence or policing, and that job descriptions in these key positions reflect the requirement for this skill set.

Numbers of key government bureaucrats and cabinet ministers who advised the prime minister regarding invoking the Emergencies Act had no background in intelligence or policing. This needs to change so that those giving advise are not doing this based on their lay experience and perceptions of what constitutes a national emergency, aided—for example—from watching the news.

- **Recommendation #4:** that the first obligation of schools of journalism and media outlets is to remind those who report the news that they have no claim on the public's attention other than in the name of democracy; that there be a public inquiry into the impact, role, and sources of misinformation and disinformation spread by the Canadian mainstream media.

The media narrative that the protesters in Ottawa were plotting a "January 6th north" blurs all distinctions between Canada and America both historically and contextually. In Ottawa, the most serious cases have been charges of mischief. Reports that an insurrection was unfolding in Ottawa were alarmist, irresponsible, and false. During the Freedom Convoy protests, the mainstream media functioned like courtiers to power, echoing the talking points of politicians without any scrutiny. The media devolved into a propaganda arm of the Liberal government. Claiming Russian actors inspired truckers to drive to Ottawa, or that the protesters were Nazis, poisoned our social discourse. The mainstream media impaired public debate surrounding the issues that inspired the Freedom Convoy protest. It failed to provide perspective and context. The pool of common facts is shrinking. The POEC failed to call to the stand anyone associated with either mainstream or independent media. It declined to ask the CEO of the CBC Catherine Tait to testify. It also neglected to accept independent reporter Viva Frei as a witness, even though he was providing live streaming from Ottawa throughout most of the protest.

- **Recommendation #5:** that any future Public Order Emergency Commission be required to present an Interim Report by the one-year anniversary of the *Act* being rescinded. As such, the Emergencies Act legislation needs to be amended to allow an Interim Report to be presented to parliament on the anniversary of the Act being rescinded.

The Emergencies Act legislation stipulates that once the government establishes a Public Order Emergency Commission, that body must present its final report to Parliament within 365 days of the Act being rescinded. This gave the POEC less than ten months to create job descriptions, interview and hire Commission staff, conduct interviews with prospective witnesses, orient all legal representatives to the work of the Commission, conduct public hearings, and write a report. The Report of over 2,100 pages was apparently written starting in mid-December 2022 and copyedited, proofread, and printed by February 17, 2023.

It takes time to convene a public commission. Under the legislation, the government of the day has two months to decide who to appoint as commissioner to head the public inquiry. This leaves just ten months to complete the following: a) Job descriptions for commission staff need to be created. b) Job searches for each prospective commission staff member need to be posted and filled. c) Commission staff need to determine who they plan to call as witnesses. d) Ahead of the inquiry, they need to take in-person statements from each witness. e) Legal teams representing interested parties have to prepare to cross examine witnesses who testify at the inquiry. f) An inquiry has to be convened and given enough time for thorough cross examination of witnesses. g) A report needs to be written and presented to parliament. Given most public inquiries are allowed more time, and Paul Rouleau identified the tight timeline as problematic, the one-year anniversary should require only an Interim Report from a POEC.

- **Recommendation #6:** that commissioner(s) may request an extension of time in order to properly document evidence brought before an inquiry prior to publishing their final Report. An additional period of time for an extension to write the Report, for example six months, should be stipulated in the revised legislation.

The POEC was convened over six weeks. During this time legal teams interviewed 76 witnesses. Cross examination for teams of lawyers representing different parties at the inquiry were often given very short timeframes for proper investigation. A witness who chose to obfuscate and dodge questions put to them could run out the clock. Since this inquiry was determining the justification for invoking the *Emergencies Act*, our democracy deserves a comprehensive examination of the matter.

- **Recommendation #7:** that documents be submitted to the inquiry before the public hearings begin. Any dumping of documents during an inquiry should trigger adjournment of proceedings to allow legal teams to review the new evidence.

The Public Order Emergency Commission is not a court of law. It has the appearance of a court. There is a judge, witnesses, lawyers, and cross-examination. Witnesses are asked to affirm or swear that they are telling the truth. However, the POEC didn't function like a court. When Government of Canada lawyers dumped hundreds of documents during the testimony of witnesses, Paul Rouleau allowed it to happen. There was no legal basis for these redactions. In addition, the documents were often relevant to witnesses who were presently taking the stand. By dumping heavily redacted documents during the hearings, Government of Canada lawyers displayed a lack of regard for the inquiry. The cost of prolonging the inquiry, based on these tactics, should result in the government of Canada paying the additional costs of legal team preparation of all who are party to a POEC.

- **Recommendation #8:** that a Public Order Emergency Commission be empowered to compel witnesses to return to testify if new key evidence is brought to the inquiries' attention that relates to a particular witness who has previously testified. Should such powers need to be granted in the Emergencies Act legislation, the Act should be amended to give a commission of inquiry such powers.

Witnesses at the POEC were asked to testify under oath and tell the truth. When additional testimony surfaces from other witnesses that shines a light on serious omissions, or even perjury, from a prior witness, that witness should return to testify and be cross examined.

- **Recommendation #9:** that each witness testifying not wear an earpiece in order to avoid any appearance that a witness is being coached in real time while they give testimony.

During her testimony, Deputy Prime Minister Chrystia Freeland was wearing an earpiece. It is plausible she was being coached about what to say under cross-examination. This undermines confidence in the inquiries' proceedings. Witnesses at a POEC should not be allowed to wear an earpiece.

- **Recommendation #10:** that a Public Order Emergency Commission have an extension of four weeks, beyond the initial six weeks, to allow for thorough cross-examination of witnesses.

There were short timeframes for cross examination of witnesses during the POEC. In addition, government lawyers routinely dumped documents related to witnesses testifying in real time. An extension of time would allow for witnesses to return to the inquiry to testify based on documents dumped by the government that required more scrutiny on the public record.

- **Recommendation #11:** that instead of one commissioner, a panel of three commissioners be appointed. This is in order to give more authority to the proceedings and report of such an inquiry. I further recommend each party with official standing in the House of Commons present the names of two candidates to the Ethics Commissioner for vetting potential conflicts of interest. After being vetted, those candidates the Ethics Commissioner determines are fit to serve as commissioners would appear on a ballot for parliamentarians to vote for in rank order. The candidates placing in the top three positions after the vote is recorded will be named to the panel of three commissioners to conduct an inquiry.

The Emergencies Act legislation states that the government appoints the commission to the public order emergency commission. The POEC is a creation of the government. It is customary for governments to appoint commissioners who head inquiries that may have ties to the governing party in power. But, in an inquiry tasked with determining if the actions of the government were unconstitutional, the appointment of commissioners needs to be nonpartisan.

- **Recommendation #12:** that Commission staff vet witnesses to determine if their testimony is based on solid evidence to learn if invoking the Emergencies Act is justified. Potential witnesses who have solid evidence that is relevant to the goals of the inquiry should be invited to take the stand. If the information a witness plans to offer before an inquiry only points to hearsay evidence, they would not be called upon to testify.

The Commission received the names of potential witnesses, including the Hon. Brian Peckford. He is the last living First Minister to sign the Patriation Agreement, the basis of the Constitution Act 1982, which includes the Charter of Rights and Freedoms. As a protester and speaker at the Freedom Convoy stage, Peckford could have testified to the right of the protesters questioning the pandemic measures to protest in Ottawa. But he and other important potential witnesses who could speak to the justification or lack of justification for invoking the Emergencies Act were denied a chance to testify on the witness stand. Meanwhile, some witnesses who did testify only provided hearsay evidence, which would never be admitted in a court of law.

- **Recommendation #13:** that the triggers for invoking the Emergencies Act be tied exclusively to the *CSIS Act* definition of a national emergency—espionage and/or foreign interference, sabotage, actual serious acts of violence, or a plot to overthrow the government.

Commissioner Rouleau stated during the public hearings that it had already been well established that the four triggers for invoking the Emergencies Act—espionage and sabotage, foreign interference, serious acts of violence, and a plot to overthrow the government—had not been met. He remarked in an effort to hurry up the public hearing on November 21, 2022, "you could have skipped (a), (b), (c), (d) (Section 2 of the Emergencies Act). It's been testified to many times that it wasn't met, but go ahead."

- **Recommendation #14:** that the public face of pandemic response not be public health officers, but the provincial and federal Minister(s) of Health, and that long-established Emergency Management Agency protocols in each province and territory be the framework for responding to any future pandemic.

Throughout the pandemic, public health officers shirked their duty to explain the basis for their mandates. The refusal to debate any doctor or scientist who questioned the pandemic measures has undermined confidence in public health in this country. Science is, by its very nature, a discipline of testing and retesting conclusions. Decades long established emergency protocols for dealing with a pandemic were placed on the shelf. Placing nonelected public health officials in charge of the pandemic was a mistake. The mantle of leadership must fall to the elected Minister of Health, the provincial Premier, and corresponding elected federal officials. The response of the government to this "pandemic" was disorienting enough for the general public. The continuity of responsible leadership is essential for unifying the nation.

- **Recommendation #15:** that Canadian military and intelligence not employ psychological techniques to compel the population to submit to policy directives issued by the government in response to a pandemic.

Our government, through the Canadian Joint Operations Command, was involved in nudging the general public to get vaccinated. What is needed during a pandemic is not a psychological operation to scare the public into complying with lockdowns, to fear asymptomatic transmission, and to treat everyone we meet as a clear and present danger to our very existence. UK health minister Matt Hancock asked a colleague "When do we deploy the next variant?" Trust in government is not earned by employing fear as a weapon to control the population. Too often press conferences by Canadian public health officials and public figures smacked of public health theatre.

- **Recommendation #16:** that a public inquiry remains a requirement of government invoking the Emergencies Act.

Was the Public Order Emergency Commission a waste of taxpayer dollars? Some people have told me as much. However, I think that the exercise of learning what witnesses said in their testimony under cross-examination is useful. It may be left to historians to show how the testimony at the inquiry did not justify the invocation of the Emergencies Act. But without that testimony and cross-examination, historians would be at a disadvantage in gaining the needed perspective to critique the Government of Canada's overreach.

- **Recommendation #17:** that false testimony given during a public order emergency commission has legal consequences, and that if the inquiry believes there are cases of perjury made by witnesses under oath, it should site these in its Report.

The testimony of a number of senior government officials and cabinet ministers contrasted with evidence entered at the inquiry and with public statements to the media. If a witness is found to have perjured themselves, this should trigger a resignation.

- **Recommendation #18:** that members of the general public practice detachment in their news consumption habits; that we ask

i.   when a breaking news story is viscerally powerful, what are we being told?

ii. what is the impact of the narrative on us mentally and emotionally?

iii. who benefits from the narrative?

iv. are there individuals or groups who are being named as scapegoats?

v.   as this narrative unfolds, what seems to be its impact on Canadian democracy and civil rights?

It's up to us as Canadian citizens to think about the kind of country we want. We need to watch our own emotional responses to startling news headlines that stampede us into supporting draconian measures. When our government and our media scapegoat a category of people in our society, we need to ask why. It appears that for many Canadians, the prospect that our government is lying to us is more frightening than being told that the barbarians are at the gate and are trying to overthrow the government. We should have been told by our media that the initial depiction of the protesters in Ottawa was slanted and inaccurate.

It's been said that citizens get the kind of government they deserve. We need to ask ourselves if we deserve better. If we do, what steps can we take as individuals to assist our better angels for the sake of Canada? What does it mean for each of us to "stand on guard" for Canadian democracy?

- **Recommendation #19:** that Canadian citizens who are charged with a crime be presumed innocent until proven guilty, have access to bail, and have a timely trial where they can defend themselves in court.

Our Charter of Rights and Freedoms guarantee "freedom from arbitrary arrest or imprisonment." If we become a nation where the police or a government lays serious charges and then throws away the key, we can no longer call ourselves a democracy. Serious allegations must be tested in a court of law. Serious charges may result in a trial that finds the accused guilty. But a trial can also find that those charged are innocent and cleared of all wrongdoing. The longer those accused remain in jail without the chance to clear their names, the more likely the court of public opinion will judge them to be guilty. Many citizens will reason that they must be guilty since they have been denied bail. And yet, the history of Western democracies is one littered with innocent people being wrongfully imprisoned.

- **Recommendation #20:** that Public Order Emergency Commissions be tasked with inquiring into the basis for events that prompt the emergency it is established to examine.

The POEC did describe the growing protests and climate of discord leading up to the Freedom Convoy protests. However, it chose to avoid any discussion about the vaccine mandates and the basis for these. If there had been no vaccine mandates there would have been no protest. The POEC would have benefitted from examining the Management and Supply Agreement between Pfizer and the Government of Canada stating the company did not know what the side effects from taking their vaccine would be. They should have sought the document containing legal advice, from the Office of the Judge Advocate General to the Chief of staff of the CAF, seeing no evidence to require all military personnel to get inoculated. They should have obtained emails between PHAC and Transport Canada officials showing a lack of documentation to support the vaccine travel mandates for air travel. The damning testimony by Dr. Celia Lourenco, Dr. Lisa Waddell, Jennifer Little and others revealed in discovery ahead of the challenge to the vaccine travel mandates was also available for the POEC to obtain. As was the testimony of Dr. Lourenco before the Federal Public Sector Labour Relations and Employment Board. However, the government dared not discuss these and other documents, given what they revealed. And as Justice Mosley ruled in his judicial review of nearly 200 pages, there was no national emergency.

French philosopher René Girard has noted it is a habit in human societies to find scapegoats when faced with a crisis. "Everywhere and always, when human beings either cannot or dare not take their anger out on the thing that has caused it, they unconsciously search for substitutes, and more often than not they find them." The depiction of Freedom Convoy protesters by the federal government, and the media, is a case study in the "habit in human societies to find scapegoats."[376] The Liberal government was in no mood to be held to account, or to justify, the basis for their pandemic measures. They stuck to the mantra of their daily talking points, "safe and effective" and "trust the science." The government wanted Canadians to accept each pandemic response as self-evident and above scrutiny.

In a democracy, it is expected that citizens can question government policy. But with the government response to the Freedom

Convoy protests of 2022, we have learned that those who question government policy can quickly become scapegoats. We have learned that false reasons, and false grounds, for accusations can flourish in a politically alarmist environment rife with media-driven hysteria. Fellow Canadians can be unjustly condemned and judged to be guilty of a host of charges. In addition to politicians and the media who point fingers at the scapegoats they create, many in the general public can be mobilized to also point fingers and pass judgement, seeking to address free-floating anxiety fueled by alarmist news stories. Peace will be restored to the nation only when the scapegoats have their bank accounts frozen, are beaten by the police, are prevented from having life-saving surgeries, are hounded in the courts, and are jailed and vilified in the media.

We have to ask if this is the kind of nation we want: a nation purged from time to time through division and scapegoating? It is far better to hold a democratic vision for a kind of Canada where all can live together harmoniously. Our collective harmony will be sustained by actions that declare to all Canadians that it is wrong to bear false witness against our neighbour. Cultivating a society where we can express our opinions, and respect our differences, has long been a cornerstone for democracy. It's a value worth preserving.

AFTERWORD

I never expected to be writing about the Freedom Convoy or the Public Order Emergency Commission.

My paternal grandfather was a farmer near Barhead, Alberta. Raised on a farm in the Eastern Townships of Quebec, he left home at the age of thirteen and travelled by boat down the St. Lawrence River and through the Great Lakes to Duluth, Minnesota. From there he took a train to Seattle. My grandpa voted for the United Farmers of Alberta party from 1921 until it dissolved in 1935. In the following years, grandpa voted for the Cooperative Commonwealth Federation and its successor, the New Democratic Party (NDP). In 1968, at the age of ten, I watched a leaders' debate between Liberal prime minister Pierre Elliott Trudeau, Conservative opposition leader Robert Stanfield, New Democratic Party leader Tommy Douglas, and Social Credit leaders from Quebec and Western Canada. If I'd been old enough to vote in 1968, I would've marked my ballot for the NDP.

My vote for Joe Clark in 1979 was an exception to my mostly voting NDP since 1980. Over the decades, I've been on the "left" in a host of political debates: against NAFTA, keeping Canada out of the Iraq War, and more. I enthusiastically supported NDP leader Jack Layton and was acquainted with him while I lived in Toronto, when he ran twice for city council and once for mayor in Toronto. When Jack Layton died of cancer in 2011 at the age of sixty-one, I lined up to sign the book of condolences at Toronto City Hall.

Still, I knew the Liberal or NDP governments weren't perfect. In the 2015 federal election, Jody Wilson-Raybould was a star Kwak'wala indigenous Liberal candidate in Vancouver riding next to mine. She was appointed both minister of justice and attorney-general by Prime Minister Justin Trudeau. But in 2019, she was expelled from the Liberal caucus over the SNC-Lavalin affair.

Canada's Ethics Commissioner Mario Dion later found that Trudeau improperly pressured Wilson-Raybould to intervene in an ongoing criminal bribery case. Trudeau's impropriety concerned the Quebec-based construction company SNC-Lavalin and pressuring Wilson-Raybould to offer the company a deferred prosecution agreement.

In her memoir, "Indian in the Cabinet," Jody Wilson-Raybould described a one-on-one meeting with Justin Trudeau at the Fairmont-Pacific Rim Hotel in Vancouver on February 11, 2019. It took place while the SNC-Lavalin affair dominated the headlines. These lines from her memoir haunted me:

> He asked if I trusted him. I could see the agitation visibly building in the prime minister. His mood was shifting. I remember seeing it. I remember feeling it. I had seen and felt this before on a few occasions, when he would get frustrated and angry. But this was different. He became strident and disputed everything I had said. He made it clear that everyone in his office was telling the truth and that I . . . and others, were not. He told me I had not experienced what I said I did. He used the line that would later become public, that I had "experienced things differently." I knew what he was really asking. What he was saying. In that moment I knew he wanted me to lie—to attest that what had occurred had not occurred.[377]

About a month into the pandemic, I spoke with some friends who were starting to question statements made by politicians and health officials. But most of my friends accepted the news about the pandemic on its face. I was shocked by accounts of people being put on ventilators. I was boggled by the daily case counts and death counts. In the early months of the pandemic, I tried to order a pair of Dr. Bonnie Henry shoes from Fluevog for my mother to wear. But they were sold out. I also banged pots on my patio at 7 p.m. each night for over a year, a practice that began in Italy during the lockdown to show support for healthcare workers.

As a writer, during the first year and a half of the pandemic, the lockdowns were inconvenient. Still, I had my home. I had my computer. In Vancouver, I could order take-out from restaurants. I was rolling with things. Not altogether comfortably. Yet, I was comfortable enough.

My comfort with the mainstream media pandemic narrative changed abruptly in June 2021. A close family friend I'd known since early childhood eagerly stepped up to get his first shot of AstraZeneca. Within eighteen hours he suffered a stroke. He couldn't speak. He couldn't walk. He couldn't work. His family doctor told his family that his recent vaccination had "accelerated" my friend's blood clotting. A team of specialists at a Vancouver hospital concurred. These new vaccines were not safe and effective for everyone in the general public—at least not for some people in my address book. Exactly how rare were serious adverse reactions? After a lightning-speed vaccine rollout after very short vaccine trials, how could pharmaceutical companies, governments, and health authorities know this new medical product would be safe for all citizens?

The Canadian mainstream media daily continued to report these new vaccines issued under Emergency Use Authorization were "safe and effective." Yet, on August 6, 2021, CDC Director Rochelle Walensky had an interview with Wolf Blitzer on CNN that undermined confidence in the healthcare ad slogan. Walensky stated that the COVID-19 vaccines did not stop, or reduce transmission, or prevent infection.[378] What was being offered as the only solution to the pandemic didn't seem to be able to deliver what it was peddled to solve.

But any off-message information that emerged in 2021 was ignored by leadership in public health, politicians, and the media. Canadians were required to get two doses. Period. By the fall of 2021, there were deadlines to get your two doses and present a vaccine passport to enter designated settings: restaurants, hospitals, airplanes, universities, etc. When I got fully vaccinated, I understood the vaccine wouldn't keep me safe from infection or injury. A mix of social obligations, a trip overseas, and social coercion played a big role.

But Canadian authorities doubled down. The penalty for refusing vaccination in Canada for many has meant getting fired with no employment insurance. In New Brunswick, the government let stores decide if they would allow the unvaccinated to buy groceries. Quebec considered regulating a special tax on anyone who was unvaccinated. The tax was not rolled out, but the threat made by the Quebec premiere promised the tax would be financially onerous.

That changed with the imposition of a vaccine requirement for truck drivers to cross our international border. It didn't make sense to me for the government to insist on a vaccine requirement when vaccinated drivers could just as easily be transmitting the virus. Why not ask for a rapid test at the border? Or just ask drivers who felt under the weather to stay home until they felt better. And what was the urgency when drivers drove alone in their trucks? In my social circle, I had one friend who drove a truck and lived in Portland, Oregon. Otherwise, truck drivers shared the same roads and highways I drove on. Until the Freedom Convoy, truck drivers were on the periphery of my life.

In British Columbia, as the Freedom Convoy left Vancouver and Prince George over the weekend of January 22–23, 2022, people were just beginning to go to restaurants again. In December 2021, a new variant was the catalyst for new lockdown measures and restrictions. As I met with several sets of friends for the first time in months in early to mid-February, I heard about their disgust regarding the protests in Ottawa. I was told it was an "insurrection." As I didn't have a television—a choice I'd made in the early 1990s—I told my friends I didn't know what to think about the allegations being made by the media. There was a mounting list of incriminating allegations. But some of them didn't make sense to me at all. Why would truck drivers, upset by a new federal government mandate, only decide to drive to Ottawa based on Russian government agent prodding?

Curious about the depiction of those opposing the mandates, I walked over to observe a bit of a protest in downtown Vancouver on February 5, 2022. In light of stories about violence, I was prepared to quickly leave if there was any trouble. But what I observed that day in Vancouver was peaceful. I heard former Global News staff Anita Krishna speak about the pandemic narrative being pushed by the media. I heard her describe the groupthink in her newsroom and the stifling of discussion and debate. I heard her tell the Vancouver protesters on Robson Street, "All you people here today, all of what you're seeing here, this is not going to happen tonight on the six o'clock news. And you know how I know that? Because I directed the news for twenty . . . years (at Global TV)."[379]

When the Emergencies Act was invoked on February 14, 2022, I was shocked. I'd watched a live stream video of the festive atmosphere among protesters the weekend of February 11–13. I saw protesters being interviewed who were Asian-Canadian women and Sikh truck drivers. There was a young Afro-Canadian man who had brought his mother down to the protest to see for herself if it was safe to attend. She didn't understand what the media were talking about on the news. "These people are so friendly," she said to her son in reference to the Ottawa protesters.

Once the government cracked down on the protesters, I discovered an interview Dr. Jordan Peterson had with Rex Murphy, former CBC host of *Cross-country Check-up*. The interview was titled "The Catastrophe of Canada." Peterson and Murphy agreed the characterization of the working-class protesters was a smear. Murphy reflected that the invocation of the Emergencies Act has "done a great injury that may not be easily repaired over time. And that's the biggest worry of all. . . . It's the nature of the country and the harmony that it once knew." Murphy wondered "where are the five or six people in his own cabinet . . . who are saying Justin, you have . . . overreached vastly. You have insulted the nature of this country, which is always the middle course, always the willingness to at least try a compromise and a talk. And you've introduced false drama. . . . Maybe the melodramatic idea of a great national emergency" motivated the prime minister to fashion himself as a hero, though in the international press the prime minister took a beating.[380]

In the months that followed, I read more and more. It became clear that the allegations against the protesters were based on lies and hyperbole. Why did I have to depend on independent reporters and footage from protesters' cell phones to reveal an ugly side to policing in Ottawa on February 18? Why weren't CBC, CTV, or Global TV covering these stories?

For decades I'd listened to *As It Happens* on the CBC. I had counted on fairness and accuracy in reporting from the CBC with the 1973 coup in Chile, political events in El Salvador and Nicaragua in the late 1970s into the 1980s, and domestic politics here in Canada. *As It Happens* hosts like Barbara Frum, Alan Maitland, Elizabeth Gray, Michael Enright, and Mary Lou Finlay were the gold standard of journalism. The same is true for *The Fifth Estate* and the CBC's evening news, *The National*, hosted for years by Knowlton Nash, Peter Mansbridge, and Pamela Wallin.

I'd voted for the Liberals in the "Sunny Ways" campaign of 2015. I lived in a safe Liberal seat. I was tired of the Harper government. But into 2021–2022, I was set adrift from my NDP and Liberal political leaders. The government depiction of the Freedom Convoy protest, and the invocation of the Emergencies Act, crossed a line.

At the same time, my cohort of centrist-liberal-progressive-left friends was drawing their own lines. It seemed the whole liberal class in Canada had reached a point of fatigue. Liberals had worked hard to listen to others. For centuries, they sought to include people who were different, to tolerate different customs and opinions. But now there was a collapse of tolerance. Fear of the virus trumped everything. A whole generation that once spouted buttons that read "Question Authority" now accepted every government claim without scrutiny. And those who wanted to debate those claims were to be cancelled.

I found the media narrative throughout the pandemic alarming. Accusing fingers were now pointed at the unvaccinated, who were to blame for everything, from keeping society getting back to 'normal.' Though I was vaccinated, I had friends who were unvaccinated, and I listened to them tell me about life on the other side of the tracks. Words like asymptomatic—meaning a person had no symptoms and correspondingly had little to no virus in them—were weaponized. Now, every healthy person—vaccinated or unvaccinated—was to be regarded as a clear and present danger to family, friend, and stranger. How would it be possible to appeal to something we all held in common? Why were people who had multiple doses of a vaccine—which they believed were safe and effective—simultaneously worried about being in the company of the unvaccinated?

Growing up, my parents were close friends with a couple who lived in Vernon, British Columbia. My family visited with them for many summer trips to the Okanagan as I grew up. Olive Woodley was a member of the Vernon City Council. In 1952, she contracted polio and walked with crutches. I had my polio vaccine sugar cube in kindergarten. My parents were not worried anyone in our family would get polio from having a visit with our friend Olive. A nurse at my school explained to me that taking my polio vaccine sugar cube would keep me from getting polio. This was the case with my vaccines for smallpox, tetanus, diphtheria, typhoid, and other vaccines I got over the years. But what did it now mean to get a vaccine promoted as "effective," but not effective enough to prevent transmission or infection?

Justin Trudeau asked if Canadians should tolerate the unvaccinated? A change in civility was on the march. Where there once was tolerance, self-described liberals became intolerant. Where there once was listening, it is now fashionable to tune others out. Where there once was understanding, people misread and misapprehended others. Foundations built for centuries to widen our societal circle were now dissolved into a campaign of exclusion. The campaign was led by politicians, public health officials, and the media.

South of the border, Dr. Anthony Fauci could not be questioned. He equated anyone who questioned him with someone who was questioning science. Fauci was "the science." One of the casualties of the pandemic was the possibility of having a conversation. Now, any sign of skepticism regarding official policies was met with postmodern shunning from a woke cancel culture. A new generation schooled to never question official claims would become a closed-down society.

During the run-up to the 2021 election, my book *Unanswered Questions: What the September Eleventh Families Asked and the 9/11 Commission Ignored* was published on the twentieth anniversary of the attacks. It was a chronicle of the efforts of the families who lost loved ones to have a proper investigation on September Eleventh. It was based on the testimony of members of the Family Steering Committee for the 9/11 Independent Commission. They presented the 9/11 Commission with over a thousand questions to pose to members of President George W. Bush's cabinet and various government agencies. Only 9 percent were seriously answered, and 70 percent were ignored. At least half of the dozen Family Steering Committee members had voted for President Bush in the 2000 election. My book did not offer any theory to explain what happened. But it was clear that many family members came to regard the 9/11 Commission as political theatre, a whitewash, and a cover-up.

In contrast to the 9/11 Commission, the Public Order Emergency Commission in Ottawa had the benefit of cross-examination. There were many documents made available. Viewers could read these online as they were presented as evidence during the inquiry in Ottawa. The 9/11 Commission was intent on writing a report that would not embarrass the president before he ran for reelection in 2004. I wondered how impartial the Rouleau Commission was. A lot of the evidence being presented at the inquiry didn't support the basis for invoking the Emergencies Act. Was the inquiry given marching orders to write a report that would confirm that the invocation of the Emergencies Act was justified? I couldn't know.

Watching the testimony of the Commission online, I sensed the importance of what was unfolding. When Tamara Lich testified in early November, there was a packed inquiry. But in the week of November 14–18, just a few people showed up. Looking around, attendance fluctuated between six and twenty, including members of the press. There was public interest in the story. Yet most Canadians were in the habit of letting the mainstream media choose what to highlight from the inquiry. Our media was not going to rock the boat. Much of the key testimony at the inquiry was off people's radar. After following the POEC and reading its Report, I count myself among the "reasonable and informed" people who disagree with its conclusions.

ACKNOWLEDGMENTS

I am grateful to Ken Whyte, publisher of Sutherland House Books. In our current era of censorship, it is refreshing to work with a publisher that is not afraid to publish books that dare scrutinize an official story of record. As well, I am indebted to the professional guidance from managing editor Shalomi Ranasinghe as we moved through the editing process.

Thank you to David Leis for believing in this book, who together with Frontier Centre for Public Policy colleagues—Peter Holle and Matthew Lane—helped me get an agreement with Sutherland House Books to publish *Unjustified* on behalf of the Frontier Centre.

After the Emergencies Act was invoked, I began to write the about the Freedom Convoy protests in Ottawa and Coutts, the POEC and its report. Angie Tibbs at dissidentvoice.org, Catte Black at off-guardian.org, Jermey Kuzmarov at *CovertAction* Magazine, Piers Robinson at Propagandainfocus. com, and Joseph Roberts at Common Ground, are among those I'm grateful to for amplifying my work.

I'm grateful to alternative media who have each given me the opportunity to engage in discussion about what has been unfolding in Canada in our 'pandemic' era. This includes Len Osanic on BlackOpRadio, Clyde Do Something, Chris Cook on Gorilla Radio, Hügo Krüger on his podcast (Paris), Jason Lavigne on The Lavigne Show, David Leis on Leaders on the Frontier, James Lowen, Domini Gordon on Open Society (UK), Marta Gamiero on Outras Evidencias (Portugal), David Craig on Return to Reason, Lt. Stephen Rogers Show, Out of the Blank podcast, Shadoe Davis on The Shadoe Davis Show, and Trish Wood on the Trish Wood is Critical show.

My unending appreciation goes to those who read *Unjustified* in advance and wrote an endorsement: Eva Chipiuk, Anna Farrow, Hügo Krüger, Dr. Aaron Kheriaty, Tamara Lich, Tom Marazzo, Brian Peckford, Dr. Julie Ponesse, Dr. Piers Robinson, Keith Wilson, Trish Wood and Elizabeth

Acknowledgments

Woodworth. I'm grateful to Scarlett Martyn and Shelley Overwater for sharing their personal accounts, Daniel Bulford for his information, and Marco Van Huigenbos for clarifying a number of details. I'm especially in debt to Rodney Palmer for his incisive, searing, foreword.

Special thanks go to Elizabeth Woodworth for suggesting I expand on my published articles and write a book. There are many other writers, physicians, scientists and commentators whose public witness has informed my perspective. Some of these have been cited in these pages. Leo Santana, Bonnie Ferguson, Brenda Reid, Peter Cameron, Heather and Jim Screaton, and Sue Cook, for your encouragement and reflections; And my mother, Alice McGinnis, who at 92—having lived through the Great Depression, World War II and so much more—reminds me to keep my eye on the prize.

A NOTE ABOUT
THE AUTHOR

Ray McGinnis is the author of *Unanswered Questions: What the September Eleventh Families Asked and the 9/11 Commission Ignored* and *Writing the Sacred: A Psalm-inspired Path to Writing and Appreciating Sacred Poetry*. He attended the Public Order Emergency Commission hearings in mid-November and heard over a dozen witnesses testify in person. Subsequently, he watched or read through the testimony of all 76 witnesses at the POEC. He also attended several days of the trial of Tamara Lich and Chris Barber. He is a senior fellow at the Frontier Centre for Public Policy. He lives in Vancouver, Canada.

WHAT IS THE FRONTIER CENTRE
FOR PUBLIC POLICY?

The Frontier Centre for Public Policy is an independent, non-profit "think tank", founded to undertake research and education in support of economic growth and social outcomes which will enhance the quality of life of all Canadians.

The Centre is non-partisan and does not accept any government funding. Frontier is supported by the generosity of our donors and is a registered charity.

Frontier's mission is to improve awareness, understanding of the fundamental institutions of a free society by analyzing and advocating the role of markets in solving economic and social challenges in Canada.

Through a variety of publications and public forums and events the Frontier Centre explores policy changes required to make Canada successful.

The Frontier Centre was founded in 1997 by a group of individuals who shared a common interest in making the prairies and Canada a better place to live, work and prosper.

The Frontier Centre has grown in size and stature with a full-time professional staff and a high quality advisory of associates and friends who research, write about, and communicate new policy ideas. These ideas are shared with the media, decision-makers and opinion leaders and with millions of Canadians.

WHY DO WE NEED NEW IDEAS?

The vision of Frontier is to build a better and more prosperous nation while respecting individuals rights and freedoms.

Canada has all the ingredients to be the most prosperous and successful nation in the world: abundant natural resources, high quality public services and hardworking, spirited citizens and a tradition of respecting individual rights and freedoms.

Our nation, more than ever, needs to renew our commitment to freedom, leadership and it needs new policy ideas to realize its full potential. The Frontier Centre for Public Policy seeks to provide these ideas based on evidence.

WHAT ARE THE FRONTIER CENTRE'S IDEAS?

The Frontier Centre conducts research and education activities in three broad areas including:

High-Performance Government – creating high-productivity public institutions via the principles of transparency, neutrality and separation in their operations; competitive vs. monopolistic service provision.

Social Policy Renewal – consumer-sensitive health care and education systems; the post- welfare state; aboriginal policy based on empowerment, not dependency.

The Open Economy – achieving the optimum size of government; adjusting with globalization; the emerging technology-driven rural renaissance, creating the value-added agriculture economy.

HOW DOES THE CENTRE SHARE ITS IDEAS?

The Frontier Centre uses various communication methods to share its policy ideas and recommendations with the community:

- Studies, reports, policy commentaries, editorials and issue updates with a wide circulation in daily and weekly newspapers, emails and across social media.
- Special guest speakers and policy experts from around the world at events and seminars.
- The Frontier Centre website (www.fcpp.org).
- Weekly media programs including Leaders on the Frontier on television and social media.
- Meetings with elected decisionmakers, public meetings, educational conferences and speaking engagements.
- Student internships, scholarships and leadership development.
- Media Interviews and news conferences.

WHAT MAKES FRONTIER CENTRE UNIQUE?

Results-Oriented

The Frontier Centre is results-oriented and produces information and ideas that offer positive, practical solutions for our public policy challenges.

Regional Focus

The Centre focuses its attention on Prairie issues at all levels of government. Its secondary focus is on national issues.

Canadians are our Audience

The Centre writes for a mass audience, the person in the street who relates rarely to complicated public policy issues. The Centre strives to present our materials in a brief and understandable format and that offers solutions to a large audience reaching several million annually.

Citizenship

Frontier recognizes that its citizens who have worked together make nations successful. This is why Frontier advocates principles in keeping with a tradition of classical liberalism with its emphasis on the rights and freedoms of individuals, a limited state, the rule of law, merit, and freedom of speech and open markets.

Frontier believes these foundational principles are essential to build a fair, peaceful society that enables prosperity for everyone with the freedom to live their lives. Frontier believes that good public policy combined with a vision of limited government and strong property rights and freedom within a democratic tradition have delivered the largest improvements in living standards and prosperity in human history.

Get involved – see www.fcpp.org

Frontier welcomes your involvement to help build our nation.

Be sure to see our website and subscribe to our newsletter to find out more about how you can volunteer, donate and support our mission.

Better ideas for a
better tomorrow

175

NOTES

1 "Rodney Palmer Testimony," National Citizens Inquiry, Ottawa, ON, May 18, 2023. https://rumble.com/v2otumu-rodney-james-palmer-nci-testimony-from-ottawa-may-18-2023.html

2 Lich, Tamara, *Hold The Line: My Story from the Heart of the Freedom Convoy,* Rebel News Network Ltd., 2023. https://www.theconvoybook.com

3 Sevunts, Levon, "Canada Ranks 6th in Global Democracy Index," Radio Canada International, January 9, 2019. https://www.rcinet.ca/en/2019/01/09/canada-ranks-6th-in-global-democracy-index/

4 Economist Intelligence Unit, "Democracy Index 2020: In Sickness and in Health," The Economist Group, February 2021. https://pages.eiu.com/rs/753-RIQ-438/images/democracy-index-2020.pdf?mkt_tok=eyJpIjoiTURZM1lXWm1aVEJsTjJWaiIsInQi OiJOS2FDeG5DTk1oOTVKQ2kwOUR3V25GVFY3SWdNQSs2blVDOXJNbk1vRU tnQk5vWFhaaWx5ZVwvVUtGbmhaQkRmUGQwQzZwNHBSeEhYVU82VWFiW GZxdjJTalkwSmFTOHV1NjdBTjU4SHB6bFFDQmNzWkRGb2ZcL0ZhMnJibUEr RUlQIn0=

5 "What's Next for Canada. 1-on-1 with Justin Trudeau," Brandon Gonez Show, May 9, 2021. https://brandongonezshow.com/episode/whats-next-for-canada-1-on-1-with-justin-trudeau-2/

6 Gray, John, *Liberalism,* University of Minnesota Press, 1995. https://www.amazon.ca/Liberalism-John-Gray/dp/0816628017

7 McCaskill, Nolan D., "Trump Promises Wall and Massive Deportation Program," Politico, August 31, 2016. https://www.politico.com/story/2016/08/donald-trump-immigration-address-arizona-227612

8 Stein, Marc, *Rethinking the Gay and Lesbian Movement* (Taylor & Francis, 2012). https://www.taylorfrancis.com/books/mono/10.4324/9780203122211/rethinking-gay-lesbian-movement-marc-stein?refId=aeb232aa-05e2-4abf-a1c9-1b51c0df4300

9 "Canada Legalizes Gay Marriage," CBC, June 20, 2005. https://www.cbsnews.com/news/canada-legalizes-gay-marriage/

10 Remnick, David, "Soviets Cancel History Tests Over Texts," *Washington Post,* June 11, 1988. https://www.washingtonpost.com/archive/politics/1988/06/11/soviets-cancel-history-tests-over-texts/f77e69c2-e882-43d9-a3f7-d539d208b1d3

11 "A Timeline of Official Apologies from the Federal Government," *National Post*, May 23, 2019. https://nationalpost.com/pmn/news-pmn/canada-news-pmn/a-timeline-of-official-apologies-from-the-federal-government

12 Gilmore, Rachel, "'Fringe Minority' in Truck Convoy with 'Unacceptable Views' Don't Represent Canadians: Trudeau," *Global News*, January 26, 2022. https://globalnews.ca/news/8539610/trucker-convoy-covid-vaccine-mandates-ottawa/

13 "Minister William Blair, Sworn," Public Order Emergency Commission, Ottawa, November 21, 2022, 220. https://publicorderemergencycommission.ca/files/documents/Transcripts/POEC-Public-Hearings-Volume-27-November-21-2022.pdf

14 Wakerell-Cruz, Roberto, "Old Trudeau Tweet Tells Canadians to #ThankATrucker," Postmellennial.com, January 25, 2022. https://thepostmillennial.com/old-trudeau-tweet-tells-canadians-to-thankatrucker

15 Heppner, Kevin, "Thousands of Truckers Prepared to Walk Due to Vaccine Mandates, Warn Canadian Trucking Groups," Real Agriculture, Altona, AB, December 13, 2021. https://www.realagriculture.com/2021/12/thousands-of-truckers-prepared-to-walk-due-to-vaccine-mandates-warn-canadian-trucking-groups/

16 Blanchfield, Mike and Taylor, Stephanie, "Business Groups Urge Feds to Reverse Vaccine Mandate for Cross-Border Truckers," *Global News*, January 24, 2022. https://globalnews.ca/news/8535295/truckers-vaccine-mandate-business-groups/

17 Ioannidis, John P. and Axfors, Catherine, "Infection Fatality Rate of COVID-19 in Community-Dwelling Populations with Emphasis on the Elderly: An Overview," Stanford University, Stanford, CA, December 23, 2021. https://www.medrxiv.org/content/10.1101/2021.07.08.21260210v2.full.pdf

18 Mahoney, Noi, "Mexican Truckers Unlikely to Protest Vaccine Rules, Industry Observers Say," Freightwaves.com, February 21, 2022 https://www.freightwaves.com/news/mexican-truckers-unlikely-to-protest-vaccine-rules

19 Kimball, Spencer, "Labor Secretary Says Most Truck Drivers Are Exempt from Covid Mandate, Handing Industry a Win," CNBC, November 5, 2021. https://www.cnbc.com/2021/11/05/labor-secretary-says-most-truck-drivers-are-exempt-from-covid-mandate-handing-industry-a-win-.html

20 Williams, Pete, "Supreme Court Blocks Biden's Covid Requirements for Businesses, Upholds Health Care Worker Mandates," CNBC, January 13, 2022. https://www.nbcnews.com/politics/supreme-court/supreme-court-blocks-biden-admin-s-covid-requirements-workplaces-allows-n1287435

21 "Mr. Tom Marazzo, Affirmed," Public Order Emergency Commission, November 2, 2022, 200-201. https://publicorderemergencycommission.ca/files/documents/Transcripts/POEC-Public-Hearings-Volume-15-November-2-2022.pdf

22 Ms. Tamara Lich, Sworn," Public Order Emergency Commission, November 3, 2022, 277. https://publicorderemergencycommission.ca/files/documents/Transcripts/POEC-Public-Hearings-Volume-16-November-3-2022.pdf

23 Dzsurdzsa, Cosmin, "Feds Ditch Interprovincial COVID-19 Vaccine Mandate for Truckers," True North, March 3, 2022. https://tnc.news/2022/03/03/feds-ditch-interprovincial-covid-19-vaccine-mandate-for-truckers/

24 "Ms. Tamara Lich, Sworn," 278–280. (See note 22).

25 "Mr. Daniel Bulford, Sworn," Public Order Emergency Commission, November 4, 2022, 222–224. https://publicorderemergencycommission.ca/files/documents/Transcripts/POEC-Public-Hearings-Volume-17-November-4-2022.pdf

26 "Ms. Margaret Hope-Braun, Sworn," Public Order Emergency Commission, November 4, 2022, 90–91ff. https://publicorderemergencycommission.ca/files/documents/Transcripts/POEC-Public-Hearings-Volume-17-November-4-2022.pdf

27 "Mr. Christopher Deering, Sworn," Public Order Emergency Commission, November 4, 2022, 87. https://publicorderemergencycommission.ca/files/documents/Transcripts/POEC-Public-Hearings-Volume-17-November-4-2022.pdf

28 Subramanya, Rupa, "What the Truckers Want: I've Spoken to 100 of the Protesters

Gathered in the Canadian Capital. What's Happening Is Far Bigger Than the Vaccine Mandates," *The Free Press*, February 10, 2022. https://www.thefp.com/p/what-the-truckers-want

29 Peckford, Brian, "In -30 Degree Weather the Canadian Truckers Convoy Is Overwhelmed with People Wanting Freedom: One Trucker's Description," Peckford42, January 27, 2022. https://peckford42.wordpress.com/2022/01/27/in-30-degree-weather-the-canadian-truckers-convey-is-overwhelmed-with-people-wanting-freedom/

30 Cousins, Ben, "'So Many Angry People': Experts Say Online Conversation Around Trucker Convoy Veering into Dangerous Territory," CTV, January 25, 2022. https://www.ctvnews.ca/canada/so-many-angry-people-experts-say-online-conversation-around-trucker-convoy-veering-into-dangerous-territory-1.5754580

31 Woolf, Marie and Bryden, Joan, "Ottawa Braces for 'Significant' Trucker Convoy Disruptions as Police Warn of Risks," Global News, January 26, 2022. https://globalnews.ca/news/8540245/ottawa-trucker-convoy-risks/

32 "Final Written Submissions of Freedom Corp. . . ., December 9, 2022, 29. https://publicorderemergencycommission.ca/files/documents/Closing-Submissions/Freedom-Corp.-et-al-Closing-Submissions.pdf

33 "CBC Issues Clarification over Claim Kremlin Behind Truckers' Protest," *Toronto Sun*, February 4, 2022. https://torontosun.com/news/national/cbc-issues-clarification-over-claim-kremlin-behind-truckers-protest

34 Wagner, David, "CBC Interview Alluding to Russian Involvement in Trucker Protests Breached Journalistic Standards: Ombudsman," *Epoch Times*, October 13, 2022. https://www.theepochtimes.com/world/cbc-interview-alluding-to-russian-collusion-with-trucker-protests-in-breach-of-journalistic-standards-ombudsman-4795325

35 Pushaw, Christina, Twitter, January 29, 11:20 AM https://twitter.com/Christina Pushaw/status/1487506015709011972?ref_src=twsrc%5etfw%7Ctwcamp%5etweetembed%7Ctwterm%5e1487506015709011972%7Ctwgr%5e%7Ctwcon%5es1_&ref_url=https%3A%2F%2Ftnc.news%2F2022%2F01%2F30%2Fthe-canadian-legacy-medias-ten-worst-spins-on-the-truckersforfreedom-convoy%2F

36 Mosleh, Omar, "Why Banning Hateful Symbols like the Swastika Is Nearly Impossible," *Toronto Star*, February 7, 2022. https://www.thestar.com/news/canada/why-banning-hateful-symbols-like-the-swastika-is-nearly-impossible/article_441c1b04-956c-54fd-9d7e-b1b682e24b7a.html

37 Baisch Beth and Isidorou, Angelo, "Indigenous Drummers Lead Crowd in O Canada in Support of Truckers' Convoy," Postmillennial.com, January 29, 2022. https://thepostmillennial.com/must-watch-indigenous-drummers-lead-crowd-in-o-canada-in-support-of-truckers-convoy/

38 Thompson, Nicole, "Anti-vaxxers Danced on Tomb of the Unknown Soldier and Desecrated National War Memorial," *National Observer*, January 29, 2022. https://www.nationalobserver.com/2022/01/29/news/anti-vaxxers-danced-tomb-unknown-soldier-and-desecrated-national-war-memorial

39 "Ottawa Police Arson Unit Investigates Fire Lit in Downtown Apartment Lobby," CBC, February 7, 2022. https://www.cbc.ca/news/canada/ottawa/ottawa-police-arson-investigation-fire-apartment-lobby-1.6342347

40 Murphy, Rex, "Will Anyone Apologize for Falsely Accusing Truckers of Attempted Arson in Ottawa?," *National Post*, April 8, https://nationalpost.com/opinion/rex-murphy-will-anyone-apologize-for-falsely-accusing-truckers-of-attempted-arson-in-ottawa

41 Wheeler, Tristan, "Ottawa Councillor Says Freedom Convoy Protesters Are 'Terrorists'

Who Are 'Torturing' Locals," *Narcity Media*, Toronto, February 6, 2022. https://www.narcity.com/ottawa-councillor-says-freedom-convoy-protestors-are-terrorists-who-are-torturing-locals

42 Bordman, Daniel, "FINTRAC Destroys Liberals' Narrative—Convoy Funding Not "Terrorism" or "Money Laundering," *National Telegraph*, March 15, 2022. https://thenationaltelegraph.com/national/fintrac-destroys-liberals-narrative-convoy-funding-not-terrorism-or-money-laundering

43 Dzsurdzsa, Cosmin, "Convoy Donations Came from Fed-up People, Not Terrorists: FINTRAC," True North, February 25, 2022. https://tnc.news/2022/02/25/convoy-donations-came-from-fed-up-people-not-terrorists-fintrac/

44 Frei, Viva, "Live Stream with Ottawa Convoy Attorney Keith Wilson!," Viva Frei Live! podcast, March 25, 2022. https://www.youtube.com/watch?v=DMvB3HiXj3k&t=22s

45 Kay, Jonathan, Twitter, February 6, 2022, 1:36 p.m. https://twitter.com/jonkay/status/1490439304224686082?ref_src=twsrc%5Etfw%7Ctwcamp%5Etweetembed%7Ctwterm%5E1490439304224686082%7Ctwgr%5E566f2eb6dac10c29054e42443132e9ed7e2a9796%7Ctwcon%5Es1_&ref_url=https%3A%2F%2Ftnc.news%2F2022%2F02%2F07%2Fanti-semitic-leaflet-was-a-hate-hoax-pushed-by-legacy-media-and-left-wing-politicians%2F

46 Connolly, Amanda and Khan, Ahmar, "Ottawa Police Issue New Warning Amid Convoy Blockade: 'Leave the Area Now'," *Global News*, February 16, 2022. https://globalnews.ca/news/8624024/ottawa-convoy-blockade-police-action/

47 McLachlin, Beverley, "The Ottawa Convoy Has Revealed the Ugly Side of Freedom," *Globe and Mail*, February 22, 2022. https://www.theglobeandmail.com/opinion/article-the-ottawa-truck-convoy-has-revealed-the-ugly-side-of-freedom/?utm_source=dlvr.it&utm_medium=twitter. Daniel Bulford emailed me on June 25, 2022. In it he stated "I can confirm that nobody associated with the Freedom Convoy has been arrested and charged with uttering threats toward PM Trudeau." This remains the case in 2024 as this book goes to print.

48 Fraser, David, "In Jail for More than 100 days, Pat King 'Beat Down,' Says Supporter," CBC, June 11, 2022. https://www.cbc.ca/news/canada/ottawa/king-billings-convoy-jail-ottawa-1.6483455

49 Subramanya, Rupa, "Justin Trudeau's Case Against the Freedom Convoy Falls on Its Face: How Are Our Elected Officials Who Purvey What Can Only Be Called Misinformation Be Held to Account?," *National Post*, October 21, 2022. https://nationalpost.com/opinion/rupa-subramanya-justin-trudeaus-case-against-the-freedom-convoy-falls-on-its-face

50 "Read Court Document: Lawyer Says Judge Sees the Freedom Convoy Protest as Peaceful and Lawful," *Farmer's Forum*, April 13, 2022. https://farmersforum.com/read-court-document-lawyer-says-judge-sees-the-freedom-convoy-protest-as-peaceful-and-lawful/

51 "Ottawa Police Breach of Charter Rights—Right to Peaceful Assembly," Justice Centre for Constitutional Freedoms, February 17, 2022. https://www.jccf.ca/wp-content/uploads/2022/02/2022-02-17-Letter-to-Chief-Bell-FINAL-003.pdf

52 Braun, Liz, "Conservative Politicians Question Sexual Assault Threat from Truckers," *Toronto Sun*, February 28, 2022. https://torontosun.com/news/national/conservative-politicians-question-sexual-assault-threat-from-truckers

53 Boutilier, Alex, and Gilmore, Rachel, "Far-right Groups Hope Trucker Protest Will Be Canada's 'January 6th,' Global News, January 25, 2022. https://globalnews.ca/news/8537433/far-right-groups-trucker-protest-jan-6/

54 Rosenthal, Peter, "The New Emergencies Act: Four Times the War Measures Act,"

Manitoba Law Journal, March 20, 1991, 573. https://www.canlii.org/en/commentary/doc/1991CanLIIDocs129#!fragment/zoupio-_Tocpdf_bk_7/BQCwhgziBcwMYgK4DsDWszIQewE4BUBTADwBdoAvbRABwEtsBaAfX2zhoBMAzZgI1TMA7AEoANMmyICEAIqJCuAJ7QA5KrERCYXAnmKV6zdt0gAynlIAhFQCUAogBl7ANQCCAOQDC9saTB80KTsIiJAA

55 "Why the Truckers' Revolt Matters: Rupa Subramanya Talks to Brendan O'Neill about the Populist Earthquake in Canada," Spiked, February 24, 2022. https://www.spiked-online.com/podcast-episode/why-the-truckers-revolt-matters/

56 Farrow, Anna, "I Saw A Mob; It Wasn't the Truckers," *Catholic Register*, January 31, 2022. https://www.catholicregister.org/opinion/guest-columnists/item/33985-i-saw-a-mob-it-wasn-t-truckers

57 Lord, Craig, "Ottawa Man Charged in February Apartment Arson, Police Dismiss Convoy Connection," Global News, March 21, 2022. https://globalnews.ca/news/8698744/ottawa-arson-freedom-convoy-arrest/

58 Wilson, Keith "We Are Making a List of the False Claims by the 'So-called Media' against the Freedom Truckers that Are Now Being Proven False . . ." Twitter, 11:08 AM, March 24, 2022. https://twitter.com/ikwilson/status/1507056697805721601?s=20&t=bH0doPBpzBJ6Hj5CRcSgIg

59 "Remarks by Chrystia Freeland, Marco Mendicino: Freeland Says Emergencies Act Begins Cracking Down ON Convoy Funds," Press Conference, Parliament Buildings, Ottawa, February 17, 2022. https://www.youtube.com/watch?v=XvMZvazmT0Q

60 See McGinnis, Ray, "Propaganda Trudeau Style," Propagandainfocus.com, June 29, 2022. https://propagandainfocus.com/propagandatrudeau-style/; And McGinnis, Ray, "Commission Reveals that Trudeau Government Lied About Nature of Truckers Protests in Ottawa Last February to Justify Invocation of Emergency Act," *Covert Action Magazine*, February 28, 2023. https://covertactionmagazine.com/2023/02/28/commission-reveals-that-trudeau-government-lied-about-nature-of-truckers-protests-in-ottawa-last-february-to-justify-invocation-of-emergencies-act/

61 "How False Testimony and a Massive U.S. Propaganda Machine Bolstered George H.W. Bush's War on Iraq," *Democracy Now!*, December 5, 2018. https://www.democracynow.org/2018/12/5/how_false_testimony_and_a_massive

62 MacArthur, John R., *Second Front: Censorship and Propaganda in the 1991 Gulf War* (University of California Press, 2004), 2nd edition, xxiv. https://books.google.ca/books/about/Second_Front.html?id=px4awQl7lT0C&redir_esc=y

63 Taube, Michael, "Will Canadian Democracy Survive Justin Trudeau? His Father Invoked Emergency Powers in 1970—But that Was against Terrorists, Not Peaceful Protesters," *Wall Street Journal*, February 21, 2022. https://www.wsj.com/articles/canadian-democracy-survive-justin-trudeau-freedom-convoy-peaceful-protest-ottawa-unacceptable-views-emergency-act-civil-liberties-11645472383

64 Editorial, "Canada's Illiberal Response to Protesters," *Financial Times*, February 18, 2022. https://www.ft.com/content/1f83d3dc-a95b-4947-92ba-4f08899228a3

65 Wilson, Pete, "Police Called Convoy Protest 'Calm, Festive' on Same Day Emergencies Act Was Invoked: Internal Memo," *Epoch Times*, November 3, 2022. https://www.theepochtimes.com/world/police-called-convoy-protest-calm-festive-on-same-day-emergencies-act-was-invoked-internal-memo-4839848

66 "Supt. Patrick Morris, Sworn," Public Order Emergency Commission, Ottawa, October 19, 2022, 291–294. https://publicorderemergencycommission.ca/files/documents/Transcripts/POEC-Public-Hearings-Volume-5-October-19-2022.pdf

67 "TDF Litigation Director Questions OPP Supt. Carson Pardy," The Democracy Fund, October 21, 2022. https://www.thedemocracyfund.ca/tdf_litigation_director_questions_opp_pardy

68 "Ms. Margaret Hope-Braun, Sworn," Public Order Emergency Commission, November 4, 2022, 90–91ff. (See note 26).

69 Faulkner, Harrison, "OPP Officer Says No Intel of Convoy Violence—Day 5 Recap of Emergencies Act Hearings," True North, Calgary, Alberta, October 19, 2022. https://tnc.news/2022/10/19/day-5-recaphearings/

70 "Can't Hide Emails: Judge," *Blacklock's Reporter*, Ottawa, February 2, 2023. https://www.blacklocks.ca/cant-hide-emails-fedjudge/

71 "Mr. Peter Sloly, Resumed," Public Order Emergency Commission, Ottawa, October 31, 2022, 91ff. https://publicorderemergencycommission.ca/files/documents/Transcripts/POEC-Public-Hearings-Volume-13-October-31-2022.pdf

72 "Comm. Thomas Carrique, Sworn," Public Order Emergency Commission, Ottawa, October 27, 2022, 231, 237. https://publicorderemergencycommission.ca/files/documents/Transcripts/POEC-Public-Hearings-Volume-11-October-27-2022.pdf

73 "Acting Supt. Marcel Beaudin, Affirmed," Public Order Emergency Commission, October 25, 2022, 191–194. https://publicorderemergencycommission.ca/files/documents/Transcripts/POEC-Public-Hearings-Volume-9-October-25-2022.pdf

74 Chartier, Noe, "Public Safety Minister's Deputy Sought Engagement with Convoy Protesters but Was Denied by Top Ministers," *Epoch Times*, October 25, 2022. https://www.theepochtimes.com/world/public-safety-ministers-deputy-sought-engagement-with-convoy-protesters-but-was-denied-4820641

75 Ivison, John, "It's Becoming Clear that the Federal Government Overreached to Shut Down the Freedom Convoy," *National Post*, October 26, 2022. https://nationalpost.com/news/canada/john-ivison-its-becoming-clear-that-the-federal-government-overreached-to-shut-down-the-freedom-convoy

76 "Comm Brenda Lucki, Sworn," Public Order Emergency Commission, November 15, 2022, 196-198. https://publicorderemergencycommission.ca/files/documents/Transcripts/POEC-Public-Hearings-Volume-23-November-15-2022.pdf

77 "Closing Submissions Ottawa Police Service," Public Order Emergency Commission, December 9, 2022, 68. https://publicorderemergencycommission.ca/files/documents/Closing-Submissions/Ottawa-Police-Service-Closing-Submissions.pdf#page=79

78 "Mr. Serge Arpin, Sworn," Public Order Emergency Commission, Ottawa, October 17, 2022, 232, 322–326. https://publicorderemergencycommission.ca/files/documents/Transcripts/POEC-Public-Hearings-Volume-3-October-17-2022.pdf

79 "Mr. Kim Ayotte, Sworn," Public Order Emergency Commission, Ottawa, October 18, 2022, 251–252. https://publicorderemergencycommission.ca/files/documents/Transcripts/POEC-Public-Hearings-Volume-4-October-18-2022.pdf

80 Phone call from Mr. Keith Wilson, May 15, 2023.

81 CSIS Director David Vigneault, Sworn," Public Order Emergency Commission, Ottawa, November 21, 2022, 89–94. https://publicorderemergencycommission.ca/files/documents/Transcripts/POEC-Public-Hearings-Volume-27-November-21-2022.pdf

82 "Emails Ridicule Mark Carney," *Blacklock's Reporter*, December 12, 2022. https://www.blacklocks.ca/emails-ridicule-mark-carney/

83 "Mr. John Ossowski, Affirmed," Public Order Emergency Commission, November 16, 2022, 42–44, 52-54. https://publicorderemergencycommission.ca/files/documents/Transcripts/POEC-Public-Hearings-Volume-24-November-16-2022.pdf

84 Batters, Senator Denise, "Senator Denise Batters Gives Riveting Speech on Public Emergency Vote," Senate of Canada Building, February 22, 2022. https://www.youtube.com/watch?v=LcWMgO8gLoY

85 Comm Brenda Lucki, Sworn," Public Order Emergency Commission, November 15, 2022, 115–116. (See note 76).

86 "Ms. Jody Thomas, Sworn," Public Order Emergency Commission, Ottawa, November 17, 2022, 270–272. https://publicorderemergencycommission.ca/files/documents/Transcripts/POEC-Public-Hearings-Volume-25-November-17-2022.pdf

87 "Final Written Submissions of Freedom Corp . . .," 18. (See note 32).

88 "Ms. Jody Thomas, Sworn," Public Order Emergency Commission, Ottawa, November 17, 2022, 282–291. (See note 86).

89 Stefanovich, Olivia, Roman, Karina, and Jones, Ryan Patrick, "Too Many First Nations Lack Clean Drinking Water and It's Ottawa's Fault, Says Auditor General," CBC, February 25, 2021. https://www.cbc.ca/news/politics/auditor-generalreports-2021-1.5927572

90 "Ms. Jody Thomas, Sworn," Public Order Emergency Commission, Ottawa, November 17, 2022, 291.(See note 86). Deputy Clerk of the Privy Council, Nathalie Drouin echoed Jody Thomas' view, testifying before the POEC . . . we considered trust in the institution as one of our criteria as part of the threat . . . a population . . . losing confidence in our public institution. (See note 97, p. 209). During her testimony, Jody Thomas agreed that the Intelligence Assessment Group concluded "The overwhelming majority of protesters have denounced violence. . . . It is unlikely premeditated violence will take place." (See note 86, p. 232-233).

91 Tasker, John Paul, "Trudeau Calls for 'Dialogue' as Blockade Cripples Rail Network, While Scheer Says Clear Out Protesters," CBC, February 14, 2020. https://www.cbc.ca/news/politics/transportminister-dialogue-blockade-1.5463960

92 Hartshorn, Max, "The Economic Nightmare that Wasn't? Border Blockades Had Little Effect on Trade, Data Reveals," Global News, April 26, 2022. https://globalnews.ca/news/8770775/borderblockades-trade-impact-data/

93 "Gov't Claim Was "Too Cute," Blacklock's Reporter, November 28, 2022. https://www.blacklocks.ca/govt-claim-was-too-cute/

94 Thomson, Carol, "Premiers Moe and Kenny and Sixteen U.S. Governors Urge for U.S. and Canada to Bring Back Trucker Vaccine Exemptions," CJWW, Saskatoon, SK, February 16, 2022. https://www.cjwwradio.com/2022/02/16/139425/

95 Leavitt, Kieran, "Diagolon Founder Jeremy MacKenzie Faces Assault, Weapon Charges in Saskatchewan," Toronto Star, August 26, 2022. https://www.thestar.com/news/canada/diagolon-founder-jeremy-mackenzie-faces-assault-weapons-charges-in-saskatchewan/article_c6d68467-e852-59c1-92e1-c44a83701c2d.html

96 "Minister David Lametti, Sworn," Public Order Emergency Commission, Ottawa, November 23, 2022, 94–101, 116-123, 135-139, 168-171, 176-178. https://publicorderemergencycommission.ca/files/documents/Transcripts/POEC-Public-Hearings-Volume-29-November-23-2022.pdf

97 "Ms. Janice Charette, Sworn, Ms. Nathalie Drouin, Affirmed," Public Order Emergency Commission, Ottawa, November 18, 2022, 126, 172-173. https://publicorderemergencycommission.ca/files/documents/Transcripts/POEC-Public-Hearings-Volume-26-November-18-2022.pdf

98 "Saw Right Wing Christians," Blacklock's Reporter, November 9, 2022 https://www.blacklocks.ca/saw-right-wing-christians/

99 Ms. Janice Charette, Sworn, Ms. Nathalie Drouin, Affirmed," 157, 216-218. (See note 97).

100 Ibid, 187.

101 "Prime Minister Justin Trudeau, Affirmed," Public Order Emergency Commission, Ottawa, November 25, 2022, 83-84 (also 3-192). https://publicorderemergencycommission.ca/files/documents/Transcripts/POEC-Public-Hearings-Volume-31-November-25-2022.pdf

102 "Ms. Janice Charette, Sworn, Ms. Nathalie Drouin, Affirmed," 242-255. (See note 97).

103 Chipiuk, Eva, Twitter, December 7, 2022. https://twitter.com/forevaeva79/status/160061 6269765832704

104 Taylor, Greg, "Why Trudeau Declaring a National Emergency Should Be a Non-starter—A Threat to the Security of Canada Is a Very High Legal Bar to Reach," *National Post*, February 14, 2022. https://nationalpost.com/opinion/greg-taylor-why-trudeau-declaring-a-national-emergency-should-be-a-non-starter

105 "Mr. Peter Sloly, Resumed," Public Order Emergency Commission, Ottawa, October 31, 2022, 91ff. (See note 71).

106 Boutilier, Alex and Gilmore, Rachel, "Far Right Groups Hope Trucker Protest Will Be Canada's 'January 6th'," January 25, 2022. https://globalnews.ca/news/8537433/far-rightgroups-trucker-protest-jan-6/

107 Gandham, Yasmin, "Salmon Arm RCMP Thank Convoy Protesters for Peaceful Event," Global News, January 24, 2022. https://globalnews.ca/news/8535449/salmon-armrcmp-convoy-protesters/

108 Lambert, Steve, "Quebec Police Admit Agents Posed as Protesters," *Toronto Star*, August 23, 2007. https://www.thestar.com/news/canada/quebec-police-admit-agents-posed-as-protesters/article_930d7140-ea3b-56b2-a64e-c49204019c4d.html

109 "Mr. Keith Wilson, Sworn," Public Order Emergency Commission, November 2, 2022, 25–27. https://publicorderemergencycommission.ca/files/documents/Transcripts/POEC-Public-Hearings-Volume-15-November-2-2022.pdf

110 Final Written Submissions of Freedom Corp. . . ., December 9, 2022, 35–37. (See note 32).

111 Ibid, 3-4.

112 Bronskill, Jim, "Legal Challenge of Emergencies Act Use Heads to Court This Week," CBC, April 3, 2023. https://www.cbc.ca/news/canada/ottawa/emergencies-act-canada-2022-ccla-legal-court-1.6799416

113 Peckford, Brian, "Freedom Convoy Speech—Canadian Charter of Rights & Freedoms," Parliament Hill, Ottawa, ON, February 15, 2022. https://www.youtube.com/watch?v=elXMwVgup60 Names of some individuals the POEC declined to have testify, who were suggested as witnesses, were been provided to me by Keith Wilson.

114 "Prime Minister Justin Trudeau, Affirmed," 3-77. (See note 101).

115 Ibid.

116 Aiello, Rachel, "Liberal MP Breaks Ranks Over Pandemic Policies," CTV, February 8, 2022. https://www.ctvnews.ca/politics/liberal-mp-breaksranks-over-pandemic-policies-1.5772722

117 Rabson, Mia and Woolf, Marie, "Some Liberal MPs Stand with Lightbound against 'Divisive' Vaccine Rhetoric," Global News, February 10, 2022. https://globalnews.ca/news/8611771/liberals-joellightbound-vaccines-rhetoric/

118 "Prime Minister Justin Trudeau, Affirmed," 42. (See note 101).

119 Fisher, Matthew and Cohen, Tobi, "'Don't Sit around Trying to Rationalize It': Harper Slams Trudeau for Response to Boston Bombing," *National Post*, April 17, 2013. https://nationalpost.com/news/politics/trudeaus-response-to-boston-marathon-bombing-was-unacceptable-made-excuses-for-terrorists-harper-says

120 Editorial, "The Orwellian Re-education of Jordan Peterson," *Toronto Sun*, January 6, 2023. https://torontosun.com/opinion/editorials/editorial-the-orwellian-re-education-of-jordan-peterson

121 Dawson, Trevor, "Jordan Peterson says he's willing to risk licence over social media training after losing court battle," National Post, January 16, 2024. https://nationalpost.com/news/canada/exclusive-jordan-peterson-loses-fight-with-psychology-college-over-mandatory-social-media-training

122 Tao, Issac, "Federal Court Rejects AG's Attempt to Dismiss Motion Seeking to Admit More Evidence Concerning Emergencies Act Invocation," *Epoch Times*, February 4, 2023. https://www2.theepochtimes.com/world/federal-court-rejects-ags-attempt-to-dismiss-motion-seeking-to-admit-more-evidence-concerning-emergencies-act-invocation-5034024

123 "Justin Trudeau Remarks," February 23, 2023. https://twitter.com/vesperdigital/status/1629023431449628673 February 23, 2023. Justin Trudeau speaking in April 2012 on the 30th anniversary of the proclamation of the Canadian Charter of Rights and Freedoms

124 Batters, Senator Denise, "Senator Denise Batters Gives Riveting Speech on Public Emergency Vote," Senate of Canada Building, February 22, 2022. (See note 84)

125 Statement by Keith Wilson, "Day 28 of Public Hearings," Public Order Emergency Commission, Webcast, November 22, 2022, 2:34:30ff. https://publicorderemergency commission.ca/public-hearings/day-28-november-22/

126 Catt, Helen, "Matt Hancock: Leaked Messages Suggest Plan to Frighten Public," BBC, March 5, 2023. https://www.bbc.com/news/uk-64848106

127 Pugliese, David, "Military Leaders Saw Pandemic as Unique Opportunity to Test Propaganda Techniques on Canadians, Forces Report Says," *Ottawa Citizen*, September 27, 2021. https://ottawacitizen.com/news/national/defencewatch/military-leaders-saw-pandemic-as-unique-opportunity-to-test-propaganda-techniques-on-canadians-forces-report-says

128 Pugliese, David, "Propaganda Program's Documents Vanished: DNND can't find papers on public manipulation," Vancouver Sun, May 12, 2023. https://www.pressreader.com/canada/vancouver-sun/20230512/281968907031730

129 Stephens, Brett, "The Mask Mandates Did Nothing. Will Any Lessons Be Learned?" *New York Times*, February 21, 2023. https://www.nytimes.com/2023/02/21/opinion/do-mask-mandates-work.html (See also Koops, Roger W., "The Year of Disguises," *American Institute for Economic Research*, October 16, 2020. https://www.aier.org/article/the-year-of-disguises/)

130 Kheriaty, M.D., Aaron, *The New Abnormal: The Rise of the Biomedical Security State* (Regenery Publishing, 2022), 195–197. https://www.regnery.com/9781684513857/the-newabnormal/

131 Agamben, Giorgio, *Where Are We Now: The Pandemic as Politics* (Roman & Littlefield, 2021), 94. https://rowman.com/ISBN/9781538157602/Where-AreWe-Now?-The-Epidemic-as-Politics

132 Finley, Allysia, "Three Years Late, the Lancet Recognizes Natural Immunity: The Public-Health Clerisy Rediscovers a Principle of Immunology It Derided throughout the Pandemic," *Wall Street Journal*, February 26, 2023. https://www.wsj.com/articles/three-years-late-the-lancet-recognizes-natural-immunity-great-barrington-declaration-tech-censor-antibodies-mandates-b3ba912c

133 "Interview with Dr. Anthony Fauci," Washington Journal, C-SPAN, October 11, 2004. (See minute 30 https://www.c-span.org/video/?183885-2/influenzavaccine)

134 Dr. John P.A. Ioannidis, Professor of Medicine/Health Research & Policy/Biomedical Data Science/Statistics, Stanford University, is the 45th most cited scientific researcher of any kind in the world, https://webometrics.info/en/hlargerthan100. He has served on the editorial board of over twenty scientific journals including Journal of the American Medical Association (JAMA), https://en.wikipedia.org/wiki/John_Ioannidis

135 Ioannidis J. "The Infection Fatality Rate of COVID-19 Inferred from Seroprevalence Data," *Bull World Health Organ.*, Epub Oct. 14, 2020 https://pubmed.ncbi.nlm.nih.gov/33716331/ The *British Medical Journal*, citing this article, reported: "Clearly, mortality is age-stratified from COVID-19. The corrected median estimates of IFP [Infection Fatality Rate] for people aged lower than 70 years is currently 0.05%, [2] which, for the population less vulnerable to deaths, is similar to influenza. However overall estimates for COVID-19 are higher [i.e., 0.23%], due to the higher fatality rate in elderly people." *BMJ* October 6, 2020. https://www.bmj.com/content/371/bmj.m3883/rr

136 Chief Public Health Officer of Canada, Dr. Theresa Tam. Biography. https://www.canada.ca/en/public-health/corporate/organizational-structure/canada-chief-public-health-officer/biography.html

137 We Are Not in a "Pandemic of the Unvaccinated," says *British Medical Journal* editor Peter Doshi," *Rio Times*, November 9, 2021. https://www.riotimesonline.com/brazil-news/modernday-censorship/we-are-not-in-a-pandemic-of-the-unvaccinated-says-british-medical-journal-editor-peter-doshi/

138 "Dr. Anthony Fauci Press Briefing," White House Press Room, January 28, 2020. https://www.youtube.com/watch?v=nTGX4crz2C0

139 Hopper, Tristin, "Lockdowns Only Reduced COVID Deaths by 0.2 Per Cent, Johns Hopkins Study Finds," *National Post*, February 2, 2022. https://nationalpost.com/news/world/johns-hopkins-university-study-covid-19-lockdowns

140 "Board Member: James C. Smith," Pfizer.com. https://www.pfizer.com/people/leadership/board-of-directors/james_smith

141 "An Interview with Carl Sagan," *Charlie Rose*, PBS, May 27, 1995. https://www.youtube.com/watch?v=U8HEwO-2L4w&t=139s

142 "In the Public Interest: An Interim Report on the COVID-19 Vaccine Authorization Process," National Citizens Inquiry, September 14, 2023, 11. https://nationalcitizensinquiry.ca/wp-content/uploads/2023/09/NCI-Interim-Report-C19-Vaccine-Authorization-Process-2023-09-14.pdf

143 Ibid, 10.

144 Ibid, 5.

145 Ibid.

146 "No Flies on Me, Thanks to DDT," Black Flag, 1947. https://www.pinterest.ca/pin/441352832225614363/

147 Gardner, Martha N. PhD, and Brandt, Allan M. PhD, "The Doctors' Choice Is America's Choice: The Physician in US Cigarette Advertisements, 1930-1953," *American Journal of Public Health*, v.96 (2), February 2006, 222-232. https://www.ncbi.nlm.nih.gov/pmc/articles/PMC1470496/

148 Brownell, Kelly D., and Kenneth E. Warner, "The Perils of Ignoring History: Big Tobacco Played Dirty. How Similar is Big Food?", *The Milbank Quarterly*, 2009 Mar; 87(1): 259–294. https://www.ncbi.nlm.nih.gov/pmc/articles/PMC2879177/ See also Whitmer, Michelle, "Asbestos Cigarette Filters," asbestos.com, September 29, 2023. https://www.asbestos.com/products/cigarette-filters/

149 "Manufacturing and Supply Agreement between Pfizer and Minister of Public Works

and Government Services Canada," October 26, 2020. https://drive.google.com/file/d/1DGIxi2gS95nt5F1fZdCnKuaMSC_Xlc-h/view

150 Campbell, Mike, "Health Canada's Contract with Pfizer Exposes their Liberal Use of the Word "Safe"," Counter Signal, November 15, 2023. https://thecountersignal.com/health-canadas-contract-with-pfizer-exposes-their-liberal-use-of-the-word-safe/

151 Kelly, Amy and Pfizer Documents Investigation Team, *War Room/Dailyclout Pfizer Documents Analysis Reports: Find Out What Pfizer, FDA Tried to Conceal,* DailyClout, 2023. 63-64, 66. https://dailyclout.io/product/war-room-dailyclout-pfizer-documents-analysis-volunteers-reports-book-paperback/

152 Ibid, 5.

153 Dowd, Edward, *Cause Unknown: The Epidemic of Sudden Deaths in 2021 and 2022,* Skyhorse Publishing, 2022, 116–117. https://www.amazon.ca/Cause-Epidemic-Sudden-Deaths-2021/dp/1510776397

154 Ibid, 119.

155 Dowd, Edward, "Bad News . . . Real Time Disability Data from US Bureau of Labor Statistics (BLS) rose 857k in June," GETTR, 12:42 PM, June 8, 2023. https://gettr.com/post/p2lk9nn2a1d

156 Tasker, John Paul, "Banks Have Started to Freeze Accounts Linked to the Protests," CBC, February 17, 2022. https://www.cbc.ca/news/politics/ottawa-protestsfrozen-bank-accounts-1.6355396

157 Murdoch, Anthony, "Canadians Withdrew Millions of Dollars from Banks after Trudeau Ordered Accounts Frozen," Lifesite, March 21, 2022. https://www.lifesitenews.com/news/canadians-withdrew-millions-of-dollars-from-banks-after-trudeau-ordered-some-accounts-frozen/

158 Frei, Viva, "Live Stream with Ottawa Convoy Attorney Keith Wilson!," Viva Frei Live! podcast, March 25, 2022. (See note 44).

159 Van Geyn, Christine and Baron, Joanna," Opinion: Even after Being Revoked, the Emergencies Act Is Creating a Chill on Charities," *National Post,* March 8, 2022. https://nationalpost.com/opinion/opinion-even-after-being-revoked-the-emergencies-act-is-creating-a-chill-on-charities?utm_term=Autofeed&utm_medium=Social&utm_source=Twitter#Echobox=1646753322 .

160 "Mr. Keith Wilson, Sworn," 25–27. (See note 109).

161 "Interview Summary: Deputy Prime Minister Chrystia Freeland," Public Order Emergency Commission, Ottawa, 2022. The document is hard to discover in a search on the POEC website; it can be found at Sheila Gunn Reid, "Deputy Prime Minister Chrystia Freeland admitted she felt the truckers had to be crushed beforehand," Rebel News, March 7, 2023. https://www.rebelnews.com/deputy_prime_minister_admitted_she_felt_the_truckers_had_to_be_crushed_beforehand

162 "Liked To Deploy the Military," Blacklock's Reporter, November 25, 2022. https://www.blacklocks.ca/liked-to-deploy-the-military/

163 Unrau, Jason, "Calgary law firm representing 20 victims of Emergencies Act measures seek $35 million in damages . . .," Twitter.com, 2:35 PM, February 14, 2024. https://twitter.com/JayUnrau/status/1757896383707713819

164 Hodgson, Jen, "Lich, other Freedom Convoy leaders file lawsuit against Trudeau Liberals," Western Standard, February 14, 2024. https://www.westernstandard.news/news/breaking-lich-other-freedom-convoy-leaders-file-lawsuit-against-trudeau-liberals/52398

165 Rouleau, The Honourable Paul S., *Report of the Public Inquiry in to the 2022 Public Order Emergency Volume 1: Overview* (His Majesty the King in Right of Canada, 2023),

23. https://publicorderemergencycommission.ca/files/documents/Final-Report/Vol-1-Report-of-the-Public-Inquiry-into-the-2022-Public-Order-Emergency.pdf

166 Ibid, 53.

167 Ibid, 72.

168 Ibid, 111.

169 Ibid, 139.

170 Ibid, 14-15.

171 Ibid, 134.

172 Ibid, 138.

173 Ibid, 147.

174 Ibid, 137.

175 "Mr. Tom Marazzo, Affirmed," 172–174. (See note 21).

176 S'ad, Caryma, and Hategan, Elisa, "The Hategate Affair: Unmasking Canada's Hate Industry," prnewswire.com, 2023, 57–58. https://mma.prnewswire.com/media/2208997/Crier_Media_DOCUMENTS_REVEAL_SHOCKING_RCMP_FAILURES_IN_THE_INVES.pdf?p=pdf

177 Kristen Little to Ashley Chen, July 14, 2021, Subject "Diagolon," in S'ad, Caryma, and Hategan, Elisa, "The Hategate Affair: Unmasking Canada's Hate Industry," prnewswire.com, 2023, 8. (See note 176).

178 Ibid.

179 Ibid, 9.

180 Ibid.

181 Ibid.

182 Proctor, Jason, "RCMP entrapment of B.C. couple in legislature bomb plot was 'travesty of justice,' court rules: John Nuttall-Amanda Korody's convictions had been stayed due to entrapment, abuse of process," CBC, December 19, 2018. https://www.cbc.ca/news/canada/british-columbia/johnnuttall-amanda-korody-2018-1.4952431

183 Proctor, Jason, "Terrorists or Targets? Appeal Court to Decide Fate of B.C. Couple Accused in Bomb Plot," CBC, December 18, 2018. https://www.cbc.ca/news/canada/britishcolumbia/nuttall-korody-entrapment-terrorism-1.4951447

184 Tieleman, Bill, "BC Terror Trial Verdict a Scathing Indictment of RCMP Management," The Tyee, August 2, 2016. https://thetyee.ca/Opinion/2016/08/02/BC-Terror-Trial-Verdict/

185 Henderson, Jennifer, "RCMP Commissioner Brenda Lucki Tried to 'Jeopardize' Mass Murder Investigation to Advance Trudeau's Gun Control Efforts," *Halifax Examiner*, June 21, 2022. https://www.halifaxexaminer.ca/policing/rcmp-commissioner-brenda-lucki-tried-to-jeopardize-mass-murder-investigation-to-advance-trudeaus-gun-control-efforts/

186 McDonald, D.C., *Commission of Inquiry Concerning Certain Activities of the Royal Canadian Mounted Police—Second Report, Volume 2: Freedom and Security under the Law,* Privy Council Office, 1981. https://publications.gc.ca/site/eng/471402/publication.html

187 Hall, Prof. Anthony J., "Commemorating January 29, 2022: Democracy, Authoritarianism and Canada's Truckers Movement: Have the Coutts 13 Been Set Up to Embody the Canadian Version of "Domestic Terrorism," Global Research.ca, February 4, 2023. https://www.globalresearch.ca/democracyauthoritarianism-canadian-truckers-movement-havecoutts-13-been-set-up-embody-canadian-versiondomestic-terrorism/5784823

188 Rouleau, *Report of the Public Inquiry . . .* , 182.

189 Ibid, 192-193.
190 Ibid, 195.
191 Ibid, 199.
192 Ibid, 200.
193 Ibid, 109.
194 Ibid, 118.
195 Ibid, 201.
196 Ibid, 203.
197 Ibid, 240.
198 Ibid, 209.
199 Ibid, 210.
200 Ibid, 213.
201 Ibid, 232.
202 Ibid, 240.
203 Ibid, 242.
204 Ibid, 261.
205 Wood, Trish, "Democracy Dies in Ottawa and East Palestine," trishwood.substack.com, February 23, 2023. https://trishwood.substack.com/p/democracy-dies-in-ottawa?utm_source=twitter&sd=pf
206 Lawton, Andrew, "Public Order Emergency Commission Defends Use of Emergencies Act," The Andrew Lawton Show, February 17, 2023. https://tnc.news/2023/02/17/alshow-poec-emergencies-act/
207 Chipiuk, Eva, 5:38PM, February 17, 2023. https://twitter.com/echipiuk/status/1626757992682229760; https://twitter.com/echipiuk/status/1626757990329253889
208 Osman, Laura, "When It Comes to Emergencies Act Justification, 'Trust Us' Is Not Enough: Ex-minister," Global News, May 8, 2022. https://globalnews.ca/news/8818746/emergencies-act-justification-canada-perrin-beatty/
209 Editorial, "The Failures of Politics, and Empathy, Before the Emergencies Act," Globe and Mail, February 20, 2023. https://www.globeandmail.com/opinion/editorials/article-the-failures-of-politics-and-empathy-before-the-emergencies-act.
210 Kline, Jesse, "Emergencies Act Report a Slap in the Face to Canadians," National Post, February 17, 2023. https://nationalpost.com/opinion/emergencies-act-report-a-slap-in-the-face-to-canadians
211 Lilley, Brian, "Rouleau Gives Trudeau a Pass on Emergencies Act with Reluctance," Toronto Sun, February 17, 2023. https://o.canada.com/opinion/columnists/lilley-rouleau-gives-trudeau-a-bare-pass-and-with-some-reluctance-heres-why
212 Bussey, Gary W., "False Accountability—Interview with Bruce Pardy," First Freedoms Foundation, Hastings, ON, March 6, 2023. https://firstfreedoms.ca/false-accountability-interview-with-bruce-pardy/
213 Mosley, the Honourable Justice Richard, Jost et al. v. Canada, Reasons for Judgment, January 23, 2024, 6-7, 124. https://www.jccf.ca/wp-content/uploads/2024/01/2024-01-23-T-306-22-T-316-22-T-347-22-T-382-22-Reasons-FINAL.pdf?mc_cid=5582064794&mc_eid=3999eed8bc
214 Ibid, 51.
215 Ibid, 48.
216 Ibid, 39.
217 Ibid, 72.
218 Ibid, 70.

219 Ibid, 84.

220 Ibid, 86.

221 Ibid, 88, 98.

222 Ibid, 98.

223 Ibid, 101.

224 Ibid, 105.

225 Ibid, 117.

226 Ibid, 33, 114.

227 Ibid, 120.

228 Ibid, 51.

229 Ibid, 53.

230 Ibid, 371.

231 "Freeland: Feds Will Appeal Court Ruling," CTV, January 23, 2024, 1:28 p.m. https://www.ctvnews.ca/video/c2852829-freeland--feds-will-appeal-court-ruling

232 Halverson, Roxanne, "Former Attorney General David Lametti Facing Lawsuit for Deleting his (X) Twitter Account," *Substack*, January 28, 2024. https://roxannehalverson.substack.com/p/former-attorney-general-david-lametti

233 Horwood, Matthew, "Attorney General, Public Safety Minister Cite Privilege in Not Disclosing Why Emergencies Act Invoked," *Epoch Times*, February 27, 2024. https://www.theepochtimes.com/world/attorney-general-refuses-to-disclose-reason-for-governments-invocation-of-emergencies-act-citing-solicitor-client-privilege-5596434

234 Carlson, Tucker, "Canadian Trucker Speaks to Tucker Carlson about Ottawa Police Violently Assaulting Him," Fox News, February 22, 2022. https://rumble.com/vvr51k-canadian-truckerspeaks-to-tucker-carlson-about-ottawa-policeviolently-ass.html

235 "Mr. Christopher Deering, Sworn,"87, 96–97. (See note 27).

236 "Mr. Keith Wilson, Sworn," Public Order Emergency Commission, November 2, 2022, 52. (See note 109).

237 Adie, Kate, "Chinese Troops Fire on Protesters in Tiananmen Square," BBC, June 4, 1989. https://www.youtube.com/watch?v=kMKvxJ-Js3A

238 Furey, Anthony, "The Emergencies Act Is Far More Dangerous than You Think: Full Comment with Anthony Furey," *National Post*, February 21, 2022. https://nationalpost.com/opinion/the-emergencies-act-is-far-more-dangerous-than-you-think-full-comment-with-anthony-furey?utm_medium=Social&utm_source=Twitter#Echobox=1645479755

239 Martin, Don, "The Trudeau Tipping Point Is Within Sight," CTV, February 28, 2023. https://www.ctvnews.ca/politics/don-martin-thetrudeau-tipping-point-is-within-sight-1.6292729

240 Woodworth, Elizabeth, "COVID-19 and the Shadowy Trusted News Initiative: How It Methodically Censors Top World Public Health Experts Using an Early Warning System," Global Research, January 22, 2022. Httpw://www.globalresearch.ca/covid-19-shadowytrusted-news-initiative/5752930

241 Wolf, Naomi, *The End of America: Letter of Warning to a Young Patriot* (Chelsea Green Publishing, 2007) 127. https://www.chelseagreen.com/product/the-end-ofamerica/

242 "Ms Zexi Li, Affirmed," Public Order Emergency Commission, October 14, 2022, 16-17, 35, 38, 48. https://publicorderemergencycommission.ca/files/documents/Transcripts/POEC-Public-Hearings-Volume-2-October-14-2022.pdf

243 "Vicious Spies and Killers under the Mask of Academic Physicians," *Pravda*, Moscow, January 13, 1953, 1. http://www.cyberussr.com/rus/vrach-ubijca-e.html

244   Brent, Jonathan and Naumov, Vladimir P., *Stalin's Last Crime: The Plot Against the Jewish Doctors, 1948-1953* (HarperCollins, 2003). https://www.harpercollins.com/products/stalins-last-crime-jonathan-brentvladimir-naumov?variant=32128871989282

245   Khrushchev, Nikita Sergeyevich, "Special Report to the 20th Congress of the Communist Party of the Soviet Union," February 24–25, 1956. https://web.archive.org/web/20051107221432/http://www.uwm.edu/Course/448-343/index12.html

246   "'Committed' to Web Censors," Blacklock's Reporter, April 3, 2023. https://www.blacklocks.ca/committed-to-web-censors/

247   *Remarks on the 20th Anniversary of the Voice of America*; Department of Health, Education, and Welfare, February 26, 1962. https://www.jfklibrary.org/asset-viewer/archives/JFKPOF/037/JFKPOF-037-020

248   Gunter, Lorne, "Feds' attempt to have story pulled from social media shows dangers of Bill C11," *Toronto Sun*, April 11, 2023. https://torontosun.com/opinion/gunter-feds-attempts-to-have-story-pulled-from-social-media-shows-dangers-of-bill-c-11

249   "Roundtable Discussion: National Security and Public Order Emergencies," Public Order Emergency Commission, November 30, 2022, 11–13. https://publicorderemergencycommission.ca/files/documents/Transcripts/POEC-Public-Hearings-Volume-34-November-30-2022.pdf

250   Horwood, Matthew, "Canadians Speak at Washington 'Covid Cartel' Forum Chaired by Senator," February 26, 2024. https://www.theepochtimes.com/world/canadians-speak-at-washington-forum-on-covid-cartel-chaired-by-senator-5595109?&utm_source=MB_article_paid_new&utm_campaign=MB_article_2024-02-27-ca&utm_medium=email&est=3U4V6gR7kM7NKDJiMG47WusLf%2Fewvn2ifBlRtaJevpSHIBlylmte0VsgksFJzQ%3D%3D&utm_content=top-news-1

251   Rodney Palmer," Trish Wood Is Critical, April 15, 2023, minute 01:10:00 ff. https://twcritical.libsyn.com/rodney-palmer

252   Nardi, Christopher, "Texts Show Feds Were Discussing Invoking Emergencies Act One Week into Freedom Convoy," *National Post*, October 27, 2022. https://nationalpost.com/news/politics/texts-discussing-invoking-emergencies-act

253   "Prime Minister's Remarks on Canada's Response to COVID-19," Prime Minister's Office, March 11, 2020. https://www.pm.gc.ca/en/news/speeches/2020/03/11/prime-ministers-remarks-canadas-response-covid-19

254   Tasker, John Paul, "The 'Measure of Last Resort:' What Is the Emergencies Act and What Does It Do?," CBC, March 23, 2020. https://www.cbc.ca/news/politics/trudeau-emergencies-act-premier-1.5507205

255   Breton, Charles and Tabbara, Mohy-Dean, "How the Provinces Compare in Their COVID-19 Responses," Policy Options, April 22, 2020. https://policyoptions.irpp.org/magazines/april-2020/how-the-provinces-compare-in-their-covid-19-responses/

256   Tunney, Catharine, Cullen, Catherine, and Cochrane, David, "Need for Emergencies Act Rejected by Premiers on Call with PM," CBC, April 10, 2020. https://www.cbc.ca/news/politics/emergencies-act-premiers-consensus-1.5529119

257   Pardy, Bruce, "Three Judges Forbear COVID's Hegemony in the Courts," *Epoch Times*, October 8, 2022. https//www.theepochtimes.com/bruce-pardythree-judges-forbear-covids-hegemony-in-thecourts_4782486.html

258   Desmet, Mattias, *The Psychology of Totalitarianism* (Chelsea Green Publishing, 2022), 176. https://www.chelseagreen.com/product/thepsychology-of-totalitarianism/

259   Ibid, 182.

260   Ibid, 187.

Notes

261 Ponesse, Dr. Julie, "Ethics Professor Dr. Julie Ponesse Threatened with Dismissal for Refusing Vaccine," YouTube.com, September 8, 2021. https://www.youtube.com/watch?v=JZMByqQOW7w

262 Siri, Aaron, Twitter, April 23, 9:25 a.m. https://twitter.com/AaronSiriSG/status/1650174117209882625

263 Kheriaty, *The New Abnormal*, 46. (See note 130).

264 Lt. Col. David Redman Testimony," National Citizens Inquiry, Red Deer, Alberta, April 25, 2023. https://rumble.com/embed/v2i5cuc/?pub=1tpa36 (Starting at 1:22:05)

265 Ibid. (Starting at 2:17:00).

266 Wolf, Naomi, *The Bodies of Others: The New Authoritarians, COVID-19 and The War Against the Human* (All Seasons Press, 2022), 61-222. https://www.allseasonspress.com/the-bodies-of-others.

267 "Episode 116: Marianne Klowak: Exclusive: CBC Journalist Speaks Out," Trish Wood is Critical, July 2, 2022. https://www.trishwoodpodcast.com/podcast/episode-116-marianne-klowak

268 "Drue Taylor Vaccine Injury Develops POTS," National Citizens Inquiry, April 27, 2023. https://rumble.com/v3pw4gg-canada-drue-taylor-vaccine-injury-develops-pots-national-citizens-inquiry.html

269 Rodney Palmer," National Citizens Inquiry, March 30, 2023. https://rumble.com/v2fs7u2-rodney-palmer-fullinterview-day-1-toronto-national-citizensinquiry.html?mref=1sktjm&mrefc=12

270 Ibid. For transcript see: https://nationalcitizensinquiry.ca/witness/rodney-palmer/#1689907599657-fefa385c-a7e7e834-2c18

271 Arendt, Hannah, "Hannah Arendt: From an Interview," *The New York Review*, October 26, 1978. https://www.nybooks.com/articles/1978/10/26/hannah-arendt-from-an-interview/

272 Nuremberg Code, 1947. https://www.fhi360.org/sites/all/libraries/webpages/fhi-retc2/Resources/nuremburg_code.pdf

273 "CUMULATIVE ANALYSIS OF POSTAUTHORIZATION ADVERSE EVENT REPORTS OF PF-07302048 (BNT162B2) RECEIVED THROUGH 28-FEB-2021," Worldwide Safety, Pfizer, April 30, 2021. https://phmpt.org/wp-content/uploads/2021/11/5.3.6-postmarketing-experience.pdf

274 Biden Targets the Unvaccinated with Widespread Plan to Mandate COVID-19 Shots: 'Our Patience is Wearing Thin, and Your Refusal has Cost Us All'" CBC, September 9, 2021. https://www.cbc.ca/news/world/biden-us-covid19-sept9-plan-coronavirus-1.6169491

275 embensadoun, "90% of Canada's COVID Cases are Among Unvaccinated, Feds Say," Global News, July 26, 2021. https://globalnews.ca/news/8059996/almost-all-recent-covid-cases-unvaccinated/

276 McElroy, Justin, "Unvaccinated in B.C. Hospitalized with COVID-19 at a Rate 17 Times Higher Than Fully Vaccinated," CBC, August 24, 2021. https://www.cbc.ca/news/canada/british-columbia/unvaccinated-vaccinated-covid-data-bc-1.6151008

277 Sullivan, Becky "US COVID Deaths are Rising Again. Experts Call It "A Pandemic of The Unvaccinated," NPR, July 16, 2021. https://www.npr.org/2021/07/16/1017002907/u-s-covid-deaths-are-rising-again-experts-call-it-a-pandemic-of-the-unvaccinated

278 Yousif, Nadine, "When It Comes to Empathy For the Unvaccinated, Many of Us Aren't Feeling It," *Toronto Star,* August 26, 2021. https://www.thestar.com/news/gta/when-it-comes-to-empathy-for-the-unvaccinated-many-of-us-aren-t-feeling-it/article_503732da-cbad-58e8-93d2-4f4f21f24407.html

279 Harding, Amanda, "'If You're Not Vaccinated, Get The F*** Out Of My House': 'The View' Co-Host Promotes Controversial Candle," DailyWire.com, December 22, 2021. https://www.dailywire.com/news/if-youre-not-vaccinated-get-the-f-out-of-my-house-the-view-co-host-promotes-controversial-candle

280 Connolly, Amanda, "Trudeau Doubles Down on Mandatory COVID-19 Vaccines for Domestic Travel," Global News, August 18, 2021. https://globalnews.ca/news/8122807/canada-election-covid-19-madatory-vaccination/

281 Cunningham, Meg, "Dr. Birx on Her Relationship with Trump: 'Respectful in Public but Very Clear in Private," ABC, December 16, 2020. https://abcnews.go.com/Politics/dr-birx-relationship-trump-respectful-public-clear-private/story?id=74760598

282 "Dr. Deborah Birx says She 'Knew' COVID Vaccines Would Not 'Protect Against Infection," FOX, July 22, 2022. https://www.foxnews.com/media/dr-deborah-birx-knew-covid-vaccines-not-protect-against-infection

283 Thakur, Ramesh, "A Pandemic of the Triple Vaccinated," Brownstone Institute, July 26, 2022. https://brownstone.org/articles/a-pandemic-of-the-triple-vaccinated/

284 "Testimony of Scarlett Martyn," National Citizens Inquiry, April 1, 2023. https://rumble.com/v2khip4-nci-toronto-day-3-scarlett-martyn.html

285 Phone call with Scarlett Martyn, November 12, 2023.

286 "Testimony of Shelley Overwater," National Citizens Inquiry, Winnipeg, Manitoba, April 14, 2023. https://rumble.com/v3d46jk-shelley-overwater-apr-14-2023-winnipeg-manitoba.html?mref=1tpa36&mrefc=2

287 Harrington, Thomas S., The Treason of the Experts, (Brownstone Institute, 2023) 63. https://www.amazon.ca/dp/B0C4G4785Y?ref_=cm_sw_r_kb_dp_CNMJWX7D624E7TR7E5MG&tag=kp066-20&linkCode=kpe

288 "Hospitalizations by Vaccination Status," Ontario Ministry of Health, June 30, 2022. https://data2.ontario.ca/en/dataset/covid-19-vaccine-data-in-ontario/resource/274b819c-5d69-4539-a4db-f2950794138c

289 "Episode 116: Marianne Klowak: Exclusive: CBC Journalist Speaks Out," Trish Wood is Critical, July 2, 2022. https://www.trishwoodpodcast.com/podcast/episo de-116-marianne-klowak

290 Subramanya, Rupa, "Court Documents Reveal Canada's Travel Ban Had No Scientific Basis," Common Sense, August 2, 2022. https://www.thefp.com/p/court-documents-reveal-canadas-travel

291 Subramanya, Rupa, "Justin Trudeau's Tyranny has Finally been Exposed – by Two Brits!" Telegraph, August 12, 2022. https://www.telegraph.co.uk/news/2022/08/12/tyranny-justin-trudeau-has-finally-exposed-two-brits-no-less/

292 Lilley, Brian, "Court Records Show Trudeau Brought in Vaccine Mandates for Travel Purely Based on Politics," Toronto Sun, August 10, 2022. https://torontosun.com/opinion/columnists/lilley-court-records-show-trudeau-brought-in-vaccine-mandates-for-travel-purely-based-on-politics

293 Frei, Viva, "Interview with Keith Wilson – Brian Peckford's Charter – the latest legal breakdown," Rumble, September 22, 2022. https://rumble.com/v1lcpal-viva-frei-interview-with-keith-wilson-brian-peckfords-charter-the-latest-le.html

294 Chartier, Noe, "Health Canada Didn't Recommend Travel Vaccine Mandate, Official Behind the Policy Testifies in Court," Epoch Times, August 2, 2022. https://www.theepochtimes.com/health-canada-did-not-recommended-travel-vaccine-mandate-official-behind-the-policy-testifies_4637758.html?utm_source=BN_article_paid&utm_campaign=breaking-2022-08-02-ca&utm_medium=email&est=NB8%2FVu

WYoe5Xt%2BWF9sk9K%2F1RKefsH166X2JcQVtkoo%2Fqtr9oXnp3vWE4. See also "Evidence on the risk of COVID-19 transmission in flight: update 3," Public Health Agency of Canada, modified April 1, 2022. https://www.canada.ca/en/public-health/services/diseases/2019-novel-coronavirus-infection/canadas-reponse/summaries-recent-evidence/evidence-risk-covid-19-transmission-flight-update-3.html

295 Chartier, Noé, "Approving Authority on COVID-19 Vaccines says Underreporting of Adverse Events a 'Common Problem'," Epoch Times, July 24, 2022. https://www.theepochtimes.com/world/approving-authority-on-covid-19-vaccines-says-underreporting-of-adverse-events-a-common-problem-5419675

296 Martin, Paul, "Report of the Auditor General of New Brunswick, Volume II," December 2023, pp. 30-54. https://www.agnb-vgnb.ca/content/dam/agnb-vgnb/pdf/Reports-Rapports/2023V2/Agrepe.pdf

297 MacKinnon, Bobbi-Jean, "Auditor General Flags Lack of Evidence-based Records to Back COVID Decisions: Department of Health Unable to Provide Documents for 33 Recommendations by Office of Chief Medical Officer," CBC, December 14, 2023. https://www.cbc.ca/news/canada/new-brunswick/auditor-general-new-brunswick-covid-19-pandemic-response-education-health-justice-1.7058576

298 Cowan, Jennifer, "BC Arbitration Ruling in Favour of Unvaccinated Workers Could Mean End of Vaccine Mandate: Former AG," Epoch Times, January 5, 2024. https://www.theepochtimes.com/world/purolator-arbitration-case-could-have-major-impact-on-bcs-vaccine-mandate-former-ag-says-5558954?utm_source=BN_article_paid&src_src=BN_article_paid&utm_campaign=breaking-2024-01-05-ca&src_cmp=breaking-2024-01-05-ca&utm_medium=email&est=RhnxbNwNUuMytIZUMNxpLMf%2FI%2ByzNLeTsdmIxNi3wPaPWc3L13iSoa9dhh4ATA%3D%3D&utm_term=news1&utm_content=1

299 Mendick, Robert, "AZ to be Sued Over 'Defective' Vaccine. Landmark Legal Action will Suggest Claims Over Jabs' Efficacy Were 'Vastly Overstated'," Daily Telegraph, London, UK, November 9, 2023. https://dailytelegraph.pressreader.com/article/281505050933445

300 Teo, Issac, "EXCLUSIVE: Canadian Military Disregarded Legal Advice in Imposing Vaccine Mandate, Internal Document Shows," Epoch Times, January 11, 2024. https://www.theepochtimes.com/world/exclusive-canadian-military-disregarded-legal-advice-in-imposing-vaccine-mandate-internal-document-shows-5561706?utm_source=MB_article_free&src_src=MB_article_free&utm_campaign=mb-2024-01-10-ca&src_cmp=mb-2024-01-10-ca&utm_medium=email&est=DY6PFOknxLD3PpL8mPSDiiu3%2FqbgBVMON5KnAU%2Fo3iA8vQHtbjxnLL0Q1jc%3D&utm_term=newstop&utm_content=1

301 "Witness 4: Dr. Gregory Chan," National Citizens Inquiry, Day 1, Red Deer, April 26, 2023. 2197-2200. https://nationalcitizensinquiry.b-cdn.net/wp-content/uploads/2023/12/FINAL-REPORT-Volume-3-Inquiry-into-the-Appropriateness-and-Efficacy-of-the-COVID-19-Response-in-Canada-December-21-2023.pdf

302 "Witness 3: Dr. Patrick Phillips," Day 1, Truro, NS, March 16, 2023. 34-53. https://nationalcitizensinquiry.b-cdn.net/wp-content/uploads/2023/12/FINAL-REPORT-Volume-1-2-3-Inquiry-into-the-Appropriateness-and-Efficacy-of-the-COVID-19-Response-in-Canada-December-21-2023.pdf. See also "Witness 6: Dr, Charles Hoffe," National Citizens Inquiry, Day 2, Vancouver, BC, May 3, 2023, 3056-3072. He submitted over a dozen adverse events to the system and they were repeatedly rejected with no explanation. https://nationalcitizensinquiry.b-cdn.net/wp-content/uploads/2023/12/FINAL-REPORT-Volume-3-Inquiry-into-the-Appropriateness-and-Efficacy-of-the-COVID-19-Response-in-Canada-December-21-2023.pdf

303 "Witness 8: Carrie Sakamoto," National Citizens Inquiry, Saskatoon, SK, April 22, 2023, 2060. https://nationalcitizensinquiry.b-cdn.net/wp-content/uploads/2023/12/FINAL-REPORT-Volume-3-Inquiry-into-the-Appropriateness-and-Efficacy-of-the-COVID-19-Response-in-Canada-December-21-2023.pdf

304 Sakamoto, Carrie, "Vaccine Class Action Statement of Claim," Rath & Company, February 29, 2024. https://rathandcompany.com/class-action-documents/

305 Kory, Dr. Pierre, *The War On Ivermectin*, (ICAN Press, 2023) 110, 114, 208-209, 212. https://www.amazon.com/War-Ivermectin-Medicine-Millions-Pandemic/dp/151077386X

306 Heffernan, Margaret, *W illful Bl ndness*, (Anchor Canada, 2011), 101-102. https://www.mheffernan.com/book-wilfulblindness.php#modal-close

307 Maybury, David, "A Night with the Untouchables," *The Reformed Physicist*, February 3, 2022. https://maybury.ca/the-reformed-physicist/2022/02/03/a-night-with-the-untouchables/

308 "Accused in Mission Double Murder Released on Bail," CBC, October 17, 2013. https://www.cbc.ca/news/canada/british-columbia/accused-in-mission-double-murder-released-on-bail-1.2101838

309 Lieberman, Caryn, "Suspect Charged in Connection with Death of Toronto Officer Granted Bail," Global News, September 22, 2021. https://globalnews.ca/news/8212220/umar-zameer-bail-jeffrey-northrup-toronto-police/

310 Geleneau, Jacqueline, "Kelowna Woman Charged with Murder Released on Bail," *Kelowna Capital News*, April 28, 2022. https://www.kelownacapnews.com/news/kelowna-woman-charged-with-murder-released-on-bail/

311 McDonald, Catherine, "Milton, Ont. Man Accused of Murdering Armed Intruder Released on Bail," Global News, March 2, 2023. https://globalnews.ca/news/9523161/milton-man-home-invasion-shooting-bail/

312 Henderson, Ernest F, "Assize of Clarendon, 1166," in *Select Historical Documents of the Middle Ages* (London, George Bell and Sons, 1896). https://avalon.law.yale.edu/medieval/assizecl.asp

313 Magna Carta, 1215, Section 38. https://magnacarta.cmp.uea.ac.uk/read/magna_carta_1215/Clause_38

314 "Canadian Charter of Rights and Freedoms," *Constitution Act of 1982*, 1982. https://laws-lois.justice.gc.ca/eng/const/page-12.html

315 Best, Donald, "Denying Bail to Coutts Four Is a Political Decision and Act," Donaldbest.ca, July 8, 2023. https://donaldbest.ca/denying-bail-to-the-coutts-four-is-a-political-decision-and-act/

316 Ibid.

317 Joannou, Ashley, "Kenney Calls for Calm, Says RCMP Officers Assaulted at Coutts Border," *Edmonton Journal*, February 2, 2022. https://edmontonjournal.com/news/local-news/kenney-calls-for-calm-says-rcmp-officers-assaulted-at-coutts-border-crossing

318 Simone, Kiane and Fizzard, Sydney, *Trucker Rebellion: The Story of the Coutts Blockade*, Rebel News, August 19, 2022. https://rumble.com/v1glv1z-trucker-rebellion-the-story-of-the-coutts-blockade.html

319 "Alberta RCMP Make Arrests at Coutts Border Blockade," RCMP, February 14, 2022. https://www.rcmp-grc.gc.ca/en/news/2022/alberta-rcmp-make-arrests-coutts-border-blockade

320 Gibson, Caley, "RCMP Arrest 13 People, Seize Weapons and Ammunition Near Coutts Border Blockade," Global News, February 14, 2022. https://globalnews.ca/news/8618494/alberta-coutts-border-protest-weapons-ammunition-seized/

321 Leavitt, Kieran and Mosleh, Omar, "Father of Accused in Alleged Coutts Blockade

Murder Conspiracy Says Son Was Radicalized Online, as Others Dispute RCMP Narrative," *Toronto Star*, February 17, 2022. https://www.thestar.com/news/canada/2022/02/17/father-of-accused-in-alleged-coutts-blockade-murder-conspiracy-says-son-was-radicalized-online-as-others-dispute-rcmp-narrative.html

322 Tran, Paula, "Anti-Hate Experts Concerned about Possible Neo-fascist Involvement at Alberta Trucker Convoy," Global News, February 15, 2022. https://globalnews.ca/news/8621125/canadian-anti-hate-network-concerned-diagolon-coutts-border-protest-diagolon/

323 Bell, Stewart, "Man Who Attended Ottawa Protest Convoy Arrested on Firearms Charges," Global News, February 3, 2022. https://globalnews.ca/news/8593064/ns-man-ottawa-convoy-protest-firearms-charge/

324 Magill, Gord, "Meet the Four Men Being Held as Political Prisoners in Canada," *Newsweek*, October 3, 2023. https://www.newsweek.com/meet-four-men-being-held-political-prisoners-canada-opinion-1831823

325 "The Coutts 13: New Details on the Men and Women Arrested at Border Blockade," Radio-Canada, February 17, 2022. https://ici.radio-canada.ca/rci/en/news/1862953/the-coutts-13-new-details-on-the-men-and-women-arrested-at-border-blockade

326 Grant, Meghan, "4 Men Accused of Conspiring to Murder RCMP Officers to Be Tried Together: Prosecutors: Chris Lysak, Chris Carbert, Anthony Olienick, Jerry Morin charged after Coutts protests," CBC, April 25, 2022. https://www.cbc.ca/news/canada/calgary/coutts-border-protest-conspiracy-to-murder-trials-1.6430369

327 Shurtz, Delon, "Bail Denied for Accused in Coutts Conspiracy Case," *Lethbridge Herald*, June 10, 2022. https://lethbridgeherald.com/news/lethbridge-news/2022/06/10/bail-denied-for-accused-in-coutts-conspiracy-case/

328 Martin, Kevin, "Arming for a Standoff Against Police," Regina Leader-Post, Regina, SK, September 8, 2022. https://www.pressreader.com/canada/regina-leader-post/20220908/281711208483474

329 Martin, Kevin, "Some Coutts Protesters Wanted to Alter Canada's Political System," *Calgary Herald*, November 30, 2022. https://calgaryherald.com/news/crime/some-coutts-protesters-wanted-to-alter-canadas-political-system-court-documents-say

330 Ward, Rachel and Grant, Meghan, "Bosses of Alberta Men Accused in Plot to Murder Mounties Still under Investigation, Court Docs Suggest," CBC, December 1, 2022. https://www.cbc.ca/news/canada/calgary/coutts-protest-blockade-border-ito-documents-unsealed-1.6670025

331 Magill (see note 324).

332 "Ms. Janice Charette, Sworn, Ms. Nathalie Drouin, Affirmed," Public Order Emergency Commission, Ottawa, November 18, 2022, p. 163. (See note 97).

333 Ibid, 183-184.

334 Ibid, 296–297.

335 "Minister Marco Mendicino, Sworn," Public Order Emergency Commission, Ottawa, November 22, 2022, 168. https://publicorderemergencycommission.ca/files/documents/Transcripts/POEC-Public-Hearings-Volume-28-November-22-2022.pdf

336 "Ms. Jody Thomas, Sworn," Public Order Emergency Commission, Ottawa, November 17, 2022, p. 225. (See note 86).

337 "Deputy PM Chrystia Freeland, Sworn," Public Order Emergency Commission, Ottawa, November 24, 2022, 112. https://publicorderemergencycommission.ca/files/documents/Transcripts/POEC-Public-Hearings-Volume-30-November-24-2022.pdf

338 "Prime Minister Justin Trudeau, Affirmed," Public Order Emergency Commission, Ottawa, November 25, 2022, 52, 76, 42. (See note 101).

339 "Mayor Jimmy Willett, Sworn," Public Order Emergency Commission, Ottawa, November 9, 2022, 29, 31–32. https://publicorderemergencycommission.ca/files/documents/Transcripts/POEC-Public-Hearings-Volume-20-November-9-2022.pdf

340 Tom Marazzo, "Jeremy MacKenzie Interview," Meet Me in the Middle Podcast, June 21, 2023. https://rumble.com/v2v7xfk-tom-marazzo-jeremy-mackenzie-pt-1-excerpt-2-meet-me-in-the-middle-podcast.html

341 "Mr. Jeremy Mitchell MacKenzie, Affirmed," Public Order Emergency Commission, Ottawa, November 4, 2022, 151–152, 157, 218. https://publicorderemergencycommission.ca/files/documents/Transcripts/POEC-Public-Hearings-Volume-17-November-4-2022.pdf

342 Ibid, 164.

343 Ibid, 176–193.

344 "The Coutts Four | Day 515," Good Morning with Jason, July 13, 2023. https://rumble.com/v2zpotm-the-coutts-four-day-515-good-morning-with-jason-july-13.html

345 Wood, Trish, "Canada's Political Prisoners: The Coutts Four," Trish Wood is Critical, November 18, 2023. https://www.trishwoodpodcast.com/podcast/episode-194-coutts-four

346 Lavigne, "The Coutts Four | Day 515" (See note 344).

347 Magill, "Meet the Four Men . . ." (see note 324).

348 Lavigne, Jason, "The Coutts Four | Day 506," Good Morning with Jason, July 4, 2023. https://rumble.com/v2xzm4i-the-coutts-four-day-506-good-morning-with-jason-july-4.html

349 Lavigne, "The Coutts Four | Day 515" (See note 344).

350 Report of the Public Inquiry into the 2022 Public Order Emergency, Volume 3: Analysis (Part 2) and Recommendations, 83, 343. https://publicorderemergencycommission.ca/files/documents/Final-Report/Vol-3-Report-of-the-Public-Inquiry-into-the-2022-Public-Order-Emergency.pdf

351 Phone call to Marco Van Huigenbos, February 9, 2024.

352 Magill, "Meet the Four Men . . ." (see note 324).

353 Wood, "Canada's Political Prisoners . . ." (See note 345).

354 Magill, Gord, "Justin Trudeau's Political Prisoners," Newsweek, July 13, 2023. https://www.newsweek.com/justin-trudeaus-political-prisoners-opinion-1812866

355 "Day 30 of Public Hearings," Public Order Emergency Commission, Ottawa, November 24, 2022. (See testimony starting at 2:50:00.) https://publicorderemergencycommission.ca/public-hearings/day-30-november-24/

356 Lavigne, Jason, "The Coutts Four | Day 509," Good Morning with Jason, July 7, 2023. https://rumble.com/v2yl1h6-the-coutts-four-day-509-good-morning-with-jason-july-7.html

357 Saïd, Carmya, and Hategan, Elisa, "The Hategate Affair: Unmasking Canada's Hate Industry," prnewswire.com, 2023, 61, 73. (See note 176).

358 Wood, "Canada's Political Prisoners . . ." (See note 345).

359 "Ms. Jody Thomas, Sworn," Public Order Emergency Commission, Ottawa, November 17, 2022, 291. (See note 86).

360 Magill, "Meet the Four Men . . ." (see note 324).

361 Bezrigan, Mocha, "BREAKING: Bail for Chris Carbert has been denied," January 15, 2024. https://www.mediabezirgan.com/post/breaking-bail-for-chris-carbert-has-been-denied

362 Carlson, Tucker, "Freedom Convoy, the Coutts Four, and Liberating Canada," The Tucker Carlson Encounter, January 24, 2024. https://tuckercarlson.com/the-tucker-carlson-encounter-freedom-convoy-the-coutts-4-and-liberating-canada/

363 Martin, Kevin, "Two suspects in Coutts border blockade plead guilty to reduced

charges," *Calgary Herald*, February 6, 2024. https://calgaryherald.com/news/crime/christopher-lysak-jerry-morin-plead-guilty-coutts-border-blockade

364 Dieterle, William, Director, *The Life of Emile Zola*, Warner Bros. Pictures, 1937. https://www.youtube.com/watch?v=ulHE1UQpOuQ&t=2122s See also Paul Read, Piers, *The Dreyfus Affair* (Bloomsbury, 2013), 86-118, 316-344.

365 Olienick, Tony, "Letter from a Canadian Political Prisoner," *Newsweek*, February 29, 2024. https://www.newsweek.com/letter-canadian-political-prisoner-opinion-1874416

366 Lawton, Andrew, "No End in Sight for Tamara Lich Trial (ft. Trish Wood)," True North, September 23, 2023. https://tnc.news/2023/09/23/lawton-lich-trial-wood/

367 "Lich Trial Highlights, October 16, 2023," The Democracy Fund, October 17, 2023. https://www.thedemocracyfund.ca/trial_day_17

368 "Update: Class action lawsuit will likely seek more than $300-million from convoy protest organizers, supporters," *Ottawa City News*, February 24, 2023. https://ottawa.citynews.ca/2022/02/24/listen-class-action-lawsuit-will-likely-seek-more-than-300-million-from-convoy-protest-organizers-supporters-5096984/

369 "Lich Trial Highlights, October 20, 2023," The Democracy Fund, October 24, 2023. https://www.thedemocracyfund.ca/trial_day_21

370 "Lich Trial Highlights, October 18, 2023," The Democracy Fund, October 19, 2023. https://www.thedemocracyfund.ca/trial_day_19

371 Stevenson, Jane, "Freedom Convoy Organizer Tamara Lich to Get award," *Toronto Sun*, April 26, 2022. https://torontosun.com/news/national/freedom-convoy-organizer-tamara-lich-to-get-award

372 Fraser, David, "Crown drops bail violation for Tamara Lich," CBC, October 23, 2023. https://www.cbc.ca/news/canada/ottawa/crown-drops-bail-violation-charge-for-tamara-lich-1.7004916

373 Helmer, Aeden, "'Freedom Convoy' Organizer Tamara Lich Denied Bail," *Ottawa Citizen*, July 8, 2022. https://ottawacitizen.com/news/local-news/freedom-convoy-organizer-tamara-lich-denied-bail

374 "Lich Trial Highlights, November 20, 2023," The Democracy Fund, November 23, 2023. https://www.thedemocracyfund.ca/trial_day_27

375 Horwood, Matthew, "Convoy Lawyers Want Police to Pay for Damages Claimed in Ottawa Residents Lawsuit," Epoch Times, February 9, 2024. https://www.theepochtimes.com/world/convoy-lawyers-want-police-to-pay-for-damages-claimed-in-ottawa-residents-lawsuit-5583996?utm_source=BN_article_paid&src_src=BN_article_paid&utm_campaign=breaking-2024-02-09-ca&src_cmp=breaking-2024-02-09ca&utm_medium=email&est=VFzao%2FpP6b6WLvLkHPz%2BowhzGtUF90JLdT6ifAAzMfL0kKpdwbxYNVB6oZfbFA%3D%3D&utm_term=news1&utm_content=1

376 Girard, René and DeBevoise, Malcolm B. (translator), *The One by Whom Scandal Comes: Studies in Violence, Mimesis & Culture* (Michigan State University Press, East Lansing, MI, 2014), 30. https://msupress.org/9781611861099/the-one-by-whom-scandal-comes/

377 Wilson-Raybould, Jody, *Indian in the Cabinet* (HarperCollins, 2021). https://www.amazon.com/Indian-CabinetSpeaking-Truth-Power/dp/1443465364

378 Blitzer, Wolf, "Interview with Dr. Rachelle Walensky," CNN, August 6, 2021. https://rumble.com/vkte8s-cdc-director-admits-tocnn-that-covid-vaccines-dont-prevent-transmission-of.html

379 "Anita Krishna Tells Vancouver Crowd 'MSM is Done,'" Rumble, February 5, 2022 https://rumble.com/vuvlvs-anita-krishna....msm-is-done.html

380 "Dr. Jordan Peterson Interview with Rex Murphy: The Catastrophe of Canada," February 19, 2022. https://www.youtube.com/watch?v=5efyUt5YDU0.